I0748460

PUERTO RICAN LITERATURE

A Bibliography of Secondary Sources

COMPILED BY
DAVID WILLIAM FOSTER

GREENWOOD PRESS
WESTPORT, CONNECTICUT • LONDON, ENGLAND

Library of Congress Cataloging in Publication Data

Foster, David William.
Puerto Rican literature.

Includes index.
1. Puerto Rican literature—History and criticism—Bibliography. I. Title.
Z1557.L56F67 [PQ7421] 016.86'09'97295 82-6198
ISBN 0-313-23419-1 (lib. bdg.) AACR2

Library of Congress Catalog Card Number: 82-6198
ISBN: 0-313-23419-1

First published in 1982

Greenwood Press
A division of Congressional Information Service, Inc.
88 Post Road West, Westport, Connecticut 06881

Printed in the United States of America

10 9 8 7 6 5 4 3 2 1

CONTENTS

PREFACE

Puerto Rican literature is unquestionably one of the key literatures of the Caribbean. Yet, despite the existence of several literary dictionaries and general bibliographies, no comprehensive critical bibliography of Puerto Rican authors has been compiled. There are partial listings of the works of major authors, and a number of authors have been studied extensively: Marqués, Palés Matos, and Arriví, for example. But with the exception of critical bibliographies for individual authors, no attempt has been made to compile a registry of representative criticism on major figures. This compilation fills that void.*

The authors presented have been chosen on the basis of their historical and aesthetic importance and on the basis of available critical references. The scope of the latter will vary in accord with the number of references available, for example, the references for Palés Matos are qualitatively more selective than those for Emilio S. Belaval, on whom only a modest amount of criticism is available. I acknowledge in advance the disappointment or surprise of the user over some of the authors not represented.

Although this compilation follows in organization and scope my *Chilean literature*, published in 1978, a comparison will reveal that the present compilation covers more authors, but that there are fewer authors on whom an extensive amount of material is available. This circumstance simply reflects the differences between Chilean and Puerto Rican literature and the extensive local and modest foreign scholarship on them.

The general criterion has been to list those items considered useful to serious scholarly research and opinion—articles in all types of scholarly

*The *Diccionario de literatura latinoamericana*, sponsored by the Pan American Union in the late fifties and early sixties, never progressed far enough to include coverage of Puerto Rico. Its goal was to provide both primary and secondary bibliographies for the authors listed. Hill's *Puerto Rican authors* (item no. A. 16) lists only works by writers and excludes criticism on them.

journals and the most important cultural ones, and all monographic studies—and those likely to be readily available in research libraries, which accounts for my not attempting to take every cultural publication into account. The distinction is difficult to make between "useful" and "nonuseful" items, and I have endeavored to sin on the side of overinclusion.

Certainly it is not the bibliographer's task to distinguish between competent and incompetent criticism, nor to restrict his compilation to essays representing a certain trend or range of trends (for example, sociological or structuralist criticism alone). Yet it would not be practical—and would constitute a misunderstanding of the task of the bibliographer of literary scholarship—to list *all* know references, especially those in general-audience magazines and newspapers. I have, accordingly, attempted the difficult task of distinguishing academic and "cultural" criticism from "journalistic" presentations, and have excluded the latter. Thus, no attempt has been made to list all known references, since it is unlikely that the demands of a serious contemporary, generally intrinsic, criticism would be served by such a vast compilation. In every case my goal has been to serve the interests, as I understand them, of the academic literary scholar.

Items in magazines, dailies, and literary supplements have, therefore, been excluded, since they rarely meet the two-fold criterion mentioned above. However, those items that have been reprinted in collected essays have been listed, not only because such collections are more readily accessible, but because reprinting in this format attests to the intrinsic importance of the essay and/or to the stature of the critic involved. All known criticism and review articles in scholarly and cultural journals have been listed.

A word about the distinction between reviews and review articles is in order. By the former I understand a relatively brief notice, ranging from the 250-500 word review published in *World literature today* (formerly *Books abroad*), to the two- or three-page presentation of more specialized journals like *Asomante* or *Revista iberoamericana*. Typically, the review is untitled and is identified by the book's pertinent bibliographic information; it is usually "signed" with the name of the reviewer at the foot of the review, although initials may be used in the case of staff reviewers. When I have cited a review for works by an author whom I deem important but for whom there is scant criticism, I have used a shortened form of the heading enclosed in brackets as the title. Clearly, any reasonable criterion of selection based on the relative merit and depth of critical notes would, in the case of authors like Marqués and Palés Matos, for example, rank reviews very low in importance. To be sure, a complete bibliography for an author would aim to present all such pertinent material (for example, the bibliographies that *Revista iberoamericana* has been publishing for the last ten years). Nevertheless, only the scholar concerned with the minutiae of the development of a writer's career could find reviews important when placed alongside extensive, in-depth critical studies meeting well-defined standards of academic methodology. Given this circumstance and the fact that to include reviews would have at least doubled the number of entries in this compilation, I feel that to exclude reviews for the majority of authors does not seriously misrepresent the criticism available on their writings that is of interest to the modern literary scholar. On the other hand, reviews may be sought by referring to the specialized bibliographies listed for each major author and to available cumulative bibliographies for Puerto Rican and Latin American publications.

Review articles, on the other hand, are generally longer than reviews—although, like the latter, they are marked by their contemporaneity with the work being discussed. Yet, because review articles are typically titled, they constitute a rough form of specialized criticism in that, as their title may announce, they tend to focus on a few salient aspects of a work in some detail. This sort of focus and detail are not regular features of reviews. Review articles, therefore, are treated in this compilation like any independently titled essay in a journal.

Although no attempt has been made to list references that are included without distinguishing headings in general treatises of Latin American literature and monographs on specific aspects of genres and movements, the scholar should always consult such works and discover pertinent passages through an index or table of contents. Latin American bibliographies, to be sure, have often listed such references as though they were monographic articles or chapters simply because there has never been a well-organized bibliography of general treatises on Spanish American literature and the various national literatures, movements periods, or genres; such a bibliography is an outstanding desideratum. However, aside from the hope that such a bibliography will soon be forthcoming, I have excluded general references of the sort described because the research libraries of most major American universities provide easy access to a block of such materials in the collection through the card catalog and/or specific class numbers (for example, the PQ7081-7082 designation of the Library of Congress system used in many large research libraries).

Finally, since these references are arranged hierarchically, beginning with a subdivided section of general topics, followed by sections on specific authors, references of a general nature that include comments on specific authors have not been repeated in the sections on the latter. If one is researching references Arriví's vanguard theater for example, he should consult the section on Twentieth Century Puerto Rican Drama, in addition to the specific references in the section on Arriví.

In general, the bibliographic formats followed are those of the U.S. Library of Congress and the Modern Language Association of America (MLA). All names of critics have been standardized to one form. Any residual errors are the combined responsibility of the compiler and the lamentably long-lived tradition in Hispanic bibliography of incomplete, confusing, and inaccurate references. Hopefully this compilation represents a step toward the sort of bibliographic control Puerto Rican literature deserves.

Methodology in Latin American literary bibliography still remains a matter of juggling incomplete bibliographies and of working out strategies for completing partial data and correcting false information. Identifying and eliminating the "phantom reference" is a special challenge—and often the case for a certain amount of harmless, pedantic pleasure.

Sources like Rela's *Guía bibliográfica de la literatura hispanoamericana,* Flores's *Bibliografía de los escritores hispanoamericanos 1609-1974,* and UNESCO's *Bibliografía general de la literatura latinoamericana* all provide basic points of departure for gathering references, both monographs and articles. All tend to complement each other rather than to overlap, and the amount of contradictory information is frequently startling. But one can assemble at least a nucleus of citations, if only partial and unreliable.

Special sources on individual authors or topics remain monographic studies along with their footnotes and/or bibliographies of references. All major monographs—and most minor ones—on Puerto Rican literature were combed for citations. Again, I found inconsistencies, inaccuracies, and contradictions that had to be checked against library catalogs (*National Union Catalog,* University of Texas, Harvard's Widener Library, and others) or, when possible, against the journals and books themselves. My goal was to double-check the data on each reference against the item itself, and this was possible for virtually all monographs and for articles in major journals.

Of course, the MLA's *International bibliography* continues to be a good source for citations, and the 1974 pilot volume of the *Hispanic American periodical index* demonstrated that *HAPI* will become a major reference source as it continues to expand coverage each year. On the other hand I found the *Index to Latin American periodical literature 1929-1960* extremely unreliable and incomplete, although the supplement volumes published through the late 1960s were more comprehensive. The *Handbook of Latin American studies,* while it served to verify some difficult references, was surprisingly not very useful: its value appears to be the annotations of items that are given, rather than the scope of journals it covers (*HLAS* also lists monographs).

There continues to be a large gap in Latin American literary bibliography between major journals and those that, although well known, seem to get lost in the shuffle. Sources such as *Asomante* and *Revista iberoamericana* are readily available in the United States and contain printed cumulative indexes. Needless to say, citations are more easily verified if the source contains a cumulative index.

Two final important sources need mentioning: bibliographies of criticism that are included as ancillary items in an author's complete or selected works, and those that appear in appendices to collections of critical essays on an author. The latter is a growing phenomenon in Latin American literature—one recalls the useful collections on Paz, Neruda, Vallejo, and Quiroga assembled by Ángel Flores—and provides an excellent opportunity for a conscientious compiler to commission such a listing.

A few miscellaneous observations concerning bibliographical standards employed in this compilation are:

1. American doctoral dissertations are cited in two fashions: if the reference in *Dissertation abstracts/Dissertation abstracts international* is known, American titles have been listed in terms of their abstract. The reason for this is that this reference is necessary to obtain the order number for the dissertation, should the researcher wish to acquire a copy from University Microfilms. For dissertations written prior to the *DA/DAI* listings, or at those few universities that do not participate in the listing, I have cited the studies as unpublished manuscripts.

2. All title citations have been made uniform despite the manner of citation in the actual article or monograph. Thus poems, short stories, and individual essays are cited with quotation marks; titles of novels, monographs, and long poems are italicized. By the same token, capitalization has been made uniform in all references, in accord with the dominant practice of Spanish. In general, the criterion for capitalization follows the rules of the Library of Congress, which explains the use of lower case with English-language titles also.

3. Sections of monographs dealing with specific authors have been listed separately only if the appropriate section is autonomous in title and content. Thus, as a general rule, sections of literary histories and other panoramic studies have not been listed separately.

CITY ABBREVIATIONS

Except for major United States and foreign cities, and unless otherwise indicated, all places of publication are in Puerto Rico.

BA	Buenos Aires
M	México, DF (Distrito Federal)
NY	New York
SJ	San Juan

KEY TO JOURNALS

ABC	American book collector. Arlington Heights, IL, 1950-.
AEA	Anuario de estudios americanos. Sevilla, 1944-.
Ahora!	Ahora! Santo Domingo, ?
AION-SR	Annali, Istituto Universitario, Napoli. Sezione Romanza. Napoli, 1959-.
ALA	American literary accents. Washington, DC, 1965-?
ALHisp	Anales de literatura hispanoamericana. Madrid, 1972-.
AM	The American Mercury. NY, 1924-.
Ambito	Ambito. SJ, 1937-?
Américas	Américas. Washington, DC, 1949-. Continues BUP, q.v.
The Americas	The Americas. Washington, DC, 1944-.
Anales	Anales, pro-Humaco. Humaco, ca. 1954.
Las antillas	Las antillas. La Habana, 1920-22?
Arbor	Arbor. Madrid, 1944-.
ASFM	Anuario de la Sociedad Folklórica de México. M, 1938/40-.
Asomante	Asomante. SJ, 1945-72. Continues RAGM, q.v.; continued by SinN, q.v.
Atenea	Atenea. Mayagüez, 1960-? n.s., 1964-.
AteneaC	Atenea. Concepción, Chile, 1924-.
Ateneo	Ateneo. Santo Domingo, 1910-13?
AtPR	Ateneo puertorriqueño. SJ, 1935-40.
Ausonia	Ausonia. Siena, 1946-.
AyL	Artes y letras. Río Piedras, 1957-.
AyLM	Armas y letras. Monterrey, Méx., 1944-.
BA	Books abroad. Norman, OK, 1927-76.
BAAC	Boletín de la Academia de Artes y Ciencias de Puerto Rico. SJ, 1965-.

BAGN	Boletín del Archivo General de la Nación. M, 1930-59, 1960-.
BANH	Boletín de la Academia Nacional de Historia. BA, 1924-.
BAPH	Boletín del Academia Puertorriqueña de la Historia. SJ, 1968-.
BAVC	Boletín de la Academia Venezolana Correspondiente de la Española. Caracas, 1934-.
BBIA	Boletín de la Biblioteca Ibero-americana de Bellas Artes. M, 1938-.
BH	Bulletin hispanique. Bordeaux, 1899-.
BHPR	Boletín histórico de Puerto Rico. SJ, 1914-27.
BHS	Bulletin of Hispanic studies. Liverpool, 1923-.
BIEA	Boletín del Instituto de Estudios Asturianos. Oviedo, 1947-.
BIS	Boletín del Instituto de Sociología. BA, 1942-.
Bohemia	Bohemia. La Habana, 1911-.
BR/RB	The bilingual review/La revista bilingüe. Jamaica, NY, etc., 1974-.
Brújula	Brújula. SJ, 1934-37.
BSBPR	Boletín de la Sociedad de Bibliotecarios de Puerto Rico. SJ, 1961-64.
BUP	Boletín de la Unión Panamericana. Washington, DC, 1911-48. Continued as Américas, q.v.
CA	Cuadernos americanos. M, 1942-.
Cam	Casa de las Américas. La Habana, 1960-.
Caravelle	Caravelle; cahiers du monde hispanique et luso-brésilien. Toulouse, 1966-.
Caribe	Caribe. Honolulu, 1976-?
CaribeSJ	Caribe. SJ, 1942-?
CarQ	Caribbean quarterly. Mona, Jamaica, 1949-.
Carteles	Carteles. La Habana, 1919-39.
CCLC	Cuadernos del Congreso por la Libertad de la Cultura. Paris, 1953-66.
CCont	Cuba contemporánea. La Habana, 1913-27.
Ceiba	Ceiba. Ponce, 1972/73-.
Centerpoint	Centerpoint. NY, 1974-.
Centro	Centro. NY, 1965-.
CHA	Cuadernos hispanoamericanos. Madrid, 1948-.
Chasqui	Chasqui. Madison, WI, etc., 1972-.
CLAJ	College Language Association journal. Baltimore, 1957-.
Claridad	Claridad. BA, 1926-41.
Clío	Clío. Santo Domingo, 1933-.
CLit	Cuadernos de literatura. Madrid, 1947-50.
CLP	Cuadernos literarios puertorriqueños. Santurce, 1965-.

Commonweal	Commonweal. NY, 1924-.
El cóndor	El cóndor. Caguas, 1976-.
Contémpora	Contémpora. BA, 1974-.
Crisis	Crisis. BA, 1973-76.
Culture	Culture. Québec, 1936-.
CuS	Cuadernos del sur. Bahía Blanca, Arg., 1964-70.
CyA	Cuba y América. NY, 1897-1912, 1913-17.
CyP	Comercio y producción. SJ, 1961-.
DA	Dissertation abstracts. Ann Arbor, MI, 1952-69. Continued as DAI, q.v.
DAI	Dissertation abstracts international. Ann Arbor, MI, 1969-. Continues DA, q.v.
DíaE	El día estético. SJ, 1941-. Continued as Insula, q.v.
EAf	Estudios afrocubanos. La Habana, 1937-.
EAm	Estudios americanos. Sevilla, 1948-.
Educación	Educación. SJ, 1951-.
Epoca	Epoca. Asunción, 1964-.
ESec	L'enseignement secondaire au Canada. Québec, 1916-.
EstLit	Estafeta literaria. Madrid, 1944-.
Estudios	Estudios. Pittsburgh, 1952-?
Europe	Europe. Paris, 1923-.
ExTL	Explicación de textos literarios. Sacramento, CA, 1972-.
La gotera	La gotera. SJ, 1969-.
Guajana	Guajana. Santurce, 1966-.
Hispamérica	Hispamérica. Takoma Park, MD, 1972-.
Hispania	Hispania. Baltimore, etc., 1919-.
Horizontes	Horizontes. SJ, 1939-.
Hostos	Hostos; revista de letras, arte, ciencia. SJ, 1928.
HR	Hispanic review. Philadelphia, 1933-.
Humanismo	Humanismo. M, 1952-60/61.
IA	Inter-América. NY, 1917-26.
IAA	Ibero Amerikanisches Archiv. Berlin, 1924-44, 1975-.
IAL	Idea; artes y letras. Lima, 1950-.
IAR	Ibero Amerikanische Rundschau. Hamburg, 1935-44.
Idearium	Idearium. SJ, 1917-18?
ILit	Isla literaria. SJ, 1969-. Continues Prensa, q.v.
IMex	Ideas de México. M, 1950-56?
Indice	Indice. SJ, 1929-31. Continues DíaE, q.v.
Insula	Insula. Madrid, 1946-.
InsulaP	Insula. Ponce, 1942-?

Inventario	Inventario. La Habana, 1948-.
InventarioF	Inventario. Firenze, 1946-.
Isla	Isla. SJ, 1939-40?
Islas	Islas. Santa Clara, Cuba, 1958-.
JAF	Journal of American folklore. Salt Lake City, 1888-.
JamJ	Jamaica journal. Kingston, Jamaica, 1967-.
JB	Juan Bobo. SJ, 1872-?
JDE	Journal of the Department of Education. SJ, 1938-?
JIAS	Journal of Inter-American studies. Coral Gables, FL, 1959-.
Kaie	Kaie. Georgetown, Guyana, 1965-.
KRQ	Kentucky Romance quarterly. Lexington, KY, 1967-.
LALR	Latin American literary review. Pittsburgh, 1972-?
Latino América	Latino América. M, 1968-.
LATR	Latin American theatre review. Lawrence, KN, 1967-.
LetrasM	Letras; publicación literaria. M, 1928-.
LitW	Literary world. Boston, 1870-1904.
Lotería	Lotería. Panamá, 1958-.
LPot	Letras potosinas. San Luis Potosí, Méx. 1943-.
Luminar	Luminar. M, 1936/37-51.
Lyceum	La Habana, 1939-.
LyP	El libro y el pueblo. M, 1922-.
Mairena	Revista Mairena. SJ, 1979-.
MAM	Memorias de la Academia Mexicana, M, 1876-91, 1905-.
MD	Modern drama. Toronto, 1958-.
MELUS	MELUS. Los Angeles, 1976-.
MHisp	Mundo hispánico. Madrid, 1948-.
MLN	MLN; modern language notes. Baltimore, 1886-.
ND	Nueva democracia. NY, 1920-63.
NNH	Nueva narrativa hispanoamericana. Garden City, NY, 1971-75.
Norte	Norte. Amsterdam, 1961-77?
Nosotros	Nosotros. BA, 1907-34, 1936-43.
Noverim	Noverim. La Habana, 1954-58.
NRP	Nueva revista del Pacífico. Valparaíso, Chile, 1976-?
Orfeo	Orfeo. Yauco, 1954-56.
Pafr	Présence africaine. Paris, 1947-.
PAm	Poesía de América. M, 1952-56.

PCL	Perspectives on contemporary literature. Louisville, KY, 1975-.
PCLS	Proceedings of the Comparative Literature Symposium. Lubbock, TX, 1970-.
Pedagogía	Pedagogía. Río Piedras, 1953-.
Pegaso	Pegaso. Santurce, 1952-.
Penélope	Penélope o el otro mundo. SJ?, 1973-.
PHisp	Poesía hispánica. Madrid, 1952-.
PLit	Prensa literaria. SJ, 1963-?
PLL	Papers on language and literature. Edwardsville, IL, 1965-.
Ploughshares	Ploughshares. Cambridge, MA, 1971-.
Plural	Plural. M, 1971-.
Prensa	Prensa. SJ, 1955-? Continued as ILit, q.v.
Prometeo	Prometeo. Río Piedras, 1962?-.
PRRM	Puerto Rico; revista mensual. NY ?, 1944-?
PSA	Papeles de Son Armadans. Madrid, 1956-79.
RABA	Revista americana de Buenos Aires. BA, 1924-?
RABN	Revista del Archivo y Biblioteca Nacional. Tegucigalpa, 1904-55.
RAm	Repertorio americano. San José, CR, 1919-59.
RAM	Revista de la Asociación de Maestros de Puerto Rico. SJ, 1942-.
RAMG	Revista de la Asociación de Mujeres Graduadas de la Universidad de Puerto Rico. Río Piedras, 1938-44. Continued as Asomante, q.v.
RAnt	Revista de las Antillas. SJ, 1913-14?
RBC	Revista bimestre cubana. La Habana, 1831-.
RBUS	Revista bimestral de la Universidad de El Salvador. San Salvador, 1890?-. Title varies.
RCAPR	Revista del Colegio de Abogados de Puerto Rico. SJ, 1935-. Title varies.
RChL	Revista chilena de literatura. Santiago, Chile, 1970-.
RCLA	Revista de ciencias, literatura y arte. Sevilla, 1855-60.
RCLL	Revista de crítica literaria latinoamericana. Lima, 1975-.
RC-R	Revista chicano-riqueña. Gary, IN, etc., 1973-.
RCS	Revista de ciencias sociales. Río Piedras, 1957-.
REduc	Revista de educación. Santo Domingo, 1910-.
REH-PR	Revista de estudios hispánicos. Río Piedras, 1928-30, 1971-.
Reintegro	Reintegro de las artes y la cultura. SJ, 1980-.
REP	Revista de estudios puertorriqueños. NY, 1971-.
RevF	Revista de filosofía. La Plata, Arg., 1950-.

RevFi	Revista de filosofía, cultura, ciencias, educación. BA, 1915-29.
RevH	Revista de humanidades. Córdoba, Arg., 1958-?
RevI	Revista/review interamericana. Hato Rey, 1971-.
Review	Review. NY, 1968-.
RevIn	Revista de Indias. Madrid, 1940-.
RevL	Revista de letras. Mayagüez, 1969-?
RevP	Revista de pedagogía. Madrid, 1920-.
RFE	Revista de filología española. Madrid, 1914-.
RFLC	Revista de la Facultad de Letras y Ciencias, Universidad de la Habana. La Habana, 1905-30.
RHI	Revista de la historia de las ideas. Quito, 1959-.
RHisp	Revue hispanique. NY, 1894-1933.
RHM	Revista hispánica moderna. NY, 1934-.
RHon	Repertorio de Honduras. Tegucigalpa, 1937-.
RI	Revista iberoamericana. M, etc., 1939-.
RIB	Revista interamericana de bibliografía/Inter-American review of bibliography. Washington, DC, 1951-.
RICP	Revista del Instituto de Cultura Puertorriqueña. SJ, 1958-.
Río Piedras	Río Piedras. Río Piedras, 1972-.
RIP	Revista de instrucción pública. La Habana, 1918-20, 1925-28?
RNC	Revista nacional de cultura. Caracas, 1938-.
Romanica	Romanica. La Plata, Arg., 1968-.
RomN	Romance notes. Chapel Hill, NC, 1959-.
RP	Revista puertorriqueña. SJ?, 1887-93.
RPIS	Revista puertorriquenña de investigaciones sociales. Hato Rey, 1976-.
RSant	Revista de Santiago. Santiago, Chile, 1872-73.
Rueca	Rueca. M, 1941-48.
RUM	Revista de la Universidad de México. M, 1959-.
RUMa	Revista de la Universidad de Madrid. Madrid, 1952-.
SAHL	Studies in Afro-Hispanic literature. Brooklyn, NY, 1977?-.
SinN	Sin nombre. Santurce, 1970-. Continues *Asomante*, q.v.
Symposium	Symposium. Syracuse, NY, 1946-.
TAH	The American hispanist. Clear Creek, IN, 1975-.
TC	Texto crítico. Xalapa, Méx., 1975-
ThA	Theatre arts. NY, 1916-.
Tiden	Tiden. Stockholm, 1909-.
La torre	La torre. Río Piedras, 1953-.

ULH	Universidad de la Habana. La Habana, 1934-.
Ultra	Ultra. La Habana, 1936-47.
Vórtice	Vórtice. Stanford, CA, 1974-.
La voz	La voz. NY, 1956?-? Title varies; also as La voz de Puerto Rico.
VUM	Vida universitaria. Monterrey, Méx., 1950-?
WLWE	World literature written in English. Arlington, TX, 1962-.
Zona	Zona de carga y descarga. SJ, 1973-.

About the Compiler

DAVID WILLIAM FOSTER is Professor of Spanish at Arizona State University in Tempe and is well known in his field for his research guide to Argentine literature and his valuable bibliographies on Chilean and Mexican literature. His critical bibliography on *Peruvian Literature* (Greenwood Press, 1981) has been cited as a significant contribution to the study of Latin American literature.

CRITICAL WORKS ON PUERTO RICAN LITERATURE: GENERAL REFERENCES

A
BIBLIOGRAPHIES

A.1 _Anuario bibliográfico puertorriqueño; índice alfabético de libros, folletos, revistas y periódicos publicados en Puerto Rico_. Río Piedras: Universidad de Puerto Rico, Biblioteca, 1950-. Imprint varies; also Departamento de Instrucción Pública.

A.2 Arana-Soto, Salvador. _Catálogo de poetas puertorriqueños_. SJ: Sociedad de Autores Puertorriqueños, 1968.

A.3 __________. __________. _Suplemento_. SJ, 1972.

A.4 "Bibliografía puertorriqueña." _RICP_, No. 1- (1958-), end of each issue.

A.5 "Bibliografía puertorriqueña." _La torre_, No. 1- (1953-).

A.6 Bravo, Enrique R. _An annotated, selected Puerto Rican bibliography_. NY: Columbia University Press, Urban Center, 1972. See Section IX. Literature.

A.7 _Catálogo por orden alfabético de autores y materias de las obras existentes en la biblioteca del Ateneo Puertorriqueño_. SJ: Ateneo Puertorriqueño, 1897.

A.8 _Catálogo por orden alfabético de autores y materias de las obras existentes en la biblioteca del Ilustre Colegio de Abogados de la isla de Puerto Rico_. SJ: González, 1882.

A.9 _Current Caribbean bibliography. Bibliografía actual del Caribe. Bibliographie courante de la Caribe_. Port-of-Spain, Trinidad: Caribbean Commission, 1951-71.

A.10 __________. __________. _Supplement_. Hato Rey, 1967-71.

A.11 Géigel Polanco, Vicente. "Bibliografía puertorriqueña (año 1945)." Asomante, 2, 1 (1946), 77-81.

A.12 Géigel y Zenón, José, and Abelardo Morales Ferrer. Bibliografía puertorriqueña, escrita en 1892-1894. Barcelona: Araluce, 1934.

A.13 González, Nilda. Bibliografía de teatro puertorriqueño (siglos XIX y XX). Río Piedras: Editorial Universitaria, Universidad de Puerto Rico, 1979.

A.14 __________. "Bibliografía mínima de teatro puertorriqueño." RICP, Nos. 76-77 (1977), 128-32.

A.15 González Padró, Pedro. Fuentes puertorriqueñas de referencia en el área de las humanidades. Río Piedras: Sociedad de Bibliotecarios de Puerto Rico, 1974.

A.16 Hill, Marnesba D., and Harold B. Schleiffer. Puerto Rican authors: a bibliographic handbook. Metuchen, NJ: Scarecrow Press, 1974.

A.17 Ledesma, Moisés. Bibliografía cultural de Puerto Rico (anotada). SJ: Plus Ultra, 1970.

A.18 Mohr, E. V. "Fifty years of Puerto Rican literature in English: 1923-1973: an annotated bibliography." RevI, 3 (1973), 290-98.

A.19 Pedreira, Antonio S. "La bibliografía puertorriqueña de Harvard." In his Aclaraciones y crítica (Río Piedras: Phi Eta Mu, Universidad de Puerto Rico, 1941), pp. 19-31. Also Río Piedras: Edil, 1969. Also in his Obras completas (SJ: Instituto de Cultura Puertorriqueña, 1970), I, 461-69. See item no. A.26.

A.20 __________. Bibliografía puertorriqueña (1493-1930). Madrid: Imprenta de la Librería y Casa Editorial Hernando, 1932. New ed., NY: B. Franklin Reprints, 1974.

A.21 Peraza, Fermín. Bibliotecas del Caribe. La Habana: Anuario Bibliográfico Cubano, 1939.

A.22 Perrier, Joseph Louis. Bibliografía dramática cubana, incluye a Puerto Rico y Santo Domingo. NY: The Phos Press, 1926.

A.23 Puerto Rico. NY: New York Public Library, 1963.

A.24 Quiles de la Luz, Lillian. "Breve historia de la colección puertorriqueña." BSBPR, 1, 3 (1962), 43-47.

A.25 __________. "Indice bibliográfico del cuento en la literatura puertorriqueña (1843-1963)." In her El cuento en la literatura puertorriqueña (SJ: Editorial Universitaria, Universidad de Puerto Rico, 1968), pp. 141-293.

A.26 Rivera, Guillermo. <u>A tentative bibliography of the belles-lettres of Porto Rico</u>. Cambridge, MA: Harvard University Press, 1931. See item no. A.19.

A.27 Rosa-Nieves, Cesáreo. <u>Indice bibliográfico para la poesía en Puerto Rico (1682-1942)</u>. M: Virginia, 1943.

A.28 Sáenz Estades, Mercedes. <u>Bibliografía anotada: revistas y periódicos de Puerto Rico en el siglo XIX</u>. Río Piedras, Sociedad de Bibliotecarios de Puerto Rico, 197?.

A.29 Sama, Manuel María. <u>Bibliografía puertorriqueña</u>. Mayagüez: Tipografía Comercial-Marina, 1887. Also Ann Arbor: University Microfilms International, 1980.

A.30 Sociedad de Bibliotecarios de Puerto Rico. <u>Guía de bibliotecas de Puerto Rico</u>; ed. rev. San Germán: Inter American University of Puerto Rico, 1975.

A.31 Toro, Josefina del. <u>A partial bibliography of Puerto Rican publications for 1938</u>. Washington, DC: Interamerican Books Exchange, 1940.

A.32 Trelles, C. M. <u>Ensayo de una bibliografía cubana de los siglos XVII y XVIII seguido de unos apuntes para la bibliografía dominicana y portorriqueña</u>. Matanzas, Cuba, 1907.

A.33 __________. __________. <u>Suplemento</u>. Matanzas, Cuba, 1907. 2. ed., 1927.

A.34 Vivó, Paquita. <u>The Puerto Ricans: an annotated bibliography</u>. Ann Arbor: Bowker, 1973.

A.35 Ward, James H. <u>Bibliografía de revistas puertorriqueñas, 1967-1968; una bibliografía de cuentos, poemas y ensayos en algunas revistas y periódicos puertorriqueños de 1967-1968 disponibles en la Sala de Autores Puertorriqueños</u>. College Station, TX: Texas A&M University, Department of Modern Languages, 1969.

A.36 Zubatsky, David S. "Annotated bibliography of Latin American author bibliographies. Part II: Central America and the Caribbean." <u>Chasqui</u>, 6, 2 (1977), 41-72.

B
GENERAL HISTORIES

B.1 Ayala Duarte, Crispín. "Historia de la literatura en Puerto Rico." BAVC, 1, 4 (1934), 310-44; 3, 12 (1936), 403-26.

B.2 Babín, María Teresa. La cultura de Puerto Rico. SJ: Instituto de Cultura Puertorriqueña, 1970. Also as The Puerto Ricans' spirit: their history, life, and culture. NY: Macmillan, 1971.

B.3 __________. Panorama de la cultura puertorriqueña. NY: Las Américas, 1958.

B.4 Belaval, Emilio S. Los problemas de la cultura puertorriqueña. Río Piedras: Cultural, 1977.

B.5 Crescioni Neggers, Gladys. Breve introducción a la cultura puertorriqueña. Madrid: Playor, 1978.

B.6 Fernández Méndez, Eugenio. Historia de la cultura en Puerto Rico (1493-1960). SJ: Rodadero, 1964. Also SJ: "El Cemi", 1970. 3. ed., 1970.

B.7 Fort, Gustavo. "La cuestión de escuelas literarias...y otras cuestiones." RAnt, 1, 3 (1913), 43-48.

B.8 González, José Luis. Literatura y sociedad en Puerto Rico; de los cronistas de Indias a la generación del 98. M: Fondo de Cultura Económica, 1976. Orig. as Proceso de la literatura puertorriqueña, de los cronistas de Indias a la generación del 98. Unpublished thesis, Universidad Nacional Autónoma de México, 1959.

B.9 __________. "La primera historia de la literatura puertorriqueña." Asomante, 13, 3 (1957), 37-47.

B.10 Grismer, Raymond Leonard, and César Arroyo. Vida y obras de autores puertorriqueños. La Habana: "Alfa", 1941-.

Also Ann Arbor: University Microfilms, 1976. Also 1978. Only vol. I ever published.

B.11 Guerra Mondragón, Miguel. "San Juan de Puerto Rico, su movimiento literario." RAnt, 2, 4 (1914), 80-85.

B.12 Henríquez Ureña, Max. "Unidad de las letras antillanas." Noverim, 2, 8 (1958), 17-54.

B.13 Henríquez Ureña, Pedro. "Puerto Rico." In Giacomo Pampolini, Historia universal de la literatura (BA: Uthea, 1941-42), XII, 86-95. 2. ed., 1955-58.

B.14 Herdeck, Donald E. Caribbean writers; a bio-bibliographical-critical encyclopedia. Washington, DC: Three Continents Press, 1979. See in particular v. 4, "Spanish language and literature from the Caribbean."

B.15 Laguerre, Enrique A. "La identidad cultural puertorriqueña." In his Polos en la cultura iberoamericana (Boston: Florentia, 1977), pp. 49-56.

B.16 López, Adalberto. "Puerto Ricans and the literature of Puerto Rico." JEthS, 1, 2 (1973), 56-65.

B.17 Maldonado-Denis, Manuel. "'El puente entre dos culturas', o el asedio de la cultura puertorriqueña." In his Puerto Rico; una interpretación histórico-social (M: Siglo XXI, 1977), pp. 199-219. Various other eds. Also Caracas: Universidad Central de Venezuela, Facultad de Ciencias Económicas y Sociales, División de Publicaciones, 1975.

B.18 Manrique Cabrera, Francisco. Apuntes para la historia literaria de Puerto Rico. SJ: Ediciones del Departamento de Instrucción Pública, 1957. Also SJ: Instituto de Cultura Puertorriqueña, 1969. Also 1972.

B.19 __________. Historia de la literatura puertorriqueña. NY: Las Américas, 1956. Also 1957. 2. ed., SJ: Cultural Puerto Rico, 1964. Also Río Piedras: Cultura, 1969. Also 1971, 1973, and 1977.

B.20 Martínez, Luis. "[Josefina Rivera de Alvarez, Historia de la literatura puertorriqueña]." Horizontes, No. 26 (1971), 79-83. See item no. B.30.

B.21 Martínez Plée, Manuel. "Literatura puertorriqueña contemporánea." In Libro de Puerto Rico (SJ: El Libro Azul, 1923), pp. 768-75. Also NY: Gordon Press, 1977. English on facing pages: "Porto Rico's present literature."

B.22 Medina, Ramón Felipe, and Juan Marey. "Chronologie littéraire et historique." Europe, Nos. 592-93 (1978), 175-84.

B.23 Meléndez, Concha. "Panorama de la cultura puertorriqueña." In her Personas y libros (SJ: Cordillera, 1970), pp. 71-83. Also in her <u>Obras completas</u> (SJ: Instituto de Cultura Puertorriqueña, 1970-72), IV, 293-305.

B.24 ________. "Sobre las historias de la literatura." In her <u>Personas y libros</u> (SJ: Cordillera, 1970), pp. 65-70. Also in her <u>Obras completas</u> (SJ: Instituto de Cultura Puertorriqueña, 1970-72), IV, 287-92.

B.25 Méndez, José Luis, and Sheila Yvonne Carter. "Problems in the creation of culture in the Caribbean." <u>CarQ</u>, 21, 1-2 (1975), 7-19.

B.26 Miller, Paul G. "Ciencias, artes y literatura." In his <u>Historia de Puerto Rico</u> (NY: Rand McNally, 1922), Ch. XXVI.

B.27 Olivera, Otto. <u>Breve historia de la literatura antillana</u>. M: de Andrea, 1957.

B.28 <u>Problemas de la cultura en Puerto Rico: foro del Ateneo Puertorriqueño, 1940</u>. Río Piedras: Editorial Universitaria, Universidad de Puerto Rico, 1976.

B.29 Rivera de Alvarez, Josefina. <u>Diccionario de literatura puertorriqueña</u>. Río Piedras: Ediciones de la Torre, Universidad de Puerto Rico, 1955. 2. ed., rev. y aum. y puesta al día hasta 1967, SJ: Instituto de Cultura Puertorriqueña, 1970-74.

B.30 ________. <u>Historia de la literatura puertorriqueña</u>. SJ: Departamento de Instrucción Pública, 1969. See item no. B.20.

B.31 ________. "Resumen panorámico de la historia literaria puertorriqueña." <u>La torre</u>, No. 9 (1955), 37-81.

B.32 ________. <u>Visión histórico-crítica de la literatura puertorriqueña: orígenes, siglos XVI, XVII, XVIII y XIX</u>. SJ: Instituto de Cultura Puertorriqueña, 1958. Also in <u>Literatura puertorriqueña; 21 conferencias</u> (SJ: Instituto de Cultura Puertorriqueña, 1960), pp. 33-64.

B.33 Rosa-Nieves, Cesáreo. "Algunas características de la literatura puertorriqueña." In his <u>La lámpara del faro: variaciones críticas sobre temas puertorriqueños; ensayos</u> (SJ: Club de la Prensa, 1957-60), II, 9-37. Vol. II carries the title <u>La lámpara del faro (ensayos para una interpretación de algunos hitos culturales del fluir puertorriqueño)</u>.

B.34 ________. <u>Historia panorámica de la literatura puertorriqueña (1589-1959)</u>. SJ: Campos, 1963.

B.35 ________. <u>Plumas estelares en las letras de Puerto Rico</u>. SJ: Ediciones de la Torre, Universidad de Puerto Rico, 1967-71. Vol. II notes as publisher Editorial Universitaria, Universidad de Puerto Rico.

B.36 __________, and Esther Melón. Biografías puertorriqueñas. Perfil histórico de un pueblo. Sharon, CT: Troutman Press, 1970.

B.37 Silva, Ana Margarita. Reseña de historia cultural y literaria de Puerto Rico. BA: W. M. Jackson, 1945.

B.38 Soto Ramos, Julio. Bocetos biográficos puertorriqueños. Barcelona: M. Parejal, 1973.

B.39 __________. "Diccionario de literatura puertorriqueña." In his Una pica en Flandes... (SJ: Club de la Prensa, 1959), pp. 19-50. See item no. B.29.

B.40 __________. Panorama literario y periodístico de Puerto Rico. Santurce: Soletero, 1955.

B.41 Vientós Gastón, Nilita. "El diccionario de literatura puertorriqueña." In her Indice cultural (Río Piedras: Ediciones de la Universidad de Puerto Rico, 1962-71), I, 219-21. See item no. B.29.

C
COLLECTED ESSAYS

C.1 Arce de Vázquez, Margot. _Impresiones; notas puertorriqueñas (ensayos)_. SJ: Yaurel, 1950.

C.2 Babín, María Teresa. _Jornadas literarias (temas de Puerto Rico)_. Barcelona: Rvmbos, 1967.

C.3 Balseiro, José A. _El vigía; ensayos_. Madrid: Mundo Latino, 1925-45. 2. ed., SJ: Biblioteca de Autores Puertorriqueños, 1956.

C.4 Braschi, Wilfredo. _Perfiles puertorriqueños_. SJ: Biblioteca de Autores Puertorriqueños, 1978.

C.5 Castro, Tomás de Jesús. _Esbozos críticos_. SJ: Baldrich, 1945-. Also Barcelona: Rumbos, 1957.

C.6 ________. _Vistos de cerca; reportajes_. SJ: Club de la Prensa, 1962.

C.7 Colberg Petrovich, Juan Enrique. _Cuatro autores clásicos contemporáneos de Puerto Rico_. SJ: Cordillera, 1966.

C.8 Coll y Toste, Cayetano. _Puertorriqueños ilustres; primera selección_. NY: Las Américas, 1952. _Segunda selección_, Barcelona: Rumbos, 1963; also 1966.

C.9 Cuchí Coll, Isabel. _Oro nativo; colección de semblanzas puertorriqueñas contemporáneas_. SJ, 1936.

C.10 Dalmau Canet, Sebastián. _Crepúsculos literarios_. SJ: Boletín Mercantil, 1903.

C.11 Diez de Andino, Juan. _Desmenuzando hechos_. Barcelona: Rvmbos, 1957.

C.12 Ferrer Canales, José. _Acentos cívicos: Martí, Puerto Rico y otros temas_. Río Piedras: Edil, 1972.

C.13 ________. Marginalia. SJ?: Venezuela?, 1939.

C.14 Fonfrías, Ernesto Juan. Sementera; ensayos breves y biografías mínimas. SJ: Club de la Prensa, 1962.

C.15 Franco Oppenheimer, Félix. Contornos; ensayos. SJ: Yaurel, 1960.

C.16 Géigel Polanco, Vicente. Valores de Puerto Rico. NY: Arno Press, 1975. Orig. SJ: Eugenio María de Hostos, 1943.

C.17 Gómez Costa, Arturo. Vendimias en prosa. Barcelona: Vosgos, 1976.

C.18 González, José Luis. El país de cuatro pisos y otros ensayos. Río Piedras: Huracán, 1980.

C.19 Guevara Castañeira, Josefina. Del Yunque a los Andes. SJ: Club de la Prensa, 1959.

C.20 Laguerre, Enrique A. Polos en la cultura iberoamericana. Boston: Florentia, 1977.

C.21 ________. Pulso de Puerto Rico, 1952-1954. SJ: Biblioteca de Autores Puertorriqueños, 1956.

C.22 Lefebre, Enrique. Paisajes mentales; estudios críticos, bocetos y perfiles, impresiones de arte, personalidades políticos, necrologías. SJ: Cantero, Fernández, 1918.

C.23 Literatura puertorriqueña; 21 conferencias. SJ: Instituto de Cultura Puertorriqueña, 1960.

C.24 Lloréns, Washington. Críticas profanas. SJ: Progreso, 1936.

C.25 Lluch Mora, Francisco. Miradero; ensayos de crítica literaria. SJ: Cordillera, 1966.

C.26 López, Julio César. Temas y estilos en ocho escritores. SJ, 1967.

C.27 Machuca, Julio. Ensayos. SJ: Venezuela, 1943.

C.28 Malaret, Augusto. Medallas de oro; 2. ed. SJ: Biblioteca de Autores Puertorriqueños, 1938. Orig. 1928. 3. ed., SJ: Cantero Fernández, 1942; 4. ed., M: Orión, 1952.

C.29 Marqués, René. Ensayos (1953-1966). Barcelona: Antillana, 1966. 2. ed. rev. y aum. as Ensayos (1953-1971). Río Piedras: Antillana, 1972. Also Barcelona: Antillana, 1972. Also as The docile Puerto Rican; essays. Philadelphia: Temple University Press, 1976.

C.30 Martín, José Luis. Arco y flecha, apuntando a la vida y a las obras; estudios de crítica literaria. SJ: Club de la Prensa, 1961.

C.31 Matos Bernier, Félix. Isla de arte. SJ: La Primavera, 1907.

C.32 Meléndez, Concha. Asomante; estudios hispanoamericanos. SJ: Universidad de Puerto Rico, 1943. Also SJ: Cordillera, 1970. Also in her Obras completas (SJ: Instituto de Cultura Puertorriqueña, 1970-72), II, 7-174.

C.33 ________. Figuración de Puerto Rico y otros temas. SJ: Instituto de Cultura Puertorriqueña, 1958. Also in her Obras completas (SJ: Instituto de Cultura Puertorriqueña, 1970-72), II, 317-538.

C.34 ________. Obras completas. SJ: Instituto de Cultura Puertorriqueña, 1970-72.

C.35 ________. Palabras para oyentes. SJ: Cordillera, 1971. Also in her Obras completas (SJ: Instituto de Cultura Puertorriqueña, 1970-72), III, 439-637.

C.36 ________. Personas y libros. SJ: Cordillera, 1970. Also in her Obras completas (SJ: Instituto de Cultura Puertorriqueña, 1970-72), IV, 225-430.

C.37 Nolasco, Sócrates. Escritores de Puerto Rico. Manzanillo, Cuba: El Arte, 1953.

C.38 Pagán, Bolívar. América y otras páginas. SJ, 1922.

C.39 Pedreira, Antonio S. Aclaraciones y crítica. Río Piedras: Phi Eta Mu, Universidad de Puerto Rico, 1941. Also Río Piedras: Edil, 1969. Also in his Obras completas (SJ: Instituto de Cultura Puertorriqueña, 1970), I.

C.40 ________. Aristas; ensayos. Río Piedras: Edil, 1969.

C.41 ________. Tres ensayos. Río Piedras: Edil, 1969.

C.42 Porras Cruz, Jorge L. Estudios y artículos. Río Piedras?: Editorial Universitaria, Universidad de Puerto Rico, 1974.

C.43 Quiñones, Samuel R. Temas y letras; 3. ed. SJ: Biblioteca de Autores Puertorriqueños, 1955. Orig. 1941.

C.44 Rodríguez Escudero, Néstor A. Ensayos escogidos (sobre autores de Europa y América). Barcelona: Rvmbos, 1960-.

C.45 ________. El mar en la literatura puertorriqueña y otros ensayos. Barcelona: Rumbos, 1967.

C.46 Rosa-Nieves, Cesáreo. Ensayos escogidos (apuntaciones de crítica literaria sobre algunos temas puertorriqueños). SJ: Academia de Artes y Ciencias de Puerto Rico, 1970?

C.47 ________. *La lámpara del faro; variaciones críticas sobre temas puertorriqueños; ensayos.* SJ: Club de la Prensa, 1957-60. Vol. II carries title *La lámpara del faro (ensayos para una interpretación de algunos hitos culturales del fluir puertorriqueño)*.

C.48 Soto Ramos, Julio. *Cumbre y remanso; ensayos de apreciación literaria y otros artículos.* SJ: Cordillera, 1963.

C.49 ________. *Una pica en Flandes; ensayos y otros artículos.* SJ: Club de la Prensa, 1959.

C.50 ________. *Yo soy yo y mi verdad; ensayos de apreciación literaria y otros artículos.* SJ: Cordillera, 1973.

C.51 Torres León, Armando. *Ensayos literarios.* Río Piedras: Editorial Universitaria, Universidad de Puerto Rico, 1977.

D

LITERARY CRITICISM, REVIEWS, AND JOURNALS

D.1 Alegría, Ricardo E. El Instituto de Cultura Puertorriqueña. Los primeros cinco años, 1955-1960. SJ: Instituto de Cultura Puertorriqueña, 1960.

D.2 ________. El Instituto de Cultura Puertorriqueña, 1955-1973. SJ: Instituto de Cultura Puertorriqueña, 1978.

D.3 "El Ateneo Puertorriqueño." RICP, No. 73 (1976), entire issue.

D.4 Azize, Yamila. "Dos revistas literarias de la década del treinta: la Revista bimestre cubana y la revista Ateneo puertorriqueño." DAI, 41 (1981), 4410A.

D.5 Babín, María Teresa. "Asomante en la cultura puertorriqueña (1945-1965)." In her Jornadas literarias (temas de Puerto Rico) (Barcelona: Rvmbos, 1967), pp. 334-51. Orig. Asomante, 21, 3 (1965), 7-18.

D.6 ________. "La crítica literaria." In her Jornadas literarias (temas de Puerto Rico) (Barcelona: Rvmbos, 1967), pp. 5-35. Also in Literatura puertorriqueña; 21 conferencias (SJ: Instituto de Cultura Puertorriqueña, 1960), pp. 553-80.

D.7 Canino Salgado, Marcelino J. "Guajana; la revolución de los poetas." Guajana, 3a época, No. 8 (1973), pagination unknown.

D.8 ________. "Notas sobre la crítica literaria en Puerto Rico." La torre, Nos. 79-80 (1973), 43-86.

D.9 Dávila, José Antonio. "La crítica como orientadora de nuestra cultura." AtPR, 4 (1940), 253-68. Also in Problemas de la cultura en Puerto Rico: foro del Ateneo Puertorriqueño, 1940 (Río Piedras: Editorial Universitaria, Universidad de Puerto Rico, 1976), pp. 160-68. Also in his Prosa:

ensayos, artículos y cartas literarias (SJ: Sociedad de Autores Puertorriqueños, 1971), pp. 53-64.

D.10 __________. "La hogaza del Ateneo." In his Prosa: ensayos, artículos y cartas literarias (SJ: Sociedad de Autores Puertorriqueños, 1971), pp. 205-207.

D.11 __________. "El premio de literatura." In his Prosa: ensayos, artículos y cartas literarias (SJ: Sociedad de Autores Puertorriqueños, 1971), pp. 135-39.

D.12 __________. "La Revista del Ateneo (julio-agosto-septiembre de 1939)." In his Prosa: ensayos, artículos y cartas literarias (SJ: Sociedad de Autores Puertorriqueños, 1971), pp. 141-44.

D.13 Davis, Lisa E. "Revista de las Antillas: el modernismo como resistencia cultural en Puerto Rico." CAm, No. 105 (1977), 54-59. Also in Actas del Simposio Internacional de Estudios Hispánicos (Budapest: Akademeia Kiadó, 1978), pp. 133-40.

D.14 Díaz de Fortier, Matilde. La crítica literaria en Puerto Rico: 1843-1915. SJ: Instituto de Cultura Puertorriqueña, 1980.

D.15 Diez de Andino, Juan. "El Certamen Poético de Ponce." In his Desmenuzando hechos (Barcelona: Rvmbos, 1957), pp. 141-44.

D.16 __________. "El libro de mérito." In his Desmenuzando hechos (Barcelona: Rvmbos, 1957), pp. 287-90. See item no. B.29.

D.17 __________. "Los poetas, las antologías y la Academia." In his Desmenuzando hechos (Barcelona: Rvmbos, 1957), pp. 243-46.

D.18 __________. "¡Ya tenemos Academia!" In his Desmenuzando hechos (Barcelona: Rvmbos, 1957), pp. 194-97.

D.19 Flórez Mejía, Luis. "Asomante." Mito, 15 (1957), 193-94.

D.20 Fonfrías, Ernesto Juan. El Instituto de Lexicografía Hispanoamericana "Augusto Malaret" y la Academia Puertorriqueña de la Lengua. Ensayos. SJ: Instituto de Lexicografía Hispanoamericana "Augusto Malaret", 1976.

D.21 Géigel Polanco, Vicente. "Prólogo." In Indice; mensuario de historia, literatura y ciencia; edición facsimilar (SJ: Editorial Universitaria, 1979), no pagination.

D.22 Gómez Costa, Arturo. "El Ateneo en el trienio." BAAC, 12, 3 (1976), 21-26.

D.23 González, José Emilio. "Los índices de Indice: revista puertorriqueña de los años treinta." SinN, 11, 2 (1980), 17-35.

D.24 "El Instituto de Cultura Puertorriqueña. Décimo Aniversario de su fundación, 1955-1965." RICP, No. 30 (1966), 19-28.

D.25 Laguerre, Enrique A. "Algunas ideas sobre la crítica." In his Pulso de Puerto Rico, 1952-1954 (SJ: Biblioteca de Autores Puertorriqueños, 1956), pp. 235-42.

D.26 __________. "Crítica y teatro en Puerto Rico: una propuesta para su revitalización." RICP, No. 59 (1973), 9-14.

D.27 Martín, José Luis. "Apuntes para una hemeroteca puertorriqueña: nuestras últimas revistas." In his Arco y flecha... (SJ: Club de la Prensa, 1961), pp. 167-74.

D.28 Martínez Capó, Juan. "Las pequeñas revistas literarias (panorama: 1930-1954)." Asomante, 11, 1 (1955), 102-23.

D.29 Medina, Ramón Felipe. "Guajana: diez años de compromiso y poesía." Guajana, 3a época, No. 8 (1973), pagination unknown.

D.30 Meléndez Muñoz, Miguel. "El Ateneo y el pueblo puertorriqueño." In his Obras completas (SJ: Instituto de Cultura Puertorriqueña, 1963), pp. 62-64.

D.31 __________. Un profano en el Ateneo Puertorriqueño. SJ: Campos, 1963.

D.32 "El XC [noveno] aniversario del Ateneo Puertorriqueño." RICP, No. 33 (1966), 25-49.

D.33 Olivera, Otto. "La literatura en La gaceta de Puerto Rico." RIB, 21 (1971), 403-18.

D.34 Rodríguez Vecchini, Hugo O. Desglose de Revista de las Antillas. Unpublished Master's thesis, Universidad de Puerto Rico, 1972.

D.35 Rosa-Nieves, Cesáreo. "La alabanza, la diatriba y la guachafita isleña: reflexiones sobre la crítica de Puerto Rico." In his La lámpara del faro... (SJ: Club de la Prensa, 1957-60), II, 77-83.

D.36 Sáenz Estades, Mercedes. Bibliografía anotada: revistas y periódicos de Puerto Rico en el siglo XIX. Río Piedras: Sociedad de Bibliotecarios de Puerto Rico, 197?

D.37 Vientós Gastón, Nilita. "El Ateneo Puertorriqueño (1876-1961)." In her Indice cultural (Río Piedras: Ediciones de la Universidad de Puerto Rico, 1962-71), IV, 63-65.

D.38 __________. "Biografía de una revista: Asomante-Sin nombre." Plural, No. 99 (1979), 37-41.

D.39 __________. "El Club del Libro de Puerto Rico." In her Indice cultural (Río Piedras: Ediciones de la Universidad de Puerto Rico, 1962-71), III, 37-38.

D.40 __________. "Diez años de Asomante." Asomante, 11, 1 (1955), 5-6.

D.41 __________. "El Instituto de Cultura Puertorriqueña (1955-1960)." In her Indice cultural (Río Piedras: Ediciones de la Universidad de Puerto Rico, 1962-71), III, 155-56.

D.42 __________. "El Instituto de Literatura Puertorriqueña." In her Indice cultural (Río Piedras: Ediciones de la Universidad de Puerto Rico, 1962-71), I, 261-66.

E

LITERATURE AND OTHER SUBJECTS

E.1 Acosta Belén, Edna. "Literature and ideology in the works of the Puerto Rican generation of 1950." DAI, 38 (1977), 6151A.

E.2 Cortina Gómez, Rodolfo. "Race and identity in Puerto Rican literature." In Minority literature and the urban experience (La Crosse, WI: University of Wisconsin-La Crosse, Institute for Minority Studies, 1975), pp. 71-73.

E.3 Cruz Monclova, Lidio. "El libro y nuestra cultura literaria." RICP, No. 42 (1969), 47-49. Also Río Piedras: Sociedad de Bibliotecarios de Puerto Rico, 197?

E.4 González, José Luis. "Literatura e identidad nacional en Puerto Rico." In his El país de cuatro pisos y otros ensayos (Río Piedras: Huracán, 1980), pp. 45-90. Also in Angel G. Quintero Rivera et al., Puerto Rico: identidad nacional y clases sociales (Coloquio de Princeton) (Río Piedras: Huracán, 1979), pp. 45-79.

E.5 Laguerre, Enrique A. "Levadura de la historia en la narrativa puertorriqueña." In his Polos en la cultura iberoamericana (Boston: Florentia, 1977), pp. 57-64.

E.6 Maldonado-Denis, Manuel. "Política y cultura puertorriqueña." RCS, 7, 1-2 (1963), 141-48.

E.7 Marqués, René. "Pesimismo literario y optimismo político: su coexistencia en el Puerto Rico actual." CA, No. 104 (1959), 43-74. Also in his Ensayos (1953-1966) (SJ: Antillana, 1966), pp. 43-80. Also in his Ensayos (1953-1971); 2. ed. rev. y aum. (Río Piedras: Antillana, 1972), pp. 45-83. Also in his Antología del pensamiento puertorriqueño (1900-1970) (Río Piedras?: Editorial Universitaria, Universidad de Puerto Rico, 1975), pp. 951-79. Also as "Literary pessimism and political optimism: their coexistence in contemporary Puerto Rico." In his The docile Puerto Rican; essays (Philadelphia: Temple University Press, 1976), pp. 3-26.

E.8 Méndez, José Luis. "La estructura social y la literatura puertorriqueña." CAm, No. 115 (1979), 38-45.

E.9 __________. "La literatura proletaria y el proletariado como tema en la literatura puertorriqueña." Vórtice, 2, 2-3 (1979), 182-95.

E.10 Silén, Juan Angel. "La literatura de la docilidad." In his Hacia una visión positiva del puertorriqueño; 4. ed. (Río Piedras: Antillana, 1976), pp. 49-64. Orig. 1970. Also as "The literature of docility." In his We, the Puerto Rican people (NY: Monthly Review Press, 1971), pp. 36-45.

F

RELATIONS WITH FOREIGN LITERATURES

F.1 Babín, María Teresa. "Presencia de Ortega y Gasset en Puerto Rico." *Asomante*, 12, 4 (1956), 83-94. Also in her *Jornadas literarias (temas de Puerto Rico)* (Barcelona: Rvmbos, 1967), pp. 270-87.

F.2 Balseiro, José A. "Letras de México y de Puerto Rico." In his *Expresión de Hispanoamérica; segunda serie* (SJ: Instituto de Cultura Puertorriqueña, 1963), pp. 141-54. 2. ed., 1970; pp. 148-62.

F.3 Cruz Monclova, Lidio. "Edgar Allan Poe y Puerto Rico." *Asomante*, 14, 4 (1958), 64-69. Also *RICP*, No. 45 (1969), 1-2.

F.4 Ferrer Canales, José. "Martí y Puerto Rico." In his *Acentos cívicos; Martí, Puerto Rico y otros temas* (Río Piedras: Edil, 1972), pp. 11-51.

F.5 Hernández Aquino, Luis. "Rubén Darío en Puerto Rico." *RICP*, No. 9 (1960), 1-4.

F.6 Méndez, José Luis. "Sartre y la literatura puertorriqueña." *SinN*, 11, 4 (1981), 68-84.

F.7 Perea, Juan Augusto, and Salvador Perea. "Horacio en Puerto Rico (historia de las reminiscencias horacianas en la lírica puertorriqueña)." *Indice*, No. 17 (1930), 317-20; No. 24 (1931), 392-94; No. 27 (1931), 23-25.

F.8 Rodríguez Velázquez, Jaime Luis. "Rubén Darío y el modernismo en Puerto Rico." *Asomante*, 23, 1 (1967), 64-70.

F.9 Rosa-Nieves, Cesáreo. "Cervantes en Puerto Rico." In his *La lámpara del faro...* (SJ: Club de la Prensa, 1957-60), I, 175-82.

F.10 __________. "José Santos Chocano." *RICP*, No. 12 (1961), 4-6.

F.11 __________. "Rubén Darío visitó a San Juan de Puerto Rico." BAAC, 4 (1968), 227-30.

G
WOMEN AUTHORS

G.1 Angelis, María Luisa de. Mujeres puertorriqueñas que se han distinguido en el cultivo de las ciencias, las letras y las artes desde el siglo XVII hasta nuestros días. SJ?: Boletín Mercantil, 1908.

G.2 Coll, Edna. "La mujer puertorriqueña en el quehacer literario." In Instituto Internacional de Literatura Iberoamericana, El ensayo y la crítica literaria en Iberoamérica (Toronto: Universidad de Toronto, 1970), pp. 75-79.

G.3 Cypess, Sandra Messinger. "Women dramatists of Puerto Rico." RevI, 9, 1 (1979), 24-41.

G.4 López-Jiménez, Ivette. "Escritoras puertorriqueñas del '70: nuevos caminos." DAI, 39 (1978), 2311A.

G.5 __________. "Poetisas puertorriqueñas del 70: nuevos caminos." Mairena, No. 5 (1980), 19-24.

G.6 Negrón Muñoz, Angela. Mujeres de Puerto Rico. SJ: Venezuela, 1935.

G.7 Pérez-Marchand, Monelisa Lina. "Poetisas puertorriqueñas." Rueca, No. 14 (1945), 30-50.

G.8 Quiñones, Samuel R. "Don Juan y el verso de una mujer." In his Temas y letras; 3. ed. (SJ: Biblioteca de Autores Puertorriqueños, 1955), pp. 125-31.

G.9 Russell, Dora Isella. "Mujeres ilustres de Puerto Rico." In her Había una vez una isla... (Río Piedras: Universidad de Puerto Rico, 1968), pp. 93-101.

G.10 Santana Maíz, Monserrate. La mujer en la literatura puertorriqueña. Unpublished thesis, Universidad de Puerto Rico, 1932.

H
SPECIAL LITERARY TOPICS

H.1 Alegría, Ricardo E. "Introducción." In his *El tema del café en la literatura puertorriqueña* (SJ: Instituto de Cultura Puertorriqueña, 1965), pp. 9-13. Orig. as "El tema del café en la literatura puertorriqueña." *RICP*, No. 27 (1965), 8-12.

H.2 Arana-Soto, Salvador. *Los médicos y la medicina en la literatura puertorriqueña*. SJ, 1969.

H.3 Babín, María Teresa. "Amor y dolor de vivir en la literatura de Puerto Rico." *RICP*, No. 9 (1960), 21-26; No. 10 (1961), 5-9. Also in her *Jornadas literarias (temas de Puerto Rico)* (Barcelona: Rvmbos, 1967), pp. 54-84.

H.4 __________. "Aristas de la esclavitud negra en la literatura de Puerto Rico." *SinN*, 4, 2 (1973), 57-65.

H.5 __________. "The 'jíbaro': symbol and synthesis." *PCLS*, 9 (1978), 433-54.

H.6 __________. "Símbolos de Borinquen." *RICP*, No. 4 (1959), 1-3.

H.7 __________. "El tema de Puerto Rico en la literatura del presente." In *Antología del pensamiento puertorriqueño (1900-1970)* (Río Piedras?: Editorial Universitaria, Universidad de Puerto Rico, 1975), pp. 938-50.

H.8 Baglin, Roger F. "The mainland experience in selected Puerto Rican literary works." *DAI*, 32 (1971), 3290A.

H.9 Canino Salgado, Marcelino J. *El cantar folklórico de Puerto Rico (estudio y florilegio)*. SJ: Editorial Universitaria, Universidad de Puerto Rico, 1975. Orig. 1974.

H.10 Cebollero, Pedro Angel. "El cantar puertorriqueño." *RAnt*, 2, 5 (1914), 141-43.

H.11 Coleman, Ben C. "The teaching of Afro-Hispanic expressions in Puerto Rican literature." RC-R, 2, 4 (1974), 35-45.

H.12 Dueño, Patricia. La sátira en la literatura puertorriqueña hasta Nemesio R. Canales. Unpublished thesis, Universidad de Puerto Rico, 1952.

H.13 Feliciano de Mendoza, Ester. Literatura infantil puertorriqueña. SJ: Instituto de Cultura Puertorriqueña, 1960. Also 1972. Also in Literatura puertorriqueña; 21 conferencias (SJ: Instituto de Cultura Puertorriqueña, 1960), pp. 429-58.

H.14 Fernández Méndez, Eugenio. "Introducción: unidad y esencia del ethos puertorriqueño." In Antología del pensamiento puertorriqueño (1900-1970) (Río Piedras?: Editorial Universitaria, Universidad de Puerto Rico, 1975), pp. ix-xvi.

H.15 Fisher, Myrtha Chabran. "Puertoricanska författare och puertoicansk politik." Tiden, 56 (1964), 538-43.

H.16 Fonfrías, Ernesto Juan Manuel. Presencia jíbara desde Manuel Alonso hasta don Florito. SJ: Club de la Prensa, 1957.

H.17 Freire de Matos, Isabel. "Mon expérience de la littérature portoricaine." Europe, Nos. 607-608 (1979), 86-94.

H.18 Homor, Susana. "Inferioridad y cambio: los personajes femeninos en la literatura puertorriqueña." RCS, 20-34 (1978), 289-304.

H.19 Laguerre, Enrique A., and Esther M. Melón. "Introducción." In their El jíbaro de Puerto Rico: símbolo y figura (Sharon, CT: Troutman Press, 1968), pp. ix-xviii.

H.20 Lloréns, Washington. El humorismo, el epigrama y la sátira en la literatura puertorriqueña. SJ: Instituto de Cultura Puertorriqueña, 1960. Also 1972. Also in Literatura puertorriqueña; 21 conferencias (SJ: Instituto de Cultura Puertorriqueña, 1960), pp. 459-512.

H.21 López Morales, Humberto. "Indigenismos en los textos cronísticos de Puerto Rico: índices de frecuencia y densidad." In Homenaje a Angel Rosenblat en sus 70 años: estudios filológicos y lingüísticos (Caracas: Instituto Pedagógico, 1974), pp. 337-46.

H.22 Maldonado-Denis, Manuel. "La temática social de la literatura puertorriqueña." La torre, No. 42 (1963), 189-208.

H.23 Manrique Cabrera, Francisco. "Literatura folklórica de Puerto Rico." In Literatura puertorriqueña; 21 conferencias (SJ: Instituto de Cultura Puertorriqueña, 1960), pp. 403-27. Orig. as "Literatura folklórica puertorriqueña." RICP, No. 4 (1959), 4-7.

H.24 Márquez, Roberto. "The politics of translation and the literature of the Caribbean." RC-R, 4, 3 (1976), 48-56.

H.25 Martínez Masden, Edgar. "El jíbaro en la literatura puertorriqueña." In Instituto Internacional de Literatura Iberoamericana, XVII Congreso (Madrid: Cultura Hispánica del Centro Iberoamericano de Cooperación, 1978), pp. 1551-59. Orig. RC-R, 4, 2 (1976), 50-57.

H.26 Mason, J. A. "Porto-Rican folklore." JAF, No. 121 (1918), 289-450.

H.27 Meléndez, Concha. "Significación de los premios del Ateneo en sus festivales de Navidad." RICP, No. 49 (1970), 11-14.

H.28 Méndez, José Luis. "Literatura e ideología en Puerto Rico." In his Sociología marxista de la literatura y problemas de la creación cultural (Río Piedras: Puerto, 1974), pp. 75-79.

H.29 __________. "El negro en la literatura y en la sociedad puertorriqueña." In his Sociología marxista de la literatura y problemas de la creación cultural (Río Piedras: Puerto, 1974), pp. 67-74.

H.30 Miranda, Luis Antonio. El negrismo en la literatura de Puerto Rico. SJ: Club de la Prensa, 1960. A portion appeared under the same title in MHisp, No. 154 (1961), 30-31.

H.31 Pedreira, Antonio S. "La actualidad del jíbaro." In his Tres ensayos (Río Piedras: Edil, 1969), pp. 13-65.

H.32 __________. "Curiosidades literarias de Puerto Rico." In his Tres ensayos (Río Piedras: Edil, 1969), pp. 67-88. Also in his Obras completas (SJ: Instituto de Cultura Puertorriqueña, 1970), I, 705-26.

H.33 Pego, Aurelio. "El humorismo en Pto. Rico; hay que aprender a reír." PLit, 1, 1 (1963), 17.

H.34 Pérez Marchand, Monelisa. "Esbozo preliminar para un estudio de las ideas históricas en la generación del 30." RCS, 7, 1-2 (1963), 169-87.

H.35 "El problema de los creadores desarraigados. The problem of the uprooted literary people." In El libro puertorriqueño de Nueva York. Handbook of the Puerto Rican community (NY/SJ: Plus Ultra Educational Publishers, 1970), pp. 183-86.

H.36 Rivera de Alvarez, Josefina. "El cultivo de la oratoria en Puerto Rico." RICP, No. 59 (1973), 1-6.

H.37 Rivera de García, Eloísa. "Primeras notas del tema jíbaro en la literatura puertorriqueña." RICP, No. 23 (1964), 55-62.

H.38 Rodríguez Escudero, Néstor. "El tema del mar en la literatura purtorriqueña." _BAAC_, 2, 4 (1966), 737-60.

H.39 Rosa-Nieves, Cesáreo. "Hombre, horizonte y canción." In his _La lámpara del faro..._ (SJ: Club de la Prensa, 1957-60), II, 39-46.

H.40 Sales, María de. _El sentimiento religioso en la lírica puertorriqueña_. Unpublished thesis, Universidad de Puerto Rico, 1964.

H.41 Santana Maíz, Monserrate. _La mujer en la literatura puertorriqueña_. Unpublished thesis, Universidad de Puerto Rico, 1932.

H.42 Silva, Ana Margarita. _El jíbaro en la literatura de Puerto Rico, comparado con el campesino de España e Hispanoamérica_. M, 1945. 2. ed. corr. y aum., SJ: Silva, 1957.

H.43 Vega, Ana Lydia. "Négritude et libération nationale dans la littérature portoricaine." _PAfr_, Nos. 99-100 (1976), 167-80.

H.44 Zenón Cruz, Isabelo. _Narciso descubre su trasero: el negro en la cultura puertorriqueña_. Humacao: Furidi, 1974-75. Vol. 2 devoted to literary materials.

I
GENERAL STUDIES ON COLONIAL LITERATURE

I.1 Babín, María Teresa. "Albores de la literatura puertorriqueña (siglos XVI y XVII)." RICP, No. 1 (1958), 8-11.

I.2 Borges, Analola. "El descubrimiento de Borinquen según las crónicas." BAAC, 5, 4 (1969), 505-15.

I.3 Coll y Toste, Cayetano. "El alborear de la literatura." PRRM, diciembre 1919, pp. 238-61.

I.4 García Díaz, Manuel. "Los neoclásicos en Puerto Rico." In Literatura puertorriqueña; 21 conferencias (SJ: Instituto de Cultura Puertorriqueña, 1960), pp. 83-117.

I.5 Santiago San Miguel, Angel M. "El andariego y el emigrante puertorriqueño: vida y literatura de los siglos XVI y XVII." DAI, 35 (1974), 3698A.

J

GENERAL STUDIES ON NINETEENTH CENTURY LITERATURE

J.1 Cadilla Colón, Francisco M. Los ochocentistas. Barcelona: Rumbos, 1961.

J.2 Cortina Gómez, Rodolfo. "Toward a literary biogram of the Puerto Rican personality 1849-1894." RC-R, 2, 4 (1974), 46-54.

J.3 Dávila, Arturo. "Un impreso puertorriqueño del año 1807 [Novena del glorioso precurso de Christo Juan Bautista]." RICP, No. 34 (1967), 48-50.

J.4 Guzmán, Julia María. Realismo y naturalismo en Puerto Rico. SJ: Instituto de Cultura Puertorriqueña, 1972.

J.5 "Literature from Porto Rico." LitW, 19 (1888), 189-90.

J.6 Rivera de Alvarez, Josefina. "Manifestaciones literarias anónimas en prosa y verso que ven la luz pública en el Diario liberal y de variedades de Puerto Rico, desde fines de 1821 hasta mediados de 1822." RICP, No. 44 (1969), 33-37.

J.7 Rivera de García, Eloísa. "Disquisiciones del primer libro impreso en Puerto Rico [Juan Rodríguez Calderón, Ocios de la juventud]." RICP, No. 11 (1961), 8-11.

J.8 Rosa-Nieves, Cesáreo. El romanticismo en la literatura puertorriqueña. SJ: Instituto de Cultura Puertorriqueña, 1960. Also in Literatura puertorriqueña; 21 conferencias (SJ: Instituto de Cultura Puertorriquña, 1960), pp. 119-48. Also as "El romanticismo en la literatura puertorriqueña (1843-1880)." In his Ensayos escogidos... (SJ: Academia de Artes y Ciencias de Puerto Rico, 1970?), pp. 13-36.

J.9 Ruiz García, Zoilo. Nuestros hombres de antaño. Mayagüez: Mayagüez Publishing Co., 1920.

J.10 Zavala, Iris M. "Puerto Rico, siglo XIX: literatura y sociedad." SinN, 7, 4 (1977), 7-26; 8, 1 (1977), 7-19.

K
GENERAL STUDIES ON TWENTIETH CENTURY LITERATURE

K.1 Acosta-Belén, Edna. "Ideología e imágenes de la mujer en la literatura puertorriqueña contemporánea." In her La mujer en la sociedad puertorriqueña (Río Piedras: Huracán, 1980), pp. 125-56. Also as "Ideology and images of women in contemporary Puerto Rican literature." In her The Puerto Rican woman (NY: Prager, 1979), pp. 85-109.

K.2 ________. "Literature and ideology in the works of the Puerto Rican generation of 1950." DAI, 38 (1978), 6151A-52A.

K.3 ________. "The literature of the Puerto Rican national minority in the United States." BR/RB, 5, 1-2 (1978), 107-16.

K.4 Alegría, José S. Cincuenta años de literatura puertorriqueña. SJ: Academia Puertorriqueña de la Lengua, 1955.

K.5 Babín, María Teresa. "Contemporary Puerto Rican literature in translation." In Dexter Fisher, Minority language and literature: retrospective and perspective (NY: Modern Language Association of America, 1976), pp. 115-20.

K.6 ________. "Expresión de Puerto Rico en la literatura contemporánea (1934-1956)." RI, No. 44 (1957), 353-58.

K.7 ________. "Landmarks in contemporary Puerto Rican letters." The Americas, 14 (1958), 247-57.

K.8 ________. "El tema de Puerto Rico en la literatura del presente." Asomante, 11, 2 (1955), 6-17. Also in her Jornadas literarias (temas de Puerto Rico) (Barcelona: Rvmbos, 1967), pp. 36-53.

K.9 Belaval, Emilio S. La literatura de transición: dos décadas de un nuevo siglo. SJ: Instituto de Cultura Puertorriqueña, 1972. Also in Literatura puertorriqueña; 21 conferencias (SJ: Instituto de Cultura Puertorriqueña, 1960), pp. 241-61.

K.10 Colberg Petrovich, Juan Enrique. Cuatro autores clásicos contemporáneos de Puerto Rico. SJ: Cordillera, 1966.

K.11 Diez de Andino, Juan. Voces de la farándula. Crítica contemporánea. Barcelona: Rvmbos, 1959.

K.12 Escritores contemporáneos de Puerto Rico. SJ: Sociedad de Autores Puertorriqueños, 1978.

K.13 Ferrer Canales, José. "Hora de Puerto Rico." CA, No. 120 (1962), 116-43.

K.14 Franco Oppenheimer, Félix. "Libros puertorriqueños." In his Contornos; ensayos (SJ: Yaurel, 1960), pp. 159-73.

K.15 Géigel Polanco, Vicente. Los ismos en la década de los veinte. SJ: Instituto de Cultura Puertorriqueña, 1960. Also in Literatura puertorriqueña; 21 conferencias (SJ: Instituto de Cultura Puertorriqueña, 1960), pp. 263-89.

K.16 Gómez Costa, Arturo. "Los lunes de Ateneo y la literatura modernista en Puerto Rico." In his Vendimias en prosa (Barcelona: Vosgos, 1976), pp. 17-44.

K.17 González, José Luis. "Plebeyismo y arte en el Puerto Rico de hoy." TC, No. 12 (1979), 84-91.

K.18 Henríquez Ureña, Max. "Puerto Rico." In his Breve historia del modernismo; 2. ed. (M: Fondo de Cultura Económica, 1962), pp. 451-71. Orig. 1954.

K.19 Hernández Aquino, Luis. Movimientos literarios del siglo XX en Puerto Rico. Unpublished dissertation, Universidad de Puerto Rico, 1951.

K.20 Jiménez Malaret, René. "Esplendor y sombras en la literatura de Puerto Rico." In his Puntos de vista (SJ: Betances, 1961), pp. 50-53.

K.21 Laguerre, Enrique A. "Literatura puertorriqueña contemporánea." In his Polos en la cultura iberoamericana (Boston: Florentia, 1977), pp. 65-73. Also as "Modern Puerto Rican literature." Kaie, 11 (1973), 16-23.

K.22 "Los libros más importantes de la literatura puertorriqueña, 1930-1954. Encuesta." Asomante, 11, 1 (1955), 124-40.

K.23 La literatura y las artes de 1980 en Puerto Rico. Río Piedras: Mairena, 1981.

K.24 López-Baralt, Mercedes. "Literatura joven de Puerto Rico." Crisis, No. 32 (1975), 58-59.

K.25 López-Jiménez, Ivette. "Escritores puertorriqueños del '70: nuevos caminos." DAI, 39 (1978), 2311A.

K.26 Marqués, René. "La función del escritor puertorriqueño en el momento actual." CA, No. 127 (1963), 55-63. Also in his Ensayos (1953-1966) (SJ: Antillana, 1966), pp. 211-22. Also in his Ensayos (1953-1971); 2. ed. rev. y aum. (Río Piedras: Antillana, 1972), pp. 217-28. Also as "The function of the Puerto Rican writer today." In his The docile Puerto Rican; essays (Philadelphia: Temple University Press, 1976), pp. 113-19.

K.27 ________. "Mensaje de un puertorriqueño a los escritores y artistas del Perú." CA, No. 84 (1955), 79-86. Also in his Ensayos (1953-1966) (SJ: Antillana, 1966), pp. 25-36. Also in his Ensayos (1953-1971); 2. ed. rev. y aum. (Río Piedras: Antillana, 1972), pp. 27-38. Also as "Message of a Puerto Rican to the writers and artists of Peru." In his The docile Puerto Rican; essays (Philadelphia: Tempel University Press, 1976), pp. 106-12.

K.28 ________. "El puertorriqueño dócil." CA, No. 120 (1962), 144-95. Also RCS, 7, 1-2 (1963), 35-78. Also as "El puertorriqueño dócil (literatura y realidad psicológica)." In his Ensayos (1952-1966) (SJ: Antillana, 1966), pp. 147-209. Also in his Ensayos (1953-1971); 2. ed. rev. y aum. (Río Piedras: Antillana, 1972), pp. 151-215. Also as "The docile Puerto Rican: literature and psychological reality." In his The docile Puerto Rican; essays (Philadephia: Temple University Press, 1976), pp. 35-73.

K.29 Menton, Seymour. "La generación puertorriqueña del cuarenta." Hispania, 44 (1961), 209-11.

K.30 Nolasco, Sócrates. "El ambiente literario en Puerto Rico hace treinta y ocho años." In his Escritores de Puerto Rico (Manzanillo, Cuba: "El Arte", 1953), pp. 11-24.

K.31 Rivera de Alvarez, Josefina. "Panorama literario de Puerto Rico durante el siglo XX." In Panorama das literaturas das Américas (Nova Lisboa: Município Nova Lisoboa, 1958-63), II.

K.32 Rosa, Samuel E. de la. "Encuesta sobre literatura puertorriqueña." Prensa, 2, 9 (1959), 9-10.

K.33 Rosa-Nieves, Cesáreo. "Breve relación de la literatura puertorriqueña." RICP, No. 24 (1964), 40-47. Also as "Breve relación de la literatura contemporánea de Puerto Rico (1921-1970)." In his Ensayos escogidos... (SJ: Academia de Artes y Ciencias de Puerto Rico, 1970?), pp. 121-39.

K.34 ________. "Los horizontes tristes del libro puertorriqueño." BSBPR, 2, 2 (1963), 104-108.

K.35 Sánchez, Luis Rafael. "Cinco problemas al escritor puertorriqueño." Vórtice, 2, 2-3 (1979), 117-21.

K.36 Silén, Juan Angel. La generación de escritores de 1970 en Puerto Rico (1950-1976). Río Piedras: Cultural, 1977.

K.37 Soto Ramos, Julio. "Nuestra aventura literaria." In his Yo soy yo y mi verdad... (SJ: Cordillera, 1973), pp. 71-98.

K.38 __________. "Peripecias del libro puertorriqueño." In his Yo soy yo y mi verdad... (SJ: Cordillera, 1973), pp. 185-89.

K.39 Turner, Faythe. "The evolution of mainland Puerto Rican writers." WLWE, 19 (1980), 74-83.

K.40 Vientós Gastón, Nilita. Indice cultural. Río Piedras: Ediciones de la Universidad de Puerto Rico, 1962-71.

K.41 Ward, James H. "A tentative inventory of young Puerto Rican writers." Hispania, 54 (1971), 924-30.

L

GENERAL STUDIES ON POETRY

L.1 Arana Soto, Salvador. Diccionario de temas regionalistas en la poesía puertorriqueña. SJ: Club de la Prensa, 1961, c1960.

L.2 Arrigoitia, Luis de. "La poesía lírica puertorriqueña." Insula, Nos. 356-57 (1976), 11-12.

L.3 Babín, María Teresa. "Introduction: the path and the voice." In María Teresa Babín, and Stan Steiner, Borinquen; an anthology of Puerto Rican literature (NY: Random House, 1964), pp. xi-xxvi.

L.4 Blanco, Tomás. "La poesía en Puerto Rico." Ultra, 3 (1937), 579-81.

L.5 Coll y Toste, Cayetano. "Historia de la poesía en Puerto Rico." BHPR, 13 (1926), 140-66; 13 (1926), 333-55; 14 (1927), 89-104.

L.6 Congreso de Poesía Puertorriqueña. 1st, Yauco, 1957. Crítica y antología de la poesía puertorriqueña; trabajos presentados o leídos en el Primer Congreso de Poesía Puertorriqueña celebrado en Yacuo, P.R., 11-25 de agosto de 1957. SJ: Instituto de Cultura Puertorriqueña, 1958.

L.7 Cortázar, Mercedes. "Larger than literature." Review, No. 14 (1975), 67-70. See item no. L.3.

L.8 Fernández Juncos, Manuel. "Origen y desarrollo de la poesía puertorriqueña." Las Antillas, 3, 2 (1921), 128. Also in Plumas amigas (SJ: Cantero Fernández, 1912), pp. 1-8.

L.9 Franco Oppenheimer, Félix. Imagen de Puerto Rico en su poesía, desde los comienzos hasta nuestros días. SJ: Editorial Universitaria, Universidad de Puerto Rico, 1972.

L.10 Gómez Tejera, Carmen. "Introducción." In her Poesía puertorriqueña (M: Orión, 1956), pp. vii-xvi. Also 1972 and 1977.

L.11 Hernández Aquino, Luis. "Panorama de la poésie portorricaine (1843-1978)." Europe, Nos. 592-93 (1978), 27-50.

L.12 ________. "Prólogo." In his Poesía puertorriqueña (Río Piedras: Universidad de Puerto Rico, 1954), pp. 7-17.

L.13 López, Julio César. Pasión de poesía; jornada crítica. SJ, 1960.

L.14 Matilla, Alfredo, and Iván Silén. "Prologue." In their The Puerto Rican poets/Los poetas puertorriqueños (NY: Bantam Books, 1972), pp. xiii-xviii.

L.15 Meléndez, Concha. Poetas hispanoamericanos diversos. SJ: Cordillera, 1971. Also in her Obras completas (SJ: Instituto de Cultura Puertorriqueña, 1970-74), IV, 11-213.

L.16 Menéndez Pelayo, Marcelino. "Puerto Rico." In his Historia de la poesía hispanoamericana (M: V. Suárez, 1911), I, 329-51.

L.17 Negroni, Héctor Andrés. "El maquinismo en la poesía puertorriqueña." RICP, No. 60 (1973), 21-24.

L.18 Rodríguez Velázquez, Jaime Luis. La poesía del romanticismo al modernismo en Puerto Rico. M: Universidad Nacional Autónoma de México, 1965.

L.19 Rosa-Nieves, Cesáreo. "Cinco generaciones estéticas en la poesía puertorriqueña (1843-1956)." In his La lámpara del faro... (SJ: Club de la Prensa, 1957-60), I, 221-44.

L.20 ________. "Dos ángulos de la poesía en Puerto Rico." Brújula, 3 (1937), 169-75. Also in Antología del pensamiento puertorriqueño (1900-1970) (Río Piedras?: Editorial Universitaria, Universidad de Puerto Rico, 1975), II, 169-75.

L.21 ________. "Observaciones para el concepto de una antología." In his La lámpara del faro... (SJ: Club de la Prensa, 1957-60), II, 69-76.

L.22 ________. La poesía en Puerto Rico; historia de los temas poéticos en la literatura puertorriqueña; 2. ed. corr. y aum. SJ: Campos, 1958. 3. ed., SJ: Edil, 1969. Orig. an unpublished thesis, Universidad Nacional Autónoma de México, 1943.

L.23 ________. "Poesía puertorriqueña (1943-1956)." EAm, No. 54 (1956), 195-211.

L.24 ________. "Prólogo." In his Aguinaldo lírico de la poesía puertorriqueña (SJ?: Campos, 1957), I, 9-29; II, 9-20; III, 9-37.

L.25 Soto Ramos, Julio. "La poesía en Puerto Rico." In his Cumbre y remanso... (SJ: Cordillera, 1963), pp. 42-57.

M
COLONIAL AND NINETEENTH CENTURY POETRY

M.1 Acevedo, Ramón Luis. "La poesía indianista puertorriqueña en el siglo XIX." _RICP_, No. 65 (1974), 24-36.

M.2 Monge, José María. "Prólogo." In his _Poetas puertorriqueños; producciones en verso_... (Mayagüez: Martín Fernández, 1879), pp. vi-vii.

M.3 Rivera-Rivera, Eloísa. _La poesía en Puerto Rico antes de 1843_. SJ: Instituto de Cultura Puertorriqueña, 1965. Orig. _DA_, 19 (1958), 329-30.

M.4 Rosa-Nieves, Cesáreo. "Lucha de fronteras estéticas: el parnasianismo en Puerto Rico." In his _La lámpara del faro_... (SJ: Club de la Prensa, 1957-60), II, 47-57.

M.5 __________. "Prólogo: fulgores aurorales del romanticismo boricua en el _Aguinaldo puertorriqueño_ del 1843." In _Aguinaldo puertorriqueño; colección de producciones originales en prosa y verso_ (SJ: Porta Coelli, 1971), pp. 5-14.

N
TWENTIETH CENTURY POETRY

N.1 Algarín, Miguel. "Volume and value of the breath in poetry." RC-R, 6, 3 (1978), 52-69.

N.2 Arroyo de Colón, María. "El elemento hispánico en el modernismo puertorriqueñno." Unpublished Ph.D. dissertation, Universidad de Puerto Rico, 1977.

N.3 Babín, María Teresa. "Ocho poetas de Puerto Rico." AyL, No. 20 (1958), 3-6.

N.4 Barradas, Efraín. "'De lejos en sueños verla': visión mítica de Puerto Rico en la poesía neoyorrican." RC-R, 7, 3 (1979), 46-56.

N.5 __________. "Palabras asediadas: situación actual de la poesía puertorriqueña." RNC, No. 235 (1978), 168-93.

N.6 __________, and Rafael Rodríguez. Herejes y mitificadores: muestra de poesía puertorriqueña en los Estados Unidos. Río Piedras: Huracán, 1980.

N.7 Callan, Richard J. "Puerto Rico's angry poets." Commonweal, 75 (1961), 276-78.

N.8 Cortina Gómez, Rodolfo. "The paradoxes of contemporary Puerto Rican poetry." In Essays on minority folklore (La Crosse, WI: University of Wisconsin-La Crosse, Institute for Minority Studies, 1977), pp. 141-47.

N.9 Esteves, José de Jesús. El modernismo en la poesía; conferencias dominicales en la Biblioteca Insular de Puerto Rico. SJ: Bureau of Supplies-Printing and Transportation, 1914.

N.10 Gil de Rubio, Víctor M. "Prefacio. Preface." In his Poemas puertorriqueños (Puerto Rican poems) (Barcelona:

Rumbos, 1968), pp. 6-11. Spanish and English on facing pages.

N.11 González, José Emilio. *La poesía contemporánea de Puerto Rico (1930-1960)*. SJ: Instituto de Cultura Puertorriqueña, 1972. Orig. an unpublished thesis, Université de Paris, 1967.

N.12 __________. "La poesía puertorriqueña de 1930 a 1954." *Asomante*, 11, 1 (1955), 69-74.

N.13 __________. "La poesía puertorriqueña 1945 a 1963." *Asomante*, 20, 3 (1964), 52-79.

N.14 __________. *Los poetas puertorriqueños de la década de 1930*. SJ: Instituto de Cultura Puertorriqueña, 1960. Also in *Literatura puertorriqueña; 21 conferencias* (SJ: Instituto de Cultura Puertorriqueña, 1960), pp. 291-318.

N.15 Hernández Aquino, Luis. *Nuestra aventura literaria*. Santo Domingo de Guzmán, PR: Arte y Cine, 1964. Also as *Nuestra aventura literaria (los ismos en la poesía puertorriqueña) 1913-1948*; 2. ed. SJ: Ediciones de la Torre, Universidad de Puerto Rico, 1966. Orig. as *Movimientos literarios del siglo XX en Puerto Rico*. Unpublished thesis, Universidad de Puerto Rico, 1951.

N.16 Labarthe, Pedro Juan. "Poesía de Puerto Rico en América." In his *Antología de poetas contemporáneos de Puerto Rico* (M: Clásico, 1946), pp. 11-26. Also in *Antología del pensamiento puertorriqueño (1900-1970)*)Río Piedras?: Editorial Universitaria, Universidad de Puerto Rico, 1975), pp. 921-37.

N.17 Laguerre, Enrique A. "El modernismo en Puerto Rico." In Instituto Internacional de Literatura Iberoamericana, *La literatura del Caribe y otros temas* (M, 1961), pp. 303-11.

N.18 __________. *La poesía modernista en Puerto Rico*. SJ: Coaquí, 1969.

N.19 Manrique Cabrera, Francisco. "Del quehacer poético en Puerto Rico." In Primer Congreso de Poesía Puertorriqueña, *Crítica y antología de la poesía puertorriqueña* (SJ: Instituto de Cultura Puertorriqueña, 1968), pp. 1-8.

N.20 Marín, Carmen Lilianne. "Introducción." In Efraín Barradas, and Rafael Rodríguez, *Herejes y mitifcadores: muestra de poesía puertorriqueña en los Estados Unidos* (Río Piedras: Huracán, 1980), pp. 11-34.

N.21 Marzán, Julio. "Introduction." In his *Inventing a word; an anthology of twentieth-century Puerto Rican poetry* (NY: Columbia University Press, 1980), pp. xi-xxvii.

N.22 Matilla, Alfredo. "'The broken dream': Puerto Rican poetry in New York." In Iris M. Zavala, and Rafael Rodríguez,

The intellectual roots of independence; an anthology of Puerto Rican political independence (NY: Monthly Review Press, 1980), pp. 299-310. Orig. REP, 1 (1971), pagination unknown. Also as "'The broken dream': poesía puertorriqueña en Nueva York." In Iris M. Zavala, and Rafael Rodríguez, Libertad y crítica en el ensayo político puertorriqueño (Río Piedras: Puerto, 1973), pp. 429-43.

N.23 Meléndez, Concha. "Introducción a la antología poética de Asomante." In her Poetas hispanoamericanos diversos (SJ: Cordillera, 1971), pp. 209-17. Also in her Obras completas (SJ: Instituto de Cultura Puertorriqueña, 1970-72), IV, 215-23. Orig. as "Introducción." In Asomante, Antología poética de Asomante, 1945-1959 (SJ: Ateneo Puertorriqueño, 1962), pp. 5-11.

N.24 Morales, Jorge Luis. "Liberación de la poesía puertorriqueña." In Primer Congreso de Poesía Puertorriqueña, Crítica y antología de la poesía puertorriqueña (SJ: Instituto de Cultura Puertorriqueña, 1958), pp. 27-35.

N.25 Puerto Rico. Universidad. Colegio de Artes y Ciencias. Seminario de Estudios Hispánicos. La naturaleza en la poesía puertorriqueña del siglo XX. Río Piedras, 1942. Same as the Boletín de la Universidad de Puerto Rico, serie XIII, no. 2.

N.26 Palés Matos, Luis. "Puerto Rico: asteriscos para lo intacto." PAm, 4, 1 (1955), 43-44.

N.27 Patterson, Helen Wohl. "La poesía y la vida: influencia mutua." ALA, 2, 9 (1965), 14-20.

N.28 "Poetas. Poetry." In El libro puertorriqueño de Nueva York. Handbook of the Puerto Rican community (NY/SJ: Plus Ultra Educational Publishers, 1970), pp. 187-89.

N.29 Puebla, Manuel de la. "La poesía de 1980 en Puerto Rico." Mairena, No. 6 (1981), 3-28. Followed, pp. 29-50, by a selection of poems.

N.30 Ramos Mimoso, Adriana. El modernismo en la lírica puertorriqueña. SJ: Instituto de Cultura Puertorriqueña, 1960. Also 1972. Also in Literatura puertorriqueña; 21 conferencias (SJ: Instituto de Cultura Puertorriqueña, 1960), pp. 179-208.

N.31 Ribera Chevremont, Evaristo, and José S. Alegría. "[Introducción]." In their Antología de poetas jóvenes de Puerto Rico (SJ: Real Hermanos, 1918), pagination unknown.

N.32 Rosa-Nieves, Cesáreo. "Literatura en la Torre." In Ramón Cancel Negrón, Antología de la joven poesía universitaria de Puerto Rico (SJ: Campos, 1959), pp. 9-20.

N.33 __________. "El modernismo en Puerto Rico." In his La lámpara del faro... (SJ: Club de la Prensa, 1957-60), II, 59-67.

N.34 __________. "Preludio al tema del modernismo en Puerto Rico." In Instituto Internacional de Literatura Iberoamericana, La literatura del Caribe y otros temas (M, 1961), pp. 297-301.

N.35 Rosario Quiles, Luis Antonio. "La poesía nueva puertorriqueña (1950-1969)." In his Poesía nueva puertorriqueña (Río Piedras?: Bondo, 1971), pp. 9-41.

N.36 Ruscalleda Bercedóniz, Jorge María. "Razón y ser de la poesía puertorriqueña (siglo XX)." Penélope, 1, 2 (1972-73), 56-58.

N.37 Soto Ramos, Julio. "Fe de erratas de la antología Nueva poesía de Puerto Rico de Angel Valbuena Briones y L. Hernández Aquino." In his Una pica en Flandes (SJ: Club de la Prensa, 1959), pp. 115-38. See item no. N.39.

N.38 __________. "Voces trascendentalistas; del tiempo y su figura." In his Una pica en Flandes (SJ: Club de la Prensa, 1959), pp. 9-17.

N.39 Valbuena Briones, Angel. "Prólogo." In Angel Valbuena Briones, and Luis Hernández Aquino, Nueva poesía de Puerto Rico (Madrid: Cultura Hispánica, 1952), pp. 11-106. See item no. 37.

O
SPECIAL TOPICS IN POETRY

O.1 Arroyo, Anita. "La poesía negroide en Puerto Rico." RICP, No. 34 (1967), 34-36.

O.2 Barradas, Efraín. "Los otros: nota sobre el cultivo de la poesía negrista en Puerto Rico." SAHL, 2-3 (1978-79), 28-40.

O.3 Cabrera Freiría, Yvette de Lourdes. La décima popular en Puerto Rico; historia, versificación, temática. M, 1960.

O.4 Cadilla de Martínez, María. La poesía popular en Puerto Rico. Madrid: Universidad de Madrid, 1933. Also SJ: Venezuela, 1953.

O.5 Canino Salgado, Marcelino J. "El amor patriótico en la lírica de Puerto Rico." RICP, No. 41 (1968), 1-8.

O.6 __________. La copla y el romance populares en la tradición oral en Puerto Rico. SJ: Instituto de Cultura Puertorriqueña, 1968.

O.7 Coulthard, G. R. "La mujer de color en la poesía antillana." Asomante, 4, 1 (1958), 35-50.

O.8 Dávila, José Antonio. "Nuestro negro y lo negroide." In his Prosa: ensayos, artículos y cartas literarias (SJ: Sociedad de Autores Puertorriqueños, 1971), pp. 209-13.

O.9 Davis, Lisa E. "Guerra Mondragón como traductor de Oscar Wilde: interpretación de la estética moderna en Puerto Rico." SinN, 6, 2 (1975), 66-81.

O.10 Escabí, Pedro C., and Elsa M. Escabí. Vista parcial del folklore: la décima; estudio etnográfico de la cultura popular en Puerto Rico. Río Piedras?: Editorial Universitaria, Universidad de Puerto Rico, 1976.

O.11 Espinosa, Aurelio M. "Romance de Puerto Rico." *RHisp*, 48 (1918), 309-64.

O.12 Franco Oppenheimer, Félix. "¿Existe una poesía genuinamente puertorriqueña?" In Primer Congreso de Poesía Puertorriqueña, *Crítica y antología de la poesía puertorriqueña* (SJ: Instituto de Cultura Puertorriqueña, 1958), pp. 87-92.

O.13 González, José Emilio. "Poeta y sociedad en Puerto Rico." *Caravelle*, No. 18 (1972), 43-58.

O.14 Gutiérrez Laboy, Roberto. "Introducción." In his *Puerto Rico: tema y motivo en la poesía hispánica (antología)* (NY: Senda Nueva de Ediciones, 1980), pp. 9-14.

O.15 Hernández Aquino, Luis. "Prólogo." In his *Poetas de Lares; antología* (SJ: Instituto de Cultura Puertorriqueña, Centro Cultural de Lares, 1966), pp. 7-11.

O.16 ________. "El tema edénico en la poesía puertorriqueña." In Primer Congreso de Poesía Puertorriqueña, *Crítica y antología de la poesía puertorriqueña* (SJ: Instituto de Cultura Puertorriqueña, 1958), pp. 9-26.

O.17 *Institución del Día del Poeta*. SJ: Sociedad de Autores Puertorriqueños, 1965.

O.18 Jiménez de Báez, Yvette. *La décima popular en Puerto Rico*. Xalapa, Méx.: Universidad Veracruzana, Cuadernos de la Facultad de Filosofía, Letras y Ciencias, 1964.

O.19 ________. *Lírica cortesana y lírica popular*. M: El Colegio de México, 1969.

O.20 ________. "El tema del amor en la décima popular puertorriqueña." *RICP*, No. 21 (1963), 1-11.

O.21 Lloréns Torres, Luis. "La décima jíbara." *BAAC*, 5, 4 (1969), 433-34.

O.22 Lluch Mora, Francisco. "La poesía modernista yaucana." In Primer Congreso de Poesía Puertorriqueña, *Crítica y antología de la poesía puertorriqueña* (SJ: Instituto de Cultura Puertorriqueña, 1958), pp. 58-75.

O.23 ________. "Visión panorámica de la creación poética yaucana con anterioridad al modernismo." *RICP*, No. 21 (1963), 14-18.

O.24 López, Julio César. *La patria en dos poetas y un paralelo modernista*. Barcelona: Ariel, 1968. Also SJ, 1968.

O.25 López Cruz, Francisco. *El aguinaldo y el villancico en el folklore puertorriqueño*. SJ: Instituto de Cultura Puertorriqueña, 1956.

0.26 Marrero, Carmen. "La décima popular puertorriqueña." In her Antología de décimas populares puertorriqueñas (SJ: Cordillera, 1974), pp. 5-30.

0.27 Millán Rivera, Pedro. "Introducción." In his Antología poética de Caguas (SJ: Club de la Prensa, 1964), pp. 7-15.

0.28 Morales, Jorge Luis. "Navegación por el tema negro." In his Poesía afroantillana y negrista (Puerto Rico, República Dominicana, Cuba) (Río Piedras: Editorial Universitaria, Universidad de Puerto Rico, 1976), pp. xv-xxiii.

0.29 Pedreira, Antonio S. "La poesía popular en Puerto Rico." In his Aclaraciones y crítica (Río Piedras: Phi Eta Mu, Universidad de Puerto Rico, 1941), pp. 111-24. Also Río Piedras: Edil, 1969. Also in his Obras completas completas (SJ: Instituto de Cultura Puertorriqueña, 1970), I, 533-42.

0.30 Pedrosa Izarra, Ciriaco. Religión y religiones en los poetas: la lírica religiosa en la literatura puertorriqueña del siglo XX. Madrid: Fax, 1973.

0.31 Roberts, Helen H. "Spanish romances from Porto Rico." JAF, No. 127 (1920), 76-79.

0.32 Rodríguez Escudero, Néstor A. "El mar en la literatura puertorriqueña." In his El mar en la literatura puertorriqueña y otros ensayos (Barcelona: Rvmbos, 1967), pp. 21-76.

0.33 Rodríguez Pagán, Juan Antonio. Presencia de Federico García Lorca en la lírica puertorriqueña del siglo XX. Unpublished doctoral dissertation, Universidad de Puerto Rico, 1977.

0.34 Rosa-Nieves, Cesáreo. "El aguinaldo navideño en Puerto Rico." CLP, No. 1 (1965), 21-30. Also in Mariana Robles de Cardona, Búsqueda y plasmación de nuestra personalidad... (SJ: Club de la Prensa, 1958), pp. 231-45.

0.35 __________. "Dos palabras para la décima en Puerto Rico." BAAC, 5, 4 (1969), 417-20.

0.36 __________. "El madrigal en Puerto Rico." Asomante, 10, 3 (1954), 65-70. Also in his La lámpara del faro... (SJ: Club de la Prensa, 1957-60), I, 165-73.

0.37 __________. "Notas para la poesía puertorriqueña. Poesía y emoción en el tema negro." Asomante, 5, 1 (1949), 84-86. Also in his La lámpara del faro... (SJ: Club de la Prensa, 1957-60), I, 183-93.

0.38 __________. "El romance 'Delgadina' en la tradición puertorriqueña." In his La lámpara del faro... (SJ: Club de la Prensa, 1957-60), I, 160-63.

0.39 __________. "El romance tradicional español en Puerto Rico." RICP, No. 3 (1959), 4-7.

0.40 __________. Tierra y lamento; rodeos de contorno para una telúrica interpretación poética de lo puertorriqueño. SJ: Club de la Prensa, 1958.

0.41 __________. Voz folklórica de Puerto Rico. Sharon, CT: Troutman, 1967.

0.42 Soto Ramos, Julio. "El niño y la poesía infantil." In his Yo soy yo y mi verdad... (SJ: Cordillera, 1973), pp. 23-29.

0.43 Thompson, Lawrence S. "Recent negroid poetry in Puerto Rico." ABC, 6, 10 (1957), 9-10.

0.44 Torre, José Ramón de la. "Comprensión y análisis de una poesía en revolución: Guajana o la guerrilla literaria." Guajana, 3a época, No. 8 (1973), pagination unknown.

P
GENERAL STUDIES ON DRAMA

P.1 Belaval, Emilio S. "Dramaturgia, ser y realidad." BAAC, 2, 2 (1966), 191-202.

P.2 __________. "El teatro en Puerto Rico, de Antonia Sáez." In his Areyto (SJ: Biblioteca de Autores Puertorriqueños, 1948), pp. 39-51. See item no. P.16.

P.3 __________. "El teatro puertorriqueño." PLit, 1, 1 (1963), 1-37.

P.4 Dauster, Frank. "Drama and theater in Puerto Rico." MD, 6 (1963), 177-86. Also as "Drama y teatro en Puerto Rico." RICP, No. 22 (1964), 1-7.

P.5 __________. "El teatro puertorriqueño." In his Historia del teatro hispanoamericano. Siglos XIX y XX (M: de Andrea, 1966), pp. 69-73. Also 1973.

P.6 Dávila, Arturo V. "La pastoral del Obisbo Arizmendi sobre las comedias." RICP, No. 12 (1961), 27-32.

P.7 Morfi, Angelina. "El teatro en Puerto Rico." In La gran enciclopedia de Puerto Rico (Madrid: Editorial R, 1976), VI, 234-44.

P.8 Pagán, Juan Bautista. Dionisios. De los orígenes del teatro; síntesis histórica del teatro en Puerto Rico. George Jean Nathan y el teatro americano. SJ: Biblioteca de Autores Puertorriqueños, 1957.

P.9 Pasarell, Emilio J. "Apuntes sobre la historia del teatro en Puerto Rico." RICP, Nos. 76-77 (1977), 2-11.

P.10 __________. Panorama teatral de Puerto Rico en el siglo XIX. SJ: Instituto de Cultura Puertorriqueña, 1960. Also 1972. Fragments appeared under the same title in CyP,

2, 2 (1964), 38-41, and in _Literatura puertorriqueña; 21 conferencias_ (SJ: Instituto de Cultura Puertorriqueña, 1960), pp. 65-81.

P.11 Pilditch, Charles. "A brief history of theater in Puerto Rico." _RevI_, 9, 1 (1979), 5-8.

P.12 Rivera de Alvarez, Josefina. "Génesis y desarrollo de la dramaturgia puertorriqueña hasta los umbrales de la generación del treinta." _RICP_, No. 49 (1970), 36-45. Also _RICP_, Nos. 76-77 (1977), 19-30.

P.13 __________. "Orígenes del teatro puertorriqueño: _La juega de gallos o el negro bozal_ de Ramón C. F. Caballero." _RICP_, No. 3 (1959), 20-25.

P.14 Rosa-Nieves, Cesáreo. "Notas para los orígenes de las representaciones dramáticas en Puerto Rico." _Asomante_, 6, 1 (1950), 63-77. Also _BAAC_, 4, 2 (1968), 409-23. Also SJ: Baldrich, 1950. Also in his _La lámpara del faro_... (SJ: Club de la Prensa, 1957-60), I, 195-219.

P.15 Sáez, Antonia. "El teatro en Puerto Rico; desde sus comienzos hasta el 1900." _RICP_, No. 12 (1961), 12-16.

P.16 __________. _El teatro en Puerto Rico (notas para su historia)_. SJ: Editorial Universitaria, Universidad de Puerto Rico, 1950. 2. ed., 1972. See item no. P.2.

Q
TWENTIETH CENTURY DRAMA

Q.1 "Anotaciones de producciones teatrales 1959-1979." RevI, 9, 2 (1979), 307-22.

Q.2 Arriví, Francisco. Areyto mayor. SJ: Instituto de Cultura Puertorriqueña, 1966. Pertinent items are listed separately.

Q.3 __________. Conciencia puertorriqueña del teatro contemporáneo, 1937-1956. SJ: Instituto de Cultura Puertorriqueña, 1967.

Q.4 __________. "El Cuarto Festival de Teatro Puertorriqueño." RICP, No. 11 (1961), 12-20. Also as "Cuarto Festival de Teatro del Instituto de Cultura Puertorriqueña." In Teatro Puertorriqueño (Cuarto Festival) (SJ: Instituto de Cultura Puertorriqueña, 1962), pp. 7-22. Also as "Cuarto Festival de Teatro Puertorriqueño, 1961." In his Areyto mayor, q.v., pp. 69-84.

Q.5 __________. "El Décimo Festival de Teatro Puertorriqueño." RICP, No. 39 (1968), 39-43.

Q.6 __________. "El Decimocuarto Festival de Teatro Puertorriqueño." RICP, No. 58 (1973), 7-15.

Q.7 __________. "El Duodécimo Festival de Teatro Puertorriqueño." RICP, No. 56 (1972), 46-49.

Q.8 __________. Entrada por las raíces (entrañamiento en prosa). SJ: Serie La Entraña, 1964. Pertinent items are listed separately.

Q.9 __________. "Evolución del autor dramático puertorriqueño a partir de 1938." In his Entrada por las raíces..., q.v., pp. 189-224. Also in El autor dramático; Primer Seminario de Dramaturgia (SJ: Instituto de Cultura Puertorriqueña, 1963), pp. 117-52.

Q.10 __________. *La generación del treinta; el teatro*. SJ: Instituto de Cultura Puertorriqueña, 1960. Also in his *Areyto mayor*, q.v., pp. 11-35. Also in *Literatura puertorriqueña; 21 conferencias* (SJ: Instituto de Cultura Puertorriqueña, 1960), pp. 377-402.

Q.11 __________. "El Noveno Festival de Teatro del Instituto de Cultura Puertorriqueña." *RICP*, No. 36 (1967), 12-17.

Q.12 __________. "El Octavo Festival de Teatro Puertorriqueño." *RICP*, No. 28 (1965), 55-63. Also as "Octavo Festival de Teatro del Instituto de Cultura Puertorriqueña." In *Teatro puertorriqueño (Octavo Festival)* (SJ: Instituto de Cultura Puertorriqueña, 1966), pp. 7-29. Also as "Octavo Festival de Teatro Puertorriqueño, 1965." In his *Areyto mayor*, q.v., pp. 187-209.

Q.13 __________. "Perspectiva de una generación teatral puertorriqueña, 1938-1956." *RICP*, No. 1 (1958), 41-47. Also in his *Conciencia puertorriqueña del teatro contemporáneo*, q.v., pp. 79-92. Also in his *Areyto mayor*, q.v., pp. 36-52. Also in his *Entrada por las raíces*, q.v., pp. 165-75.

Q.14 __________. "El Primer Festival del Teatro Puertorriqueño." *RICP*, No. 2 (1959), 38-42. Also in his *Areyto mayor*, q.v., pp. 211-14.

Q.15 __________. "El Quinto Festival de Teatro." *RICP*, No. 15 (1962), 41-48. Also as "Quinto Festival de Teatro Puertorriqueño, 1962." In his *Areyto mayor*, q.v., pp. 119-30.

Q.16 __________. "Segundo Festival de Teatro Puertorriqueño." *RICP*, No. 4 (1959), 10-14. Also as "Segundo Festival de Teatro Puertorriqueño, 1959." In his *Areyto mayor*, q.v., pp. 53-58.

Q.17 __________. "El Séptimo Festival de Teatro Puertorriqueño, 1964." *RICP*, No. 23 (1964), 30-40. Also as "Séptimo Festival de Teatro Puertorriqueño, 1964." In his *Areyto mayor*, q.v., pp. 148-86. Also as "Séptimo Festival del Instituto de Cultura Puertorriqueña." In *Teatro puertorriqueño; Séptimo Festival* (SJ: Instituto de Cultura Puertorriqueña, 1965), pp. 7-44.

Q.18 __________. "El Sexto Festival de Teatro." *RICP*, No. 20 (1963), 46-55. Also as "Sexto Festival de Teatro Puertorriqueño, 1963." In his *Areyto mayor*, q.v., pp. 131-47.

Q.19 __________. "El Tercer Festival de Teatro Puertorriqueño." *RICP*, No. 7 (1960), 37-44. Also as "Tercer Festival de Teatro del Instituto de Cultura Puertorriqueña." In *Teatro puertorriqueño (Tercer Festival)* (SJ: Instituto de Cultura Puertorriqueña, 1961), pp. 7-16. Also as "Tercer Festival de Teatro Puertorriqueño, 1960." In his *Areyto mayor*, q.v., pp. 59-68.

Q.20 __________. "El Undécimo Festival de Teatro Puertorriqueño." RICP, No. 41 (1968), 35-45. Also in Programa para el Undécimo Festival de Teatro Puertorriqueño (SJ, 1968), pp. 3-17.

Q.21 Arroyo, Anita. "Instantánea del teatro en Puerto Rico." RICP, No. 32 (1966), 17-22.

Q.22 El autor dramático: Primero Seminario de Dramaturgia. SJ: Instituto de Cultura Puertorriqueña, 1963.

Q.23 Babín, María Teresa. "Veinte años de teatro puertorriqueño (1945-1964)." Asomante, 20, 4 (1964), 7-20. Also in her Jornadas literarias (temas de Puerto Rico) (Barcelona: Rvmbos, 1967), pp. 198-219.

Q.24 Balbuena, Aidil. "El teatro puertorriqueño actual, 10mo. Festival." Epoca, 5, 22 (1968), 12-13.

Q.25 Belaval, Emilio S. "Lo que podría ser un teatro puertorriqueño." AtPR, 3 (1939), 34-48. Also in his Areyto (SJ: Biblitoeca de Autores Puertorriqueños, 1948), pp. 55-62. Also in Francisco Arriví, Areyto mayor, q.v., pp. 245-90.

Q.26 __________. "El teatro." In Problemas de la cultura en Puerto Rico... (Río Piedras: Editorial Universitaria, Universidad de Puerto Rico, 1976), pp. 69-77.

Q.27 Boudet, Rosa Ileana. "Colectivo Nacional de Teatro de Puerto Rico." In Recopilación de textos sobre el teatro latinoamericano de creación colectiva (La Habana: Casa de las Américas, 1978?), pp. 411-20.

Q.28 Braschi, Wilfredo. Apuntes para la historia crítica del teatro puertorriqueño contemporáneo. Unpublished thesis, Universidad de Puerto Rico, 1952. Also as Apuntes sobre el teatro puertorriqueño. SJ: Coquí, 1970.

Q.29 __________. "Nuevas tendencias en la literatura puertorriqueña." In Literatura puertorriqueña; 21 conferencias (SJ: Instituto de Cultura Puertorriqueña, 1960), pp. 539-52.

Q.30 __________. "Treinta años de teatro en Puerto Rico." Asomante, 9, 1 (1955), 95-101.

Q.31 Castillo, Susana D., and María Elena Sandoz Montalvo. "Festival Latinoamericano de Teatro y I Muestra Internacional." LATR, 7, 1 (1973), 49-70.

Q.32 Collins, James A. "Puerto Rican theater today." RevI, 4 (1974), 322-29.

Q.33 "Dramaturgos. Dramatists." In El libro puertorriqueño de Nueva York. Handbook of the Puerto Rican community (NY/SJ: Plus Ultra Educational Publishers, 1970), pp. 192-95.

Q.34 Fernández de Lewis, Piri. "Temas del teatro puertorriqueño de hoy." In El autor dramático, q.v., pp. 153-82.

Q.35 Fumero de Colón, Odette. Las obras de los Festivales de Teatro del Instituto de Cultura Puertorriqueña. Unpublished thesis, Universidad de Puerto Rico, 1967.

Q.36 Galich, Manuel. "Boceto puertorriqueño." Conjunto, No. 25 (1975), 3-16.

Q.37 González, José Emilio. "La literatura dramática contemporánea de Puerto Rico." Insula, Nos. 356-57 (1976), 6.

Q.38 Green, William. "Puerto Rican portrait." ThA, 40, 3 (1956), 79-80, 93-95.

Q.39 Guerrero Zamora, Juan. "Historia del teatro contemporáneo [de Puerto Rico]." BAAC, 1 (1968), 465-96.

Q.40 Laguerre, Enrique A. "El teatro puertorriqueño del presente." In his Pulso de Puerto Rico, 1952-1954 (SJ: Biblioteca de Autores Puertorriqueños, 1956), pp. 293-304.

Q.41 Márquez, Juan L. "Crítica y teatro en Puerto Rico; una propuesta para su revitalización." RICP, No. 59 (1973), 9-14.

Q.42 Márquez, Rosa Luisa. "Cuarenta años después de 'Lo que podría ser un teatro puertorriqueño' (1939-1979)." RevI, 9 (1979), 300-306. See item no. Q.25.

Q.43 Martínez, Iris. "El teatro en Puerto Rico, arma de sobrevivencia de nuestra América." CAm, No. 123 (1980), 126-30.

Q.44 Monleón, José. "Visión rápida del teatro en Puerto Rico y México." In Popular theater for social change in Latin America (Los Angeles: University of California at Los Angeles, Latin American Center, 1978), pp. 77-84. Orig. 1974.

Q.45 Morales, María Victoria. "La actividad teatral en Puerto Rico." Horizontes, 5, 10 (1962), 92-102.

Q.46 Morfi, Angelina. "Evasión, reflejo y polémica en el teatro puertorriqueño." RevI, 7 (1977-78), 564-73.

Q.47 __________. "El teatro en Puerto Rico en el primer tercio del siglo XX." RevI, 9 (1979), 255-99.

Q.48 Pasarell, Emilio J. "Guía para la producción dramática de Puerto Rico en el siglo XX." RICP, No. 27 (1965), 50-60.

Q.49 Phillips, Jordan B. Contemporary Puerto Rican drama. NY: Plaza Mayor, 1972. Also Madrid: Playor, 1973. Orig. as "Thirty years of Puerto Rican drama: 1938-1968." DAI, 31 (1971), 6626A.

Q.50 Rivera, Margarita. "Teatro nuevo." RICP, Nos. 76-77 (1977), 92-101.

Q.51 Rivera de Alvarez, Josefina. "Génesis y desarrollo de la dramaturgia puertorriqueña hasta los umbrales de la generación del treinta." RICP, No. 49 (1970), 36-45.

Q.52 Rosa-Nieves, Cesáreo. "Notas para el origen de las representaciones dramáticas en Puerto Rico." Asomante, 6, 1 (1950), 63-77. Also BAAC, 4 (1968), 409-23.

Q.53 Sáez, Antonia. "El teatro en Puerto Rico." RICP, Nos. 76-77 (1977), 12-18.

Q.54 "El teatro. The theatre." In El libro puertorriqueño de Nueva York. Handbook of the Puerto Rican community (NY/SJ: Plus Ultra Educational Publishers, 1970), pp. 201-205.

R
SPECIAL TOPICS IN DRAMA

R.1 Arriví, Francisco. "El antiguo San Juan y el Teatro Tapia." <u>RICP</u>, No. 45 (1969), 40-44.

R.2 __________. "Espiritualidad del teatro 'La Perla'." In his <u>Entrada por las raíces</u>... (SJ: Serie La Entraña, 1964), pp. 21-25.

R.3 __________. <u>Informe de la Oficina de Fomento Teatral: año fiscal 1967-68</u>. SJ: Instituto de Cultura Puertorriqueña, 1968.

R.4 __________. "Primer Seminario de Dramaturgia 1961." In his <u>Areyto mayor</u> (SJ: Instituto de Cultura Puertorriqueña, 1966), pp. 85-118.

R.5 __________. "Teatros del Borikén. Caguana y el 'teatro' ceremonial indígena." <u>RICP</u>, No. 49 (1970), 7-9.

R.6 Belaval, Emilio S. "Cultura de la esencialidad humana: dramaturgia, ser y realidad." <u>RICP</u>, No. 2 (1959), 25-28.

R.7 Casas, Myrna. "Theatrical production in Puerto Rico from 1700-1824: the role of the government and of the Roman Catholic church." <u>DAI</u>, 35 (1974), 1279A.

R.8 Fragoso, Víctor. "Notas sobre la expresión teatral de la comunidad puertorriqueña de Nueva York." <u>RICP</u>, No. 70 (1976), 21-26.

R.9 Márquez, Rosa Luisa. "The Puerto Rican Traveling Company: the first ten years." <u>DAI</u>, 39 (1978), 26A.

R.10 Ornes, Maricusa. "El teatro infantil en Puerto Rico." <u>RICP</u>, Nos. 76-77 (1977), 102-109.

R.11 Pasarell, Emilio J. <u>Orígenes y desarrollo de la afición</u>

<u>teatral en Puerto Rico: siglo XX</u>. Río Piedras: Editorial Universitaria, Universidad de Puerto Rico, 1951-67. 2. ed., 1967. Also SJ: Editorial del Departamento de Instrucción Pública, 1970.

R.12 Sáez, Antonia. "Teatro puertorriqueño. Obras de ambiente político y social (1880-1927)." <u>RICP</u>, No. 25 (1964), 8-10.

R.13 Suárez Radillo, Carlos Miguel. "El areyto de Marojo, festival de la tierra puertorriqueña." <u>MHisp</u>, No. 282 (1971), 46-51.

R.14 __________. "Comentario y consideraciones en torno al 'Proyecto para el Fomento de las Artes Teatrales en Puerto Rico'." <u>RICP</u>, No. 26 (1965), 14-19.

S

GENERAL STUDIES ON PROSE FICTION

S.1 Acosta-Belén, Edna. "Notes on the evolution of the Puerto Rican novel." LALR, No. 16 (1980), 183-95.

S.2 Coll, Edna. "Novelista puertorriqueños." In her Indice informativo de la novela hispanoamericana (Río Piedras?: Editorial Universitaria, Universidad de Puerto Rico, 1974-), I, 27-167.

S.3 Gómez Tejera, Carmen. La novela en Puerto Rico; apuntes para su historia. SJ: Junta Editora, Universidad de Puerto Rico, 1947.

S.4 Hernández de Norman, Isabel. La novela criolla en las Antillas. NY: Plus Ultra, 1977.

S.5 Laguerre, Enrique A. "Prólogo." In his Antología de cuentos puertorriqueños (M: Orión, 1971), pp. 7-16.

S.6 __________. "Resumen histórico del relato en Puerto Rico." RICP, No. 1 (1958), 12-14.

S.7 Meléndez, Concha. El arte del cuento en Puerto Rico. NY: Las Américas, 1961.

S.8 __________. "El cuento en Cuba y Puerto Rico: estudio sobre dos antologías." RHM, 24 (1958), 201-12. Also in her Literatura de ficción en Puerto Rico: cuento y novela (SJ: Cordillera, 1971), pp. 75-96. Also in her Obras completas (SJ: Instituto de Cultura Puertorriqueña, 1970-72), IV, 501-22.

S.9 __________. "El cuento en Puerto Rico." In Antología de autores puertorriqueños. III. El cuento; primera parte (SJ: Ediciones del Gobierno, Estado Libre Asociado de Puerto Rico, 1957), pp. vii-xli.

S.10 ________. "El cuento puertorriqueño y cubano." In Instituto Internacional de Literatura Iberoamericana, La literatura del Caribe y otros temas (M, 1961), pp. 41-49.

S.11 ________. Literatura de ficción en Puerto Rico: cuento y novela. SJ: Cordillera, 1971. Also in her Obras completas (SJ: Instituto de Cultura Puertorriqueña, 1970-72), IV, 431-621.

S.12 Onís, Federico de. "El cuento en Puerto Rico." In his España en América... (Río Piedras?: Ediciones de la Universidad de Puerto Rico, 1955), pp. 586-88. Also 1968.

S.13 Quiles de la Luz, Lillian. El cuento en la literatura puertorriqueña. Río Piedras: Editorial U.P.R., Universidad de Puerto Rico, 1968.

S.14 Rivera de Alvarez, Josefina. "La novela puertorriqueña desde sus orígenes hasta el presente." In La gran enciclopedia de Puerto Rico (Madrid: Editorial R, 1976), V, 39-40, 109-17.

S.15 Romeu, José A. "Panorama de la prosa puertorriqueña." BAAC, 11, 1-2 (1975), 75-87.

S.16 Rosa-Nieves, Cesáreo, and Félix Oppenheimer. "El cuento en Puerto Rico." In their Antología general del cuento puertorriqueño; 2. ed. (SJ: Edil, 1970), I, 15-35. Orig. 1959.

S.17 Vázquez, Margarita, and Daisy Caraballo. "El cuento en Puerto Rico." In La gran enciclopedia de Puerto Rico (Madrid: Editorial R, 1976), IV, 111, 121-29.

T

NINETEENTH CENTURY PROSE FICTION

T.1 Ara, Guillermo. "Puerto Rico." In his La novela naturalista hispanoamericana (BA: EUDEBA, 1965), pp. 60-62.

T.2 Coll, Edna. "La novela del siglo XIX en Puerto Rico." In Instituto Internacional de Literatura Iberoamericana, La literatura iberoamericana del siglo XIX (Tucson, AZ: Universidad de Arizona, 1974), pp. 245-49.

T.3 Guzmán, Julia María. "Realismo y naturalismo en Puerto Rico." In Literatura puertorriqueña; 21 conferencias (SJ: Instituto de Cultura Puertorriqueña, 1960), pp. 149-77.

T.4 Hernández Norman, Isabel. La novela romántica en las Antillas. NY: Ateneo Puertorriqueño de Nueva York, 1969, c1967. Orig. DA, 27 (1967), 253A.

T.5 Matos Bernier, Félix. "La novela en Puerto Rico." In his Isla de arte (SJ: La Primavera, 1907), pp. 17-20.

T.6 Rivera, Modesto. "El modernismo.--La prosa." In Literatura puertorriqueña; 21 conferencias (SJ: Instituto de Cultura Puertorriqueña, 1960), pp. 209-39.

T.7 Suárez-Murias, Marguerite C. "Los iniciadores de la novela en Puerto Rico." Asomante, 18, 3 (1962), 43-48.

T.8 __________. "Puerto Rico." In her La novela romántica en Hispanoamérica (NY: Hispanic Institute in the United States, 1963), pp. 41-51.

U
TWENTIETH CENTURY PROSE FICTION

U.1 Acarón Ramírez, Marlene. "El cuento y la novela puertorriqueña de los últimos veinticinco años." RevL, No. 2 (1969), 330-59.

U.2 Arana de Love, Francisca. Los temas fundamentales de la novela puertorriqueña durante la primera década de Puerto Rico como Estado Libre Asociado a los Estados Unidos (1952-1962). Washington, DC, 1969. Also as La novela de Puerto Rico durante la primera década del Estado Libro Asociado: 1952-1962; 2. ed. Barcelona: Vosgos, 1976.

U.3 Arroyo, Anita. "Instantánea del cuento en Puerto Rico." RICP, No. 30 (1966), 1-4.

U.4 __________. "La novela en Puerto Rico." RICP, No. 28 (1965), 48-54.

U.5 Babín, María Teresa. "El cuento puertorriqueño de hoy." In her Jornadas literarias (temas de Puerto Rico) (Barcelona: Rvmbos, 1967), pp. 247-55.

U.6 Barradas, Efraín. "La figura en la alfombra: nota sobre dos generaciones de narradores puertorriqueños." Insula, Nos. 356-57 (1976), 5.

U.7 Beauchamp, José Juan. "La novela puertorriqueña: una estructura de resistencia, ruptura y recuperación." CAm, No. 124 (1981), 67-82.

U.8 Canino Salgado, Marcelino. "Apuntes sobre la novela actual en Puerto Rico." Penélope, 1, 1 (1972), 29-33.

U.9 Cruz, José Angel. "Realismo y literatura en el cuento de la 'generación del cuarenta' en Puerto Rico." DAI, 33 (1973), 6349A.

U.10 Díaz Valcárcel, Emilio. "Apuntes para el desarrollo histórico del cuento literario puertorriqueño y la generación del 40." RICP, No. 43 (1969), 11-17.

U.11 Gómez Lance, Betty Rita. "¿Existe una 'promoción del cuarenta' en el cuento puertorriqueño?" RI, No. 58 (1964), 283-92.

U.12 Gómez Tejera, Carmen. "Nuestra retardación novelística." Indice, No. 12 (1930), 224-25.

U.13 Laguerre, Enrique A. "La novela." In Problemas de la cultura en Puerto Rico... (Río Piedras: Editorial Universitaria, Universidad de Puerto Rico, 1976), pp. 64-68.

U.14 __________. "[Prólogo]." In his Antología de cuentos puertorriqueños (M: Orión, 1956), pp. 7-16. Various other editions.

U.15 López-Jiménez, Ivette. "El cuento al día." Reintegro, 1, 2 (1980), 15-17.

U.16 Manrique Cabrera, Francisco. "Notas sobre la novela puertorriqueña de los últimos veinticinco años." Asomante, 11, 1 (1955), 20-38.

U.17 Marqués, René. "El cuento puertorriqueño en la promoción del cuarenta." In his Cuentos puertorriqueños de hoy; 3. ed. (Río Piedras: Cultural, 1971), pp. 13-36. Orig. 1959. Also in his Ensayos (1953-1966) (SJ: Antillana, 1966), pp. 81-111. Also in his Ensayos (1953-1971); 2. ed. rev. y aum. (Río Piedras: Antillana, 1972), pp. 85-115. Also as "The Puerto Rican short story of the forties generation." In his The docile Puerto Rican; essays (Philadelphia: Temple University Press, 1976), pp. 74-89.

U.18 Meléndez, Concha. "Cuentistas de ahora en Puerto Rico." In her Palabras para oyentes (SJ: Cordillera, 1971), pp. 187-201. Also in her Obras completas (SJ: Instituto de Cultura Puertorriqueña, 1970-72), III, 623-37.

U.19 __________. "El cuento contemporáneo en Puerto Rico." Caravelle, No. 18 (1972), 77-90. Also Penélope, 1, 2 (1972), 4-11. Also as "Le conte contemporain à Porto Rico." Europe, Nos. 592-93 (1978), 76-89.

U.20 __________. "El cuento en la edad de Asomante, 1945-1955." Asomante, 11, 1 (1955), 39-68. Also in her Literatura de ficción en Puerto Rico: cuento y novela (SJ: Cordillera, 1971), pp. 11-49. Also in her Obras completas (SJ: Instituto de Cultura Puertorriqueña, 1970-72), IV, 437-75.

U.21 __________. "La generación del treinta: cuento y novela." In Literatura puertorriqueña; 21 conferencias (SJ: Instituto de Cultura Puertorriqueña, 1960), pp. 341-76. Also in her Literatura de ficción en Puerto Rico: cuento y novela

(SJ: Cordillera, 1971), pp. 97-134. Also in her Obras completas (SJ: Instituto de Cultura Puertorriqueña, 1970-72), IV, 523-60.

U.22 __________. "La literatura de ficción en Puerto Rico (1955-1963)." Asomante, 20, 3 (1964), 7-23. Also as "La literatura de ficción en Puerto Rico: cuento y novela, 1955-1963." In her Literatura de ficción en Puerto Rico: cuento y novela (SJ: Cordillera, 1971), pp. 51-73. Also in her Obras completas (SJ: Instituto de Cultura Puertorriqueña, 1970-72), IV, 477-99.

U.23 "Los prosistas. Puerto Rican writers." In El libro puertorriqueño de Nueva York. Handbook of the Puerto Rican community (NY/SJ: Plus Ultra Educational Publishers, 1970), pp. 190-92.

U.24 Puerto Rico. Universidad. Facultad de Humanidades. Seminario de Estudios Hispánicos. El cuento puertorriqueño en el siglo XX. Río Piedras: Editorial Universitaria, Universidad de Puerto Rico, 1963.

U.25 Rivera Avilés, Sotero. La generación del 60: aproximación a tres autores. SJ: Instituto de Cultura Puertorriqueña, 1976. Carmelo Rodríguez Torres, Jorge María Ruscalleda Bercedóniz, and Salvador López González.

U.26 Rodríguez, Rafael. "Apuntes sobre el último decenio de narrativa puertorriqueña: el cuento." NNH, 2, 1 (1972), 179-91. Also REP, 2, 1 (1972), 16-25.

U.27 Rodríguez de Laguna, Asela. "Balance novelístico del trienio 1976-1978: conjunción de signos tradicionales y rebeldes en Puerto Rico." Hispamérica, Nos. 23-24 (1979), 133-42.

U.28 Rodríguez-Seda, Asela. "Puerto Rican narratives: aspects of frustration." PCL, 2, 1 (1976), 53-62.

U.29 __________. "La trayectoria de la novelística puertorriqueña contemporánea (1950-1973)." RC-R, 4, 1 (1976), 34-45.

U.30 Rodríguez Torre, Carmelo. "La nueva novela puertorriqueña." Penélope, 1, 3-4 (1973), 31-39.

U.31 Ruffinelli, Jorge. "Entre el gueto y la locura." In his Crítica en marcha; ensayos sobre literatura latinoamericana (M: Premia, 1979), pp. 150-54.

U.32 Vientós Gastón, Nilita. "Una antología del cuento puertorriqueño." In her Indice cultural (Río Piedras: Ediciones de la Universidad de Puerto Rico, 1962-71), II, 41-43.

U.33 __________. "Prólogo [al número dedicado al cuento puertorriqueño actual]." SinN, 5, 4 (1975), 5-8.

V
SPECIAL TOPICS IN PROSE FICTION

V.1 Cruz López, David. *La lengua del jíbaro en la novela costumbrista puertorriqueña.* Unpublished thesis, Universidad de Puerto Rico, 1950.

V.2 Hansen, Terrence L. *The types of the folktale in Cuba, Puerto Rico, the Dominican Republic, and Spanish South America.* Unpublished Ph.D. dissertation, Stanford University, 1952.

V.3 Miller, John C. "The emigrant and New York City: a consideration of four Puerto Rican writers." *MELUS*, 5, 3 (1978), 82-99.

W

GENERAL STUDIES ON THE ESSAY

W.1 Alegría, José S. "El periodismo puertorriqueño desde su aparción hasta los comienzos del siglo XX." In Literatura puertorriqueña; 21 conferencias (SJ: Instituto de Cultura Puertorriqueña, 1960), pp. 513-37.

W.2 Arce de Vázquez, Margot, and Mariana Robles de Cardona. "Veinticinco años del ensayo puertorriqueño." Asomante, 11, 1 (1955), 7-19.

W.3 López González, Julio César. El ensayo y su enseñanza: dos ejemplos puertorriqueños. Río Piedras: Editorial Universitaria, Universidad de Puerto Rico, 1980.

W.4 Pedreira, Antonio S. El periodismo en Puerto Rico; bosquejo histórico desde su iniciación hasta el 1930. La Habana: Ucar, García, 1941. Also in his Obras completas (SJ: Instituto de Cultura Puertorriqueño, 1970), II, 7-552.

W.5 Pérez-Marchand, Monelisa Lina. "La historia de las ideas en Puerto Rico." In Literatura puertorriqueña; 21 conferencias (SJ: Instituto de Cultura Puertorriqueña, 1960), pp. 581-616.

W.6 Robles de Cardona, Mariana. Antología crítica del ensayo en Puerto Rico. Unpublished thesis, Universidad de Puerto Rico, 1951.

W.7 __________. "Concepción orgánica del ensayo puertorriqueño." In Armando Torres León, Ensayos en torno a Puerto Rico (SJ: Departamento de Instrucción Pública, 1968), pp. 1-4.

W.8 __________. "El ensayo en la generación del treinta." In Literatura puertorriqueña; 21 conferencias (SJ: Instituto de Cultura Puertorriqueña, 1960), pp. 319-40.

W.9 __________. "El ensayo puertorriqueño en los últimos veinte años." Asomante, 20, 3 (1964), 24-51.

W.10 __________. "Introducción: concepción orgánica del ensayo puertorriqueño." In her Búsqueda y plasmación de nuestra personalidad; antología crítica del ensayo puertorriqueño desde sus orígenes hasta la generación del 30 (SJ: Club de la Prensa, 1958), pp. 13-35.

W.11 Tirado Mercado, Pablo. Anatomía del periodismo puertorriqueño. M: Costa-Amic, 1974.

W.12 Torner, Florentino N. "Prólogo." In his Antología de ensayos (M: Orión, 1953), pp. 11-23.

W.13 Zavala, Iris M. "Introducción." In Iris M. Zavala, and Rafael Rodríguez, Libertad y crítica en el ensayo político puertorriqueño (Río Piedras: Puerto, 1973), pp. 5-38. Also as "Prologue." In Iris M. Zavala, and Rafael Rodríguez, The intellectual roots of independence: an anthology of Puerto Rican political essays (NY: Monthly Review Press, 1980), pp. 11-42.

CRITICAL WORKS ON PUERTO RICAN LITERATURE: AUTHORS

1

ALEGRÍA, JOSÉ S. (1887-1965)

Critical Essays

1.1 Belaval, Emilio S. "Contestación de don Emilio S. Belaval." In José S. Alegría, Cincuenta años de literatura puertorriqueña; discurso de ingreso (SJ: Academia Puertorriqueña de la Lengua Correspondiente de la Española, 1955), pp. 31-65.

1.2 __________. "Presentación del puertorriqueño José S. Alegría." In José S. Alegría, El alma de la aldea... (SJ, 1972), pp. 7-28. Also SJ: Colección de Estudios Puertorriqueños, 1972; pp. 7-26. Orig. 1956. Also Barcelona: M. Pareja, 1972.

1.3 Braschi, Wilfredo. "José S. Alegría." In his Perfiles puertorriqueños (SJ: Biblioteca de Autores Puertorriqueños, 1978), pp. 133-35.

1.4 Géigel Polanco, Vicente. "Una voz insobornable: José S. Alegría." RICP, No. 28 (1965), 36-37.

1.5 Gómez Costa, Arturo. "José S. Alegría." In his Vendimias en prosa (Barcelona: Vosgos, 1976), pp. 47-51.

1.6 "José S. Alegría. 1886-1965." RICP, No. 28 (1965), 18.

1.7 Meléndez, Concha. "José S. Alegría." In her Personas y libros (SJ: Cordillera, 1970), pp. 51-64. Also in her Obras completas (SJ: Instituto de Cultura Puertorriqueña, 1970-72), IV, 273-86. Orig. RICP, No. 28 (1965), 19-23.

1.8 __________. "Prólogo." In José S. Alegría, Retablos de la aldea...; 8. ed. (SJ, 1974), pp. 7-19. Also Barcelona: M. Pareja, 1971? Various other editions.

1.9 Meléndez Muñoz, Miguel. "José S. Alegría." RICP, No. 28 (1965), 33-35.

2

ALONSO, MANUEL ANTONIO (1822-1889)

Critical Monographs and Dissertations

2.1 Rivera, Modesto. El gíbaro, Manuel A. Alonso: su vida y su obra. Unpublished thesis, Universidad de Puerto Rico, 1947. Revised as Concepto y expresión del costumbrismo en Manuel A. Alonso Pacheco, el gíbaro. Unpublished doctoral dissertation, Universidad Nacional Autónoma de México, 1952.

2.2 ________. Manuel A. Alonso: su vida y su obra. SJ: Coquí, 1966.

Critical Essays

2.3 Bothwell Travieso, Louis C. "Manuel Alonso: costumbrismo y nacionalismo." CAm, No. 110 (1978), 54-62.

2.4 Brau, Salvador. "Al que leyere." In Manuel Antonio Alonso, El jíbaro (Río Piedras: Cultural, 1970), pp. ix-xxvi. Various other editions.

2.5 Coll y Toste, Cayetano. "Manuel Alonso." In his Puertorriqueños ilustres; segunda selección (Barcelona: Rumbos, 1966), pp. 96-100.

2.6 Fernández Juncos, Manuel. "Don Manuel Alonso." In his Semblanzas puertorriqueñas (SJ: J. González Font, 1888), pp. 9-30.

2.7 ________. "Manuel A. Alonso." In his Antología puertorriqueña (NY: Hinds, Hayden & Eldredge, 1913), pp. 19-20. Various other editions.

2.8 González, José Emilio. "En torno a El jíbaro de Manuel A. Alonso." Asomante, 7, 3 (1951), 48-63.

2.9 López, Julio César. "Concepto de la patria en Manuel Alonso (dos cuadros de El jíbaro)." In his Temas y estilos en ocho escritores (SJ, 1967), pp. 79-90.

2.10 Manrique Cabrera, Francisco. "Palabra inicial." In Manuel Antonio Alonso, El jíbaro (Río Piedras: Cultural, 1974), pp. v-vii. Various other editions.

2.11 Morales Carrión, Arturo. "El jíbaro y su época (reflexiones mínimas)." Asomante, 6, 2 (1950), 84-86. Also in his Ojeada al proceso histórico y otros ensayos (SJ: Cordillera, 1971), pp. 120-23. Also 1974.

2.12 Porras Cruz, Jorge Luis. "Un costumbrismo puertorriqueño del siglo XIX (Manuel A. Alonso)." Asomante, 1, 2

(1945), 59-65. Also in his Estudios y artículos (Río Piedras?: Editorial Univesitaria, Universidad de Puerto Rico, 1974), pp. 15-26.

2.13 Rosa-Nieves, Cesáreo. "Manuel A. Alonso (1822-1889). Jibaridad, lengua y propósito." Prensa, 2a época, No. 7 (1959), 27-30. Also in his La lámpara del faro... (SJ: Club de la Prensa, 1957-60), II, 165-83.

2.14 ________. "Manuel A. Alonso Pacheco (1822-1889)." In his Plumas estelares en las letras de Puerto Rico (SJ: Ediciones de la Torre, Universidad de Puerto Rico, 1967), I, 55-70.

2.15 Zayas Micheli, Luis O. "La trascendencia como conyuntura de El jíbaro." In Manuel Antonio Alonso, El jíbaro (Río Piedras: Edil, 1974), pp. 5-19.

3

ALVAREZ MARRERO, FRANCISCO (1847-1881)

Critical Essays

3.1 Brau, Salvador. "Otra víctima." In his Ecos de la batalla (SJ: J. González Font, 1886), pp. 121-25.

3.2 Coll y Toste, Cayetano. "Francisco Alvarez y Marrero (1846-1881)." In his Puertorriqueños ilustres; segunda selección (Barcelona: Rumbos, 1966), pp. 309-11.

3.3 Fernández Juncos, Manuel. "Francisco Alvarez." In Francisco Alvarez Marrero, Obras literarias (SJ: González, 1882), pp. v-xv.

3.4 ________. "Francisco Alvarez." In his Antología puertorriqueña (NY: Hinds, Hayden & Eldredge, 1913), pp. 176-78. Various other editions.

3.5 Pérez Losada, José. "Francisco Alvarez." In Plumas amigas (SJ: Cantero Fernández, 1912), pp. 44-55.

3.6 Rosa-Nieves, Cesáreo. "Francisco Alvarez Marrero (1847-1881)." In his Plumas estelares en las letras de Puerto Rico (SJ: Ediciones de la Torre, Universidad de Puerto Rico, 1967), I, 153-68.

3.7 ________. "Vereda hacia el poeta: notas y rasgos sobre la vida y obra de Francisco Alvarez Marrero (1847-1881)." In Francisco Alvarez Marrero, Antología (SJ: Ateneo Puertorriqueño, 1966), pp. 9-25.

3.8 ________. "Vida y obra de Francisco Alvarez, poeta y romántico." In his Ensayos escogidos... (SJ: Academia de Artes y Ciencias de Puerto Rico, 1970?), pp. 37-51. Orig. RICP, No. 36 (1967), 18-24.

4

ANDREU IGLESIAS, CÉSAR (1915-)

Critical Monographs and Dissertations

4.1 Fromm, G. H. César Andreu Iglesias. Aproximación a su vida y su obra. Río Piedras: Huracán, 1977.

4.2 Sánchez Boudy, José. Las novelas de César Andreu Iglesias y la problemática puertorriqueña actual. Barcelona: Bosch, 1968.

Critical Essays

4.3 González, José Luis. "[Una gota de tiempo]." Asomante, 14, 3 (1958), 89-91.

4.4 Guevara Castañeira, Josefina. "Los derrotados de César Andreu Iglesias." In her Del Yunque a los Andes (SJ: Club de la Prensa, 1959), pp. 203-207.

4.5 Kite, Ralph B. "Socialist realism in the Puerto Rican nationalist novel: Andreu Iglesias' Los derrotados." RevI, 4 (1974), 434-45.

4.6 Rivera de Alvarez, Josefina. "César Andreu Iglesias." RICP, No. 72 (1976), 16-17. Followed by "Cronología sumaria de César Andreu Iglesias," pp. 18-19.

4.7 Vientós Gastón, Nilita. "Una novela puertorriqueña: Los derrotados." In her Indice cultural (Río Piedras: Ediciones de la Universidad de Puerto Rico, 1962-71), I, 287-90.

4.8 ________. "La segunda novela de Andreu Iglesias [Una gota de tiempo]." In her Indice cultural (Río Piedras: Ediciones de la Universidad de Puerto Rico, 1962-71), II, 239-40.

5

ARCE DE VÁZQUEZ, MARGOT (1904-)

Bibliographies

5.1 Arrigoitia, Luis de. "Bibliografía de Margot Arce de Vázquez." REH-PR, 2, 1-4 (1972), 283-92.

Critical Essays

5.2 Arrigoitia, Luis de. "Margot Arce de Vázquez." In Escritores contemporáneos de Puerto Rico (SJ: Sociedad de Autores Puertorriqueños, 1978), pp. 175-200.

5.3 __________. "Margot Arce de Vázquez y la crítica literaria en Puerto Rico." REH-PR, 2, 1-4 (1972), 269-82.

5.4 __________. "Margot Arce de Vázquez y su libro sobre José de Diego." RICP, No. 37 (1967), 40-49. See item no. 31.2.

5.5 Córdova de Braschi, Julia. "Impresiones de Margot Arce: una obra ejemplar puertorriqueña." REH-PR, 2, 1-4 (1972), 255-61.

5.6 Cuchí Coll, Isabel. "Margot Arce." In her Oro nativo; colección de semblanzas puertorriqueñas contemporáneas (SJ, 1936), pp. 51-63.

5.7 Feliciano Fabre, M. A. "Margot Arce y un ensayo ejemplar [El paisaje de Puerto Rico]." REH-PR, 2, 1-4 (1972), 263-68.

5.8 Ferrer Canales, José. "Margot Arce y Gabriel Mistral." In his Acentos cívicos... (Río Piedras: Edil, 1972), pp. 103-18.

5.9 López González, Julio César. "[Margot Arce de Vázquez]." In his El ensayo y su enseñanza (dos ejemplos puertorriqueños) (Río Piedras: Editorial Universitaria, Universidad de Puerto Rico, 1980), pp. 104-12.

5.10 Martín, José Luis. "Visión de la Dra. Margot Arce." In his Arco y flecha... (SJ: Club de la Prensa, 1961), pp. 105-109.

5.11 Meléndez, Concha. "Figuración de Puerto Rico [Impresiones]." In her Figuración de Puerto Rico y otros ensayos (SJ: Instituto de Cultura Puertorriqueña, 1958), pp. 1-6. Also in her Obras completas (SJ: Instituto de Cultura Puertorriqueña, 1970-72), II, 323-29.

5.12 Negrón Muñoz, Angela. "Margot Arce." In her Mujeres de Puerto Rico (SJ: Venezuela, 1935), pp. 254-57.

5.13 Rosa-Nieves, Cesáreo. "Margot Arce de Vázquez (1904-)." In his Plumas estelares en las letras de Puerto Rico (SJ: Ediciones de la Torre, Universidad de Puerto Rico, 1967), II, 477-94.

5.14 _________. "Prólogo." In Margot Arce de Vázquez, Impresiones (SJ: Yaurel, 1950), pp. 9-13. Also as "Impresiones." In his La lámpara del faro... (SJ: Club de la Prensa, 1957-60), I, 129-34.

6

ARRIVÍ, FRANCISCO (1915-)

Critical Essays

6.1 Arriví, Francisco. "Sobre Bolera y plena." In his Entrada por las raíces (entrañamiento en prosa) (SJ: Serie La Entraña, 1964), pp. 121-25.

6.2 _________. "Sobre Sirena." In his Entrada por las raíces (entrañamiento en prosa) (SJ: Serie La Entraña, 1964), pp. 177-82.

6.3 Dauster, Frank. "El concepto de Puerto Rico en algunas obras de Francisco Arriví." In Estudios de literatura hispanoamericana en honor a José J. Arrom (Chapel Hill, NC: North Carolina Studies in the Romance Languages and Literatures, 1974), pp. 257-66.

6.4 _________. "Francisco Arriví: the mask and the garden." Hispania, 45 (1962), 637-43. Also as "Francisco Arriví: la máscara y el jardín." RICP, No. 14 (1962), 37-41.

6.5 _________. "Francisco Arriví y la entrada por las raíces." RICP, No. 50 (1971), 25-30. Also RICP, Nos. 76-77 (1977), 54-60.

6.6 Fernández de Lewis, Piri. "Francisco Arriví (1915)." In Escritores contemporáneos de Puerto Rico (SJ: Sociedad de Autores Puertorriqueños, 1978), pp. 115-30.

6.7 Ferrer Canales, José. "Un drama de Francisco Arriví [Vejigantes]." RICP, No. 27 (1965), 1-4. Also in Instituto Internacional de Literatura Iberoamericana, El teatro en Iberoamérica (M, 1966), pp. 127-34. See commentary by Wilberto Cantón, pp. 123-25.

6.8 Martínez Capó, Juan. "[Isla y nada]." Asomante, 15, 2 (1959), 70-71.

6.9 Montes Huidobro, Matías. "*Vejigantes*: síntesis erótica de la historia puertorriqueña." *RICP*, No. 75 (1977), 33-40.

6.10 Morfi, Angelina. "*Cóctel de don Nadie*. Guiñol absurdo de la actualidad puertorriqueña." *RICP*, No. 47 (1970), 12-14. Also as "*Cóctel de don Nadie* (guiñol absurdo de la actualidad puertorriqueña)." In her *Temas del teatro* (Santo Domingo: Caribe, 1969), pp. 113-19.

6.11 Neglia, Erminio G. "La 'conscientização' de Paulo Freire y su aplicación al teatro." *RCEH*, 5, 2 (1981), 157-66. Arriví and Egon Wolff.

6.12 Padilla, Nieves. "*Teatro* de Francisco Arriví." *Asomante*, 9, 4 (1953), 97-99.

6.13 Pereira, Teresinha Alves. "Sobre el tema de *María Soledad*." *VUM*, 26-XI-1972, p. 11.

6.14 Pérez-Marchand, Monelisa Lina. "La poesía de Francisco Arriví: dos pulsos y una misma trayectoria creadora." *RICP*, No. 9 (1960), 27-33.

7

ASTOL, EUGENIO (1868-1948)

Critical Essays

7.1 Braschi, Wilfredo. "Eugenio Astol." In his *Perfiles puertorriqueños* (SJ: Biblioteca de Autores Puertorriqueños, 1978), pp. 97-99.

7.2 Calderón Aponte, José. "Eugenio Astol." In his *Estados de alma* (SJ: Boletín Mercantil, 1907), pp. 211-14.

7.3 Carreras, Carlos N. "Eugenio Astol." In his *Hombres y mujeres de Puerto Rico* (M: Orión, 1974), pp. 175-83. Orig. 1957.

7.4 Collado Martell, A. "Eugenio Astol: nuestro idealista estoico." *Indice*, No. 8 (1929), 117-18.

7.5 Grismer, Raymond Leonard, and César Arroyo. "Eugenio Astol." In their *Vida y obras de autores puertorriqueños* (La Habana: "Alfa", 1941-), I, 51-53. Also Ann Arbor: University Microfilms, 1976. Also 1978.

7.6 Lloréns, Washington. "Donde el autor juzga a su protagonista." In his *Críticas profanas* (SJ: Progreso, 1936), pp. 91-94.

7.7 Matos Bernier, Félix. "*Cuentos y fantasías* (Eugenio Astol)." In his *Isla de arte* (SJ: La Primavera, 1907), pp. 121-25.

7.8 Meléndez Muñoz, Miguel. "Palabras del Presidente del Ateneo Puertorriqueño en el homenaje que el Club Eugenio María de Hostos tributa hoy a don Eugenio Astol." In his *Obras completas* (SJ: Instituto de Cultura Puertorriqueña, ñ963), III, 58-61.

7.9 __________. "Silueta de un hombre y perfil de una época." In his *Obras completas* (SJ: Instituto de Cultura Puertorriqueña, 1963), III, 48-53.

7.10 Padró, Humberto. "Eugenio Astol, faro." *Indice*, No. 8 (1929), 118.

7.11 Quiñones, Samuel R. "Lo que no es Eugenio Astol: una ligera apuntación impresionista." *Indice*, No. 8 (1929), 119. Also as "Lo que no es Eugenio Astol." In his *Temas y letras* (SJ: Biblioteca de Autores Puertorriqueños, 1955), pp. 155-59.

7.12 Rivera Matos, Manuel. "Eugenio Astol." *Indice*, No. 8 (1929), 124.

7.13 Romeu, José A. "Eugenio Astol, orientador de multitudes." *Indice*, No.8 (1929), 126.

7.14 Rosa-Nieves, Cesáreo. "Eugenio Astol Bussatti (1868-1948)." In his *Plumas estelares en las letras de Puerto Rico* (SJ: Ediciones de la Torre, Universidad de Puerto Rico, 1967), II, 151-62.

8

BALBUENA, BERNARDO DE (1568-1627)

Critical Monographs and Dissertations

8.1 Fernández Juncos, Manuel. *Don Bernardo de Balbuena, obispo de Puerto Rico*. SJ: Las Bellas Artes, 1884.

8.2 Mireles Malpica, Guadalupe. *La significación de Balbuena, Alarcón y Altamirano dentro de la evolución de la cultura literaria mexicana*. Unpublished thesis, Universidad Nacional Autónoma de México, Escuela de Verano, 1954.

8.3 Rojas Garcidueñas, José. *Bernardo de Balbuena: la vida y obra*. M: Universidad Nacional Autónoma de México, Instituto de Investigaciones Estéticas, 1958.

8.4 Van Horne, John. Bernardo de Balbuena; biografía y crítica. Guadalajara, Méx.: Font, 1946.

8.5 ________. El Bernardo of Bernardo de Balbuena. A study of the poem with particular attention to its relation to the epics of Boiardo and Ariosto and to its significance in the Spanish renaissance. Urbana, IL: University of Illinois Press, 1927.

Critical Essays

8.6 Arroyo, Anita. "Balbuena y sus grandezas." RICP, No. 19 (1963), 51-56.

8.7 Banks, Russell. "The New World." Ploughshares, 3, 2 (1976), 8-35.

8.8 Bellini, Giuseppe. "Presenze italiane nell'opera di Balbuena." In his Storia delle relazioni litterarie tra l'Italia e l'America di lingua spagnola (Milano: Cisalpino, 1977), pp. 39-44.

8.9 Castro Leal, Antonio. "La naturaleza americana en Bernardo de Balbuena y Salvador Díaz Mirón." LPot, Nos. 149-50 (1963), 16-17. Also in Instituto Internacional de Literatura Iberoamericana, Literatura iberoamericana; influjos locales (M, 1965), pp. 151-55.

8.10 Corbató, Hermenegildo. "La emergencia de la idea de la nacionalidad en el México colonial." RI, No. 12 (1943), 377-92.

8.11 Domínguez, Luis Adolfo. "Estudio preliminar." In Bernardo de Balbuena, La grandeza mexicana y Compendio apologético en alabanza de la poesía (M: Porrúa, 1971), pp. ix-xl.

8.12 Entrambasaguas, Joaquín. "Los sonetos de Bernardo de Balbuena." RevL, 1, 4 (1969), 483-504.

8.13 Forcadas M., Alberto. "La grandeza mexicana, de Bernardo de Balbuena, en el 'Canto a la Argentina', de Rubén Darío." CA, No. 198 (1975), 229-47.

8.14 Fucilla, Joseph G. "Bernardo de Balbuena." In his Estudios sobre el petrarquismo en España (Madrid: C.S.I.C., 1960), pp. 258-59.

8.15 ________. "Bernardo de Balbuena's Siglo de oro and its sources." HR, 15 (1947), 101-19. Also as "El Siglo de oro de Balbuena y sus fuentes." In his Relaciones hispanolatinas (Madrid: C.S.I.C., 1953), pp. 77-99.

8.16 ________. "Glosses on El Bernardo of Bernardo de Balbuena." MLN, 49 (1934), 20-24.

8.17 García Icazbalceta, Joaquín. "La grandeza mexicana de Balbuena." MAM, 3, 1 (1886), 94-112; 3, 2 (1889), 113-16. Also in his Obras (M: V. Agüeros, 1896), II, 187-215.

8.18 Leal, Luis. "El siglo de oro de Balbuena: primera novela americana." In Homenaje a Andrés Iduarte... (Clear Creek, IN: American Hispanist, 1976), pp. 217-28.

8.19 Lista, Alberto. "Examen del Bernardo de Balbuena." RCLA, 3 (1856), 81-92, 133-43.

8.20 López Estrada, Francisco. "Un libro pastoril mexicano, El siglo de oro de Bernardo de Balbuena." AEA, No. 27 (1970), 787-813.

8.21 Mateo, L. "Centenario de Bernardo de Balbuena." BAAC, 5 (1969), 43-52.

8.22 Medina, José Toribio. "Don Bernardo de Balbuena." In his Escritores hispanoamericanos celebrados por Lope de Vega en el "Laurel de Apolo" (Santiago de Chile, 1922), pp. 49-80.

8.23 Méndez Plancarte, Gabriel. "Dr. Francisco Cervantes de Salazar. Bernardo de Valbuena. Sor Juana Inés de la Cruz." In his Horacio en México (M: Universidad Nacional, 1937), pp. 3-10.

8.24 Millán, María del Carmen. "Dos aspectos de la obra de Bernardo de Balbuena." Rueca, No. 10 (1943), 27-31.

8.25 ________. "El paisaje hiperbólico (Bernardo de Balbuena)." In her El paisaje en la poesía mexicana (M: Universitaria, 1952), pp. 35-36.

8.26 Monterde García Icazbalceta, Francisco. "Balbuena y su alabanza de México." In his Cultura mexicana (M: Intercontinental, 1946), pp. 1-41.

8.27 ________. "Prólogo." In Bernardo de Balbuena, Grandeza mexicana y fragmentos del Siglo de oro y El Bernardo (M: Universidad Nacional Autónoma de México, 1941), pp. vii-xxxvii. 2. ed., 1954.

8.28 Pascual Buxó, José. "Bernardo de Balbuena y el manierismo novohispano." In Studi ispanici (Pisa: Giardini, 1977), pp. 143-62.

8.29 Pierce, Frank. "L'allégorie poétique au XVIe siècle, son évolution et son traitement par Bernardo de Balbuena." BH, 51 (1949), 381-406; 52 (1950), 191-228.

8.30 ________. "El Bernardo of Balbuena, a Baroque fantasy." HR, 13 (1945), 1-23.

8.31 ________. "Descripción de los poemas y estudio de las declaraciones de los mismos poetas. Balbuena." In his

La poesía épica del siglo de oro (Madrid: Gredos, 1961), pp. 276-80.

8.32 Pirotto, Armando D. "Balbuena y Ojeda." In his La literatura en América. El coloniaje (BA: Sociedad Amigos del Libro Rioplatense, 1937), pp. 102-97.

8.33 Porras Muñoz, G. "Nuevos datos sobre Bernardo de Balbuena." RevIn, 10 (1950), 591-97.

8.34 Rivera de Alvarez, Josefina. "Bernardo de Balbuena: reflejo en Puerto Rico de las letras españolas del siglo de oro." RICP, No. 39 (1968), 20-21.

8.35 Roggiano, Alfredo A. "Instalación del barroco hispánico en América: Bernardo de Balbuena." In Homage to Irving A. Leonard... (East Lansing, MI: Michigan State Unviersity, Latin American Studies Center, 1977), pp. 61-74.

8.36 Rubio Mañe, Jorge Ignacio. "Bernardo de Balbuena y su Grandeza mexicana." BAGN, 2a serie, 1, 1 (1960), 87-100.

8.37 __________. "Noticias biográficas adicionales de Bernardo de Balbuena." BAGN, 2a serie, 7, 4 (1966), 857-62.

8.38 Sánchez, Luis Alberto. "Bernardo de Balbuena." In his Escritores representativos de América; 1ª serie (Madrid: Gredos, 1963), I, 39-48.

8.39 Tirri, Néstor. "Bernardo de Balbuena y la comunidad barroca hispanoamericana." CuS, Nos. 8-9 (1967-68), 45-54.

8.40 Triviños, Gilberto. "Bernardo del Carpio desencantado por Bernardo de Balbuena." RChL, Nos. 16-17 (1980-81), 315-38.

8.41 Van Horne, John. "Bernardo de Balbuena y la literatura de la Nueva España." Arbor, 3, 8 (1945), 205-14.

8.42 __________. "Introduction." In Bernardo de Balbuena, La grandeza mexicana (Urbana, IL: University of Illinois, 1930), pp. 11-19.

8.43 __________. "El nacimiento de Bernardo de Balbuena." RFE, 20 (1933), 160-68.

8.44 Villegas García, Carlos. "Bernardo de Balbuena." VUM, No. 398 (1958), 5.

8.45 Wyuter, Silvia. "Bernardo de Balbuena, epic poet and abbot of Jamaica 1562-1627." JamJ, 4, 1 (1970), 11-19.

8.46 Zertuche, Francisco M. "Bernardo de Balbuena y la Grandeza mexicana." In his Literatura mexicana de los siglos XVI, XVII y XVIII (Monterrey, Méx.: Centenario del Colegio Civil, Universidad de Nuevo León, 1957), pp. 87-106.

9

BALSEIRO, JOSÉ A. (1900-)

Critical Essays

9.1 Adams, Nicholson B. "Prefacio." In José A. Balseiro, Cuatro individualistas de España (Chapel Hill, NC: University of North Carolina Press, 1949), pp. vii-ix.

9.2 Babín, María Teresa. "Una obra de Balseiro [El vigía]." In her Jornadas literarias (temas de Puerto Rico) (Barcelona: Rumbos, 1967), pp. 263-69.

9.3 Camejo, Rafael W. "José A. Balseiro." In his Florecían los rosales (Caracas: Hernández, 1952), pp. 237-43.

9.4 Colberg Petrovich, Juan Enrique. "El caso literario de José A. Balseiro." In his Cuatro autores clásicos contemporáneos de Puerto Rico (SJ: Cordillera, 1966), pp. 161-211.

9.5 Colorado, Antonio J. "[En vela mientras el mundo duerme]." La torre, No. 3 (1953), 192-93.

9.6 Cuchí Coll, Isabel. "José A. Balseiro." In her Oro nativo; colección de semblanzas puertorriqueñas contemporáneas (SJ, 1936), pp. 7-24.

9.7 "Fragmentos de algunas opiniones acerca del tomo I de Expresión de Hispanoamérica." In José A. Balseiro, Expresión de Hispanoamérica; segunda serie (SJ: Instituto de Cultura Puertorriqueña, 1963), pp. 187-95.

9.8 García Blanco, Manuel. "Prólogo." In José A. Balseiro, Saudades de Puerto Rico. La pureza cautiva (Madrid: Aguilar, 1957), pp. 15-26.

9.9 Grismer, Raymond Leonard, and César Arroyo. "José A. Balseiro." In their Vida y obras de autores puertorriqueños (La Habana: "Alfa", 1941-), I, 7-10. Also Ann Arbor: University Microfilms, 1976. Also 1978. Only vol. I ever published.

9.10 Marañón, Gregorio. "Prólogo." In José A. Balseiro, Vigía; 2. ed. (SJ: Biblioteca de Autores Puertorriqueños, 1956), II, 13-24. Orig. 1928.

9.11 Monterde, Francisco. "Prólogo." In José A. Balseiro, Expresión de Hispanoamérica; primera serie (SJ: Instituto de Cultura Puertorriqueña, 1960), pp. 7-10.

9.12 Pagán, Bolívar. "Flores de primavera." In his América y otras páginas (SJ, 1922), pp. 163-64.

9.13 Reyes, Alfonso. "Prólogo." In José A. Balseiro, La pureza cautiva (La Habana: Lex, 1946), pp. 11-15. Also in

José A. Balseiro, Saudades de Puerto Rico. La pureza cautiva (Madrid: Aguilar, 1957), pp. 145-47.

9.14 Ribera Chevremont, Evaristo. "Prólogo." In José A. Balseiro, Las palomas de Eros (Madrid: Editorial-América, 192?), pp. 11-19.

9.15 Rosa-Nieves, Cesáreo. "José A. Balseiro (1900-)." In his Plumas estelares en las letras de Puerto Rico (SJ: Ediciones de la Torre, Universidad de Puerto Rico, 1967), II, 277-99.

9.16 ________. "La pureza cautiva." In his La lámpara del faro... (SJ: Club de la Prensa, 1957-60), I, 117-21.

10

BAUZÁ, OBDULIO (1907-)

Critical Essays

10.1 Castro, Tomás de Jesús. "Obdulio Bauzá." In his Esbozos (Barcelona: Rumbos, 1957), II, 124-27.

10.2 Defendini, Pablo. "Prólogo." In Obdulio Bauzá, La canción de los olivos (Barcelona: Rumbos, 1958), pp. 9-17.

10.3 Diez de Andino, Juan. "La canción de los olivos." In his Voces de la farándula (Barcelona, 1959), pp. 306-309.

10.4 ________. "Un poeta en Puerto Rico." In his Desmenuzando hechos (Barcelona: Rvmbos, 1957), pp. 84-87.

10.5 Meléndez, Concha. "Prólogo: tiempo y recuerdo en la poesía de Obdulio Bauzá." In Obdulio Bauzá, Selected poems (Madrid: Escelier, 1961), pp. 7-20. Also as "Tiempo y recuerdo en la poesía de Obdulio Bauzá." In her Poetas hispanoamericanos diversos (SJ: Cordillera, 1971), pp. 165-73. Also in her Obras completas (SJ: Instituto de Cultura Puertorriqueña, 1970-72), IV, 171-79.

11

BELAVAL, EMILIO S. (1903-)

11.1 Lugo de Marichal, Flavia. "Bibliografía." SinN, 4, 4 (1974), 105-10.

Critical Monographs and Dissertations

11.2 Lugo de Marichal, Flavia. Belaval y sus Cuentos para fomentar el turismo. SJ: Coquí, 1972.

11.3 Sánchez, Luis Rafael. Fabulación e ideología en la cuentística de Emilio S. Belaval. SJ: Instituto de Cultura Puertorriqueña, 1979.

Critical Essays

11.4 Arriví, Francisco. "Emilio Belaval: conciencia capital de teatro." RICP, Nos. 76-77 (1977), 31-36.

11.5 Belaval, Emilio S. "Documento epistolar: carta a María Teresa Babín sobre 'La muerte'." SinN, 4, 4 (1974), 101-1-4.

11.6 Dávila, José Antonio. "A Emilio S. Belaval." In his Prosa: ensayos, artículos y cartas literarias (SJ: Sociedad de Autores Puertorriqueños, 1971), pp. 277-78.

11.7 "Emilio S. Belaval: biografía mínima." SinN, 4, 4 (1974), 7-8.

11.8 Géigel Polanco, Vicente. "Emilio S. Belaval." In his Valores de Puerto Rico (NY: Arno Press, 1975), pp. 125-30. Orig. SJ: Eugenio María de Hostos, 1943.

11.9 González, José Emilio. "Visiones del ensayo en Emilio S. Belaval." SinN, 4, 4 (1974), 37-53.

11.10 González, Nilda. "La vida de Emilio S. Belaval." Asomante, 16, 3 (1960), 70-71.

11.11 Guerrero Zamora, Juan. "Teatro de Emilio S. Belaval." RICP, No. 55 (1972), 24-28.

11.12 Marqués, René. "Apuntes para una interpretación: un autor, un intríngulis y una obra." Asomante, 9, 4 (1953), 35-40. Also as "Un autor, un intríngulis y una obra." In his Ensayos (1953-1966) (SJ: Antillana, 1966), pp. 15-24. Also in his Ensayos (1953-1971); 2. ed. rev. y aum. (Río Piedras:

Antillana, 1972), pp. 15-25.

11.13 Martínez Capó, Juan. "Entrada en la temática de los cuentos de Emilio S. Belaval." SinN, 4, 4 (1974), 9-36.

11.14 Meléndez, Concha. "Ficciones narrativas de Emilio S. Belaval." RICP, No. 55 (1972), 2-6.

11.15 Pedreira, Antonio S. "Los cuentos de la universidad." In his Aclaraciones y crítica (Río Piedras: Phi Eta Mu, Universidad de Puerto Rico, 1941), pp. 241-47. Also Río Piedras: Edil, 1969. Also in his Obras completas (SJ: Instituto de Cultura Puertorriqueña, 1970), I, 631-35.

11.16 Rosa-Nieves, Cesáreo. "Emilio S. Belaval (1903-)." In his Plumas estelares en las letras de Puerto Rico (SJ: Ediciones de la Torre, Universidad de Puerto Rico, 1967), II, 387-98.

11.17 Sánchez, Luis Rafael. "Prólogo." In Emilio S. Belaval, Los problems de la cultura puertorriqueña (Río Piedras: Cultural, 1977), pp. 7-21.

11.18 ________. "El teatro de Emilio S. Belaval." SinN, 4, 4 (1974), 54-61.

12

BENÍTEZ Y DE ARCE DE GAUTIER, ALEJANDRINA (1819-1879)

Critical Monographs and Dissertations

12.1 Acosta, José J. Alejandrina Benítez y Arce de Gautier. Puerto-Rico [sic]: Imprenta y Librería de Acosta, 1886. Also SJ: Acosta, 1899.

12.2 Girón de Segura, Socorro. Vida y obra de María Bibiana y Alejandrina Benítez. Palma de Mallorca: Mossén Alcover, 1967.

Critical Essays

12.3 Angelis, María Luisa de. "Alejandrina Benítez y de Arce de Gautier." In her Mujeres puertorriqueñas que se han distinguido en el cultivo de las ciencias, las letras y las artes desde el siglo XVII hasta nuestros días (SJ: Boletín Mercantil, 1908), pp. 17-26.

12.4 Fernández Juncos, Manuel. "Alejandrina Benítez." In his Antología puertorriqueña (NY: Hinds, Hayden & Eldredge, 1913), pp. 88-89. Various other editions.

12.5 Negrón Muñoz, Angela. "Alejandrina Benítez de Arce y de Gautier." In her Mujeres de Puerto Rico (SJ: Venezuela, 1935), pp. 31-33.

12.6 Rosa-Nieves, Cesáreo. "Alejandrina Benítez y de Arce de Gautier (1819-1879)." In his Plumas estelares en las letras de Puerto Rico (SJ: Ediciones de la Torre, Universidad de Puerto Rico, 1967), I, 71-82.

12.7 Torres, José Antonio. "Alejandrina Benítez." Asomante, 7, 4 (1951), 54-60.

13

BERNAOLA, PEDRO (1916-1972)

Critical Essays

13.1 Belaval, Emilio S. "Prólogo al trémolo." In Pedro Bernaola, Trémolo de angustias (Barcelona: Rumbos, 1961), pp. 7-15.

13.2 Díaz Mesón, Juan. "Pedro Bernaola ha muerto." RICP, No. 57 (1972), 27-29.

13.3 Meléndez, Concha. "Premio a la poesía de Pedro Bernaola." In Pedro Bernaola, Diario (Barcelona: Rumbos, 1965), pp. 7-17. Also in her Poetas hispanoamericanos (SJ: Cordillera, 1971), pp. 185-95. Also in her Obras completas (SJ: Instituto de Cultura Puertorriqueña, 1970-72), IV, 191-201.

13.4 ________. "El recto perfil buscado; notas sobre la poesía de Pedro Bernaola." In her Poetas hispanoamericanos diversos (SJ: Cordillera, 1971), pp. 175-83. Also in her Obras completas (SJ: Instituto de Cultura Puertorriqueña, 1970-72), IV, 181-89.

13.5 Ramírez de Arellano. Diana. "En torno a una estética: la poesía de Pedro Bernaola." RICP, No. 47 (1970), 37-44.

14

BETANCES, RAMÓN EMETERIO (1827-1898)

Critical Monographs and Dissertations

14.1 Carreras, Carlos N. Betances, el antillano proscrito. SJ: Club de la Prensa, 1961.

14.2 Imagen de Betances. SJ: Partido Nacionalista de Puerto Rico, 1967.

14.3 Suárez Díaz, Ada. El doctor Ramón Betances: su vida y su obra. SJ: Ateneo Puertorriqueño, 1968.

14.4 Todd, Roberto Henry. Génesis de la bandera puertorriqueña. Betances, Henna, Arillaga; 2. ed. Madrid: Iberoamericanas, 1967.

Critical Essays

14.5 Coll y Toste, Cayetano. "Puertorriqueños ilustres. Betances (1827-1898)." BHPR, 4 (1917), 294-96. Also as "Ramón Emeterio Betances (1827-1898)." In his Puertorriqueños ilustres; primera selección (NY: Las Américas, 1952), pp. 183-86.

14.6 __________. "Ramón Emeterio Betances (1827-1898)." In his Puertorriqueños ilustres; segunda selección (Barcelona: Rumbos, 1966), pp. 136-39.

14.7 Estrade, Paul. "Cómo Betances defendió al negro hatiano: carta a Jules Auguste (1882)." SinN, 4, 2 (1973), 70-77.

14.8 Ferrer Canales, José. "Martí y Betances." CA, No. 200 (1975), 130-37.

14.9 Figueroa, Loida. "Betances, el irreductible." Atenea, 9, 3-4 (1972), 29-39.

14.10 Fonfrías, Ernesto Juan. "A puertas abiertas (para el libro de Betances)." In his Sementera; ensayos breves y biografías mínimas (SJ: Club de la Prensa, 1962), pp. 27-31.

14.11 __________. "Ramón Emeterio Betances." In his Sementera; ensayos breves y biografías mínimas (SJ: Club de la Prensa, 1962), pp. 61-71.

14.12 Géigel Polanco, Vicente. "Betances." AtPR, 3 (1939), 189-95.

14.13 __________. "Betances, una voz de todos los tiempos." In his El despertar de un pueblo (SJ: Biblioteca de Autores Puertorriqueños, 1942), pp. 105-16.

14.14 Gilard, Jacques. "Betances en Toulouse, 1839-1846." SinN, 6, 4 (1976), 42-58.

14.15 Hostos, Adolfo de. "Ramón Emeterio Betances (1827-1898)." In his Hombres representativos de Puerto Rico (SJ, 1961), pp. 53-57.

14.16 Lugo Filippi, Carmen. "Betances y Voltaire." RICP, No. 40 (1968), 28-33.

14.17 Maldonado-Denis, Manuel. "Vigencia de Betances." RICP, No. 59 (1973), 53-58.

14.18 Meléndez, Concha. "Día y noche de Betances." In her Personas y libros (SJ: Cordillera, 1970), pp. 101-106. Also in her Obras completas (SJ: Instituto de Cultura Puertorriqueña, 1970-72), IV, 323-28. Orig. RICP, No. 40 (1968), 48-51.

14.19 Neumann Gandía, Eduardo. "Doctor Ramón E. Betances." In his Benefactores y hombres notables de Puerto-Rico (Ponce: "Listín Comercial", 1899), II, 221-30.

14.20 Pagán, Bolívar. "Betances." In his América y otras páginas (SJ, 1922), pp. 89-96.

14.21 ________. "Betances, Betances, Betances." ILit, Nos. 2-3 (1969), 25.

14.22 Rama, Carlos M. "Prólogo." In Ramón Emeterio Betances, Las Antillas para los antillanos (SJ: Instituto de Cultura Puertorriqueña, 1975), pp. v-lxiv.

14.23 Rodríguez Otero, Eladio. "El grito de Lares, Betances y Pablo Serrano." ILit, Nos. 2-3 (1969), 23-24.

14.24 ________. "Tres imágenes de Betances." RICP, No. 70 (1976), 27-29.

14.25 Ruiz García, Zoilo. "Dr. Ramón Emeterio Betances." In his Nuestros hombres de antaño (Mayagüez: Mayagüez Publishing Co., 1920), pp. 57-59.

14.26 Suárez Díaz, Ada. "Betances en Nueva York y Haití." RICP, No. 43 (1969), 27-34.

14.27 ________. "Introducción." In Ramón Emeterio Betances, Obras...; epistolario, año 1885 (Río Piedras: Huracán, 1978), pp. 7-9.

15

BLANCO, ANTONIO NICOLÁS (1887-1945)

Critical Monographs and Dissertations

15.1 Rivera Quiñones, Eladio. Antonio Nicolás Blanco: su vida y su obra. Unpublished thesis, Universidad de Puerto Rico, 1961.

Critical Essays

15.2 Hernández Aquino, Luis. "La poesía de Antonio Nicolás Blanco." In Antonio Nicolás Blanco, Antología (SJ?: Ateneo Puertorriqueño, 1959?), pp. 5-11.

15.3 Lefebre, Enrique. "El jardín de Pierrot." In his Paisajes mentales (SJ: Cantero, Fernández, 1918), pp. 151-60.

15.4 Massanet, Agustina. "Antonio Nicolás Blanco." In Puerto Rico. Universidad. Colegio de Artes y Ciencias. Seminario de Estudios Hispánicos, La naturaleza en la poesía puertorriqueña del siglo XX (Río Piedras, 1942), pp. 8-21. Same as the Boletín de la Universidad de Puerto Rico, serie XIII, no. 2.

15.5 Rosa-Nieves, Cesáreo. "Antonio Nicolás Blanco (1887-1945)." In his Plumas estelares en las letras de Puerto Rico (SJ: Ediciones de la Torre, Universidad de Puerto Rico, 1967), II, 235-44.

15.6 Samalea Iglesias, Luis. "Algunas palabras a manera de proemio." In Antonio Nicolás Blanco, El jardín de Pierrot (SJ: Antillana, 1914), pp. 7-14.

16

BLANCO, TOMÁS (1897-)

Critical Monographs and Dissertations

16.1 Frau Alou, María A. Estudio estilístico; los vates de Tomás Blanco. Unpublished thesis, Universidad de Puerto Rico, 1964.

Critical Essays

16.2 Arce de Vázquez, Margot. "[Los aguinaldos del infante]." Asomante, 10, 4 (1954), 96-98.

16.3 __________. "[Los cinco sentidos]." Asomante, 12, 3 (1956), 105-108.

16.4 __________. "Los cuentos de Tomás Blanco." In Tomás Blanco, Cuentos sin ton ni son (SJ: Instituto de Cultura Puertorriqueña, 1970), pp. 5-10.

16.5 __________. "La obra literaria de Tomás Blanco." Insula, Nos. 356-57 (1976), 3. Also RICP, No. 67 (1975), 3-11.

16.6 __________. "Tomás Blanco, ensayista. Primer asedio." RICP, No. 18 (1963), 1-5.

16.7 Arrillaga, Zayda M. "'Naufragio' de Tomás Blanco." In Puerto Rico. Universidad. Facultad de Humanidades. Seminario de Estudios Hispánicos, El cuento puertorriqueño en el siglo XX (Río Piedras: Editorial Universitaria, Universidad de Puerto Rico, 1963), pp. 43-71.

16.8 Braschi, Wilfredo. "Tomás Blanco." In his Perfiles puertorriqueños (SJ: Biblioteca de Autores Puertorriqueños, 1978), pp. 58-60.

16.9 Pedreira, Antonio S. "Prontuario histórico de Puerto Rico." In his Obras completas (SJ: Instituto de Cultura Puertorriqueña, 1970), I, 611-20.

16.10 Rodríguez Otero, Eladio. "Elogio de Tomás Blanco." RICP, No. 63 (1974), 11-14-

16.11 Rosa-Nieves, Cesáreo. "Tomás Blanco (1897-)." In his Plumas estelares en las letras de Puerto Rico (SJ: Ediciones de la Torre, Universidad de Puerto Rico, 1967), II, 461-76.

16.12 Vientós Gastón, Nilita. "Un libro de Tomás Blanco [Los cinco sentidos]." In her Indice cultural (Río Piedras: Ediciones de la Universidad de Puerto Rico, 1962-71), I, 201-202.

BRAU, SALVADOR (1842-1912)

Critical Monographs and Dissertations

17.1 Córdova Landrón, Arturo. Salvador Brau, su vida, su obra, su época; ensayo histórico biográfico crítico. Río Piedras: Universidad de Puerto Rico, 1949. 2. ed., SJ: Coquí, 1968.

17.2 Cortón, Antonio. A Salvador Brau y Frasquito Oller. Madrid: Enrique Teodoro, 1895.

17.3 Encarnación Caparrós, Marie. Salvador Brau, vida y obra. Unpublished thesis, Universidad de Puerto Rico, 1961.

17.4 Fernández Méndez, Eugenio. Salvador Brau y su tiempo; drama y paradoja de una sociedad. Río Piedras: Universidad de Puerto Rico, 1956. Same as item no. 17.15.

17.5 Real, Cristóbal. Salvador Brau: estudio biográfico-crítico. SJ, 1910.

Critical Essays

17.6 Abril, Mariano. "Un antillano ilustre: Salvador Brau." RAnt, 1, 1 (1913), 127-28.

17.7 Babín, María Teresa. "Una época y su hombre. Salvador Brau: 1842-1912." In her Jornadas literarias (temas de Puerto Rico) (Barcelona: Rvmbos, 1967), pp. 256-62.

17.8 Córdova Landrón, Arturo. "Salvador Brau, maestro de periodistas." Asomante, 5, 3 (1949), 49-51.

17.9 Cortón, Antonio. "Salvador Brau." In Salvador Brau, Un poema de Brau [Mi campo santo] (SJ: Boletín Mercantil, 1905), pp. 3-13.

17.10 Dalmau Canet, Sebastián. "D. Salvador Brau." In his Crepúsculos literarios (SJ: Boletín Mercantil, 1903), pp. 19-23.

17.11 Diez de Andino, Juan. "La estatua del patricio." In his Desmenuzando hechos (Barcelona: Rvmbos, 1957), pp. 153-56.

17.12 Fernández Juncos, Manuel. "Salvador Brau." In his Semblanzas puertorriqueñas (SJ: J. González Font, 1888), pp. 97-122.

17.13 __________. "Salvador Brau." In Salvador Brau, Ecos de la batalla (primera serie) (SJ: J. González Font, 1886), pp. v-xviii.

17.14 Fernández Méndez, Eugenio. "Elogio a Salvador Brau." RICP, No. 60 (1973), 29-31.

17.15 _________. "Introducción." In Salvador Brau, Disquisiciones sociológicas y otros ensayos (Río Piedras: Universidad de Puerto Rico, 1956), pp. 7-120. Same as item no. 17.4.

17.16 _________. "Salvador Brau, precursor de una sociología americana." La torre, No. 14 (1956(, 159-77.

17.17 González, José Luis. "Tres fundadores de la literatura puertorriqueña [Hostos, Brau, Zeno Gandía]." Humanismo, Nos. 48-49 (1958), 96-115.

17.18 González, Nilda. "El teatro de Salvador Brau." RICP, No. 18 (1963), 15-24.

17.19 Hostos, Adolfo de. "Salvador Brau (1842-1912)." In his Hombres representativos de Puerto Rico (SJ, 1961), pp. 72-78.

17.20 Malaret, Augusto. "Salvador Brau." In his Medallas de oro; 2. ed. (SJ: Biblioteca de Autores Puertorriqueños, 1938), pp. 27-61. 3. ed., SJ, 1942; pp. 29-65. 4. ed., M: Orión, 1952; pp. 35-84.

17.21 Matos Bernier, Félix. "Triángulo equilátero (Brau, Padilla, Valle)." In his Isla de arte (SJ: La Primavera, 1907), pp. 224-28.

17.22 Mauría, José María. "Salvador Brau y la historia." Latino América, 9 (1976), 211-19.

17.23 Pagán, Juan Bautista. "Don Salvador Brau." In his Dionisios; de los orígenes del teatro... (SJ: Biblioteca de Autores Puertorriqueños, 1957), pp. 154-67.

17.24 Rosa-Nieves, Cesáreo. "Salvador Brau y Asencio 1842-1912)." In his Plumas estelares en las letras de Puerto Rico (SJ: Ediciones de la Torre, Universidad de Puerto Rico, 1967), I, 307-25.

17.25 Sáez, Antonia. "Salvador Brau, dramaturgo." RAMG, 1, 3 (1939), 26-33.

18

BURGOS, JULIA DE (1914-1953)

Critical Monographs and Dissertations

18.1 Cabrera Freiría, Yvette de Lourdes. Vida y poesía de Julia de Burgos. Unpublished thesis, Universidad de Puerto Rico, 1957.

18.2 Cuchí Coll, Isabel. Dos poetisas de América: Clara Lair, Julia de Burgos. Barcelona: Manuel Pareja, 1970. Orig. SJ: Departamento de Instrucción, 1965.

18.3 Jiménez de Báez, Yvette. Julia de Burgos; vida y poesía. SJ: Borinquen, 1966.

18.4 Quiroga, Carmen Lucila. "Julia de Burgos: el desarrollo de la conciencia femenina en la expresión poética." DAI, 41 (1981), 5117A.

Critical Essays

18.5 Arce de Vázquez, Margot. "Los últimos versos de Julia de Burgos." AyL, No. 5 (1953), 5.

18.6 Arroyo, Anita. "Julia de Burgos, diosa del agua." RICP, No. 38 (1968), 20-23.

18.7 Braschi, Wilfredo. "Julia de Burgos." In his Perfiles puertorriqueños (SJ: Biblioteca de Autores Puertorriqueños, 1978), pp. 23-25.

18.8 "La crítica contemporánea y Julia de Burgos." In Julia de Burgos, Poemas de 20 surcos (SJ: Venezuela, 1938), pp. 3-7.

18.9 Dávila, José Antonio. "La verdad sencilla de Julia de Burgos." In his Prosa: ensayos, artículos y cartas literarias (SJ: Sociedad de Autores Puertorriqueños, 1971), pp. 165-70.

18.10 "Dos cartas inéditas de Julia de Burgos." SinN, 7, 3 (1976), 86-100.

18.11 Ferré, Rosario. "Carta a Julia Burgos." In her Sitio a Eros: trece ensayos literarios (M: Joaquín Mortiz, 1980), pp. 127-32.

18.12 Gale, Leonore. "Julia de Burgos: visión y expresividad." RICP, No. 57 (1972), 31-42.

18.13 González, José Emilio. "Algo más sobre la vida y la poesía de Julia de Burgos." La torre, No. 51 (1965), 151-74.

18.14 __________. "Estudio preliminar." In Julia Burgos, Obra poética (SJ: Instituto de Cultura Puertorriqueña, 1961), pp. 9-59.

18.15 __________. "La individualidad poética de Julia de Burgos." Río Piedras, Nos. 3-4 (1973-74), 47-59.

18.16 __________. "Julia de Burgos: intensa siempreviva." Asomante, 9, 4 (1953), 23-34.

18.17 __________. "Julia de Burgos: la mujer y la poesía." SinN, 7, 3 (1976), 86-104.

18.18 __________. "La poesía de Julia de Burgos." In Julia de Burgos, Obra poética (SJ: Instituto de Cultura Puertorriqueña, 1957), pp. 11-59.

18.19 Jiménez, Ivette de Lourdes. "Del dolor-vivir en Julia de Burgos." Educación, 13, 9 (1963), 129-39.

18.20 "Julia de Burgos." In El libro puertorriqueño de Nueva York. Handbook of the Puerto Rican community (NY/SJ: Plus Ultra Educational Publishers, 1970), pp. 223-29.

18.21 Laguerre, Enrique A. "Julia de Burgos." In his Pulso de Puerto Rico, 1952-1954 (SJ: Biblioteca de Autores Puertorriqueños, 1956), pp. 274-82.

18.22 Laguna Díaz, Elpidio. "Dos instantes de Julia de Burgos: su concepción del tiempo." Asomante, 25, 3 (1969), 38-49.

18.23 __________. "The phenomenology of nothingness in the poetry of Julia de Burgos." In Latin American woman writers: yesterday and today (Pittsburgh: Latin American Literary Review, 1977), pp. 127-33.

18.24 López Jiménez, Ivette. "Julia de Burgos: los textos comunicantes." SinN, 10, 1 (1979), 47-68.

18.25 Matos Paoli, Francisco. "El río y el mar en Julia de Burgos." RICP, No. 67 (1975), 28-32.

18.26 Mir, Pedro. "Julia del agua." RICP, No. 59 (1973), 42-43.

18.27 Neggers, Gladys. "Clara Lair y Julia de Burgos: reminiscencias de Evaristo Ribera Chevremont y Jorge Font Saldaña." RevI, 4 (1974), 258-63.

18.28 Quiñones, Samuel R. "Canción de la verdad sencilla." In his Temas y letras; 3. ed. (SJ: Biblioteca de Autores Puertorriqueños, 1955), pp. 161-66.

18.29 Ramírez de Arellano, Diana. "Conocimiento artístico de un hecho artístico: Julia de Burgos." RICP, No. 6 (1960), 1-5.

18.30 __________. "Homenaje a Julia de Burgos, capítulo de avanzada en la poesía de Puerto Rico." In her Poesía contemporánea en lengua española (Madrid: Murillo, 1961), pp. 277-355.

18.31 Rivera Matos, Manuel. "Los motivos del río en la poesía de Julia de Burgos." AtPR, 4, 1 (1940), 31-41.

18.32 Rivero, Eliana. "Dialéctica de la persona poética en la obra de Julia de Burgos." RCLL, No. 4 (1976), 31-41.

18.33 __________. "Julia de Burgos: y su visión poética del ser." SinN, 11, 3 (1980), 51-57.

18.34 Santos, Nelly E. "El itinerario temático de Julia de Brugos: el amor y la muerte." CA, No. 203 (1975), 234-46.

18.35 __________. "Love and death: the thematic journey of Julia de Burgos." In Latin American women writers: yesterday and today (Pittsburgh: Latin American Literary Review, 1977), pp. 134-47.

18.36 Torres Morales, José A. "Palabra y creación poética." In his Ensayos literarios (Río Piedras: Editorial Universitaria, Universidad de Puerto Rico, 1977), pp. 25-34.

19

CADILLA DE MARTÍNEZ, MARÍA (1884-1951)

Critical Essays

19.1 Arce de Vázquez, Margot. "María Cadilla de Martínez, la incansable hilandera." In her Impresiones (SJ: Yaurel, 1950), pp. 35-37.

19.2 Carreras, Carlos N. "María Cadilla de Martínez." In his Hombres y mujeres de Puerto Rico (M: Orión, 1957), pp. 231-38. Various subsequent editions.

19.3 Castro, Tomás de Jesús. "María Cadilla de Martínez." In his Esbozos críticos (SJ: Baldrich, 1945), pp. 53-58.

19.4 Dávila, José Antonio. "Juegos y canciones infantiles de María Cadilla de Martínez." In his Prosa: ensayos, artículos y cartas literarias (SJ: Sociedad de Autores Puertorriqueños, 1971), pp. 131-33.

19.5 Figueroa de Cifredo, Patria. "Presencia de tres mujeres en la investigación en Puerto Rico." BAAC, 14, 3-4 (1978), 121-39. Cadilla de Martínez inter alias.

19.6 Grismer, Raymond Leonard, and César Arroyo. "María Cadilla de Martínez." In their Vida y obras de autores puertorriqueños (La Habana: "Alfa", 1941-), I, 43-46. Also Ann Arbor: University Microfilms, 1976. Also 1978. Only vol. I ever published.

19.7 Guevara Castañeira, Josefina. "Obra y personalidad de la doctora Cadilla de Martínez." In her Del Yunque a los Andes (SJ: Club de la Prensa, 1959), pp. 155-76.

19.8 Lima, Sílvio Júlio de Albuquerque. "O folclore na obra de María Cadilla de Martínez." In his História, literatura e folclore de América espanhola (Rio de Janeiro: A. Coelho Branco, 1945), pp. 145-203. Signed Júlio Sílvio.

19.9 Limón de Arce, José. "María Cadilla de Martínez (Liana)." In his Poetas arecibeños, 1832-1904 (Arecibo?: Harry C. del Pozo, 1926), pp. 73-75. Followed by a selection of her poetry.

19.10 Mendoza, Vicente T. "Doña María Cadilla de Martínez. Diciembre 21 de 1886 - agosto 23 de 1951." ASFM, 8 (1954), 117-98.

19.11 Morales, Angel Luis. "[Hitos de la raza]." Asomante, 1, 4 (1945), 117-19.

19.12 Negrón Muñoz, Angela. "María Cadilla de Martínez." In her Mujeres de Puerto Rico (SJ: Venezuela, 1935), pp. 174-76.

19.13 Rosa-Nieves, Cesáreo. "María Cadilla de Martínez (seud. Liana: 1884-1951)." In his Plumas estelares en las letras de Puerto Rico (SJ: Ediciones de la Torre, Universidad de Puerto Rico, 1967), II, 179-98.

20

CANALES, NEMESIO R. (1878-1923)

Critical Monographs and Dissertations

20.1 Babín, María Teresa. Genio y figura de Nemesio R. Canales. SJ: Biblioteca de Autores Puertorriqueños, 1978.

20.2 Montaña Peláez, Servando. Nemesio Canales: lenguaje y situación. Río Piedras: Editorial Universitaria, Universidad de Puerto Rico, 1973.

20.3 Montes de Rodríguez, Encarnita. Nemesio R. Canales

(1878-1923). Vida y obra. Unpublished thesis, Universidad de Puerto Rico, 1967.

20.4 Quiñones, Samuel R. Nemesio R. Canales, el humorista de Puerto Rico. SJ: Senado de Puerto Rico, 1961.

Critical Essays

20.5 "Apreciaciones y comentarios: la personalidad de Canales." Indice, No. 6 (1929), 89.

20.6 Carreras, Carlos N. "Nemesio R. Canales." In his Hombres y mujeres de Puerto Rico (M: Orión, 1957), pp. 213-38. Various subsequent editions.

20.7 Colorado, Antonio J. "Prólogo." In Nemesio R. Canales, Paliques (SJ?: Universidad de Puerto Rico, Editorial Phi Eta Mu, 1952), pp. v-xi. 4. ed., SJ: Coquí, 1967; pp. 9-16.

20.8 Diez de Andino, Juan. "Perdigones contra luceros." In his Desmenuzando hechos (Barcelona: Rvmbos, 1957), pp. 42-49.

20.9 Géigel Polanco, Vicente. "Nemesio R. Canales." In his Valores de Puerto Rico (NY: Arno Press, 1975), pp. 99-110. Also SJ: Eugenio María de Hostos, 1943.

20.10 __________. "Nemesio R. Canales." Asomante, 1, 3 (1945), 69-70.

20.11 __________. "Ubicación de Canales." Indice, No. 6 (1929), 87.

20.12 Jesús, Antonio de. "Nemesiones R. Canales." Brújula, 1, 2 (1934), 40-42.

20.13 Pedreira, Antonio S. "El héroe galopante." In his Aclaraciones y crítica (SJ: Venezuela, 1941), pp. 227-32. Also in his Obras completas (SJ: Instituto de Cultura Puertorriqueña, 1970), I, 621-24.

20.14 Quiñones, Samuel R. "El humorismo en la obra de Nemesio R. Canales." Indice, No. 6 (1929), 88.

20.15 __________. "Humorismo en Nemesio R. Canales." In his Temas y letras; 3. ed. (SJ: Biblioteca de Autores Puertorriqueños, 1955), pp. 95-117.

20.16 __________. "Nemesio R. Canales, el humorista de Puerto Rico." Educación, 11, 4 (1962), 83-96. Also in Nemesio R. Canales, Paliques (SJ: Isla, 1967), pp. v-xxviii.

20.17 Rodríguez-Seda, Asela. "Arms and the man y El héroe

galopante: la desmitificación del heroismo." LATR. 9, 2 (1976), 63-67.

20.18 ________. "G. Bernard Shaw y Nemesio R. Canales: relaciones e influencias." SinN, 8, 2 (1977), 34-45.

20.19 Rosa-Nieves, Cesáreo. "Nemesio R. Canales Rivera (1878-1923)." In his Plumas estelares en las letras de Puerto Rico (SJ: Ediciones de la Torre, Universidad de Puerto Rico, 1967), II, 163-78.

20.20 Soto Ramos, Julio. "Nemesio R. Canales, el humorista de Puerto Rico." In his Cumbre y remanso... (SJ: Cordillera, 1963), pp. 58-68.

21

CESTERO, FERDINAND R. (1864-1945)

Critical Essays

21.1 Braschi, Wilfredo. "Ferdinand Cestero." In his Perfiles puertorriqueños (SJ: Biblioteca de Autores Puertorriqueños, 1978), pp. 17-19.

21.2 Carreras, Carlos N. "Ferdinand R. Cestero." In his Hombres y mujeres de Puerto Rico (M: Orión, 1974), pp. 163-72. Orig. 1957 etc.

21.3 Castro, Tomás de Jesús. "Ferdinand R. Cestero." In his Esbozos críticos (SJ: Baldrich, 1945), pp. 108-109.

21.4 Negrón Flores, Ramón. "Prólogo." In Ferdinand R. Cestero, Sueños y quimeras (SJ: Casa Baldrich, 1939), pp. i-vii.

21.5 Rosa-Nieves, Cesáreo. "Ferdinand R. Cestero, un poeta de transición." Rumbos, No. 39 (1959), 70-80. Also as "Ferdinand R. Cestero, un poeta de transición romántico-modernista." In Ferdinand R. Cestero, San Juan...mi ciudad amada (SJ: Campos, 1960), pp. 11-29.

21.6 ________. "Ferdinand R. Cestero (1864-1945)." In his Plumas estelares en las letras de Puerto Rico (SJ: Ediciones de la Torre, Universidad de Puerto Rico, 1967), II, 137-49.

21.7 Soto Ramos, Julio. "Ferdinand R. Cestero." In his Cumbre y remanso... (SJ: Cordillera, 1963), pp. 140-43.

22

COLL Y TOSTE, CAYETANO (1850-1930)

Critical Monographs and Dissertations

22.1 Arana Soto, Salvador. Las poesías del doctor Cayetano Coll y Toste (incluyendo su traducción del "Rubaiyat" de Omar Khayyam, y otros escritos sobre el ilustre médico). SJ, 1970.

22.2 Coll, Edna. Cayetano Coll y Toste; síntesis de estímulos humanos. SJ: Editorial Universitaria, Universidad de Puerto Rico, 1970.

Critical Essays

22.3 Alegría, Ricardo E. "Introducción." In Cayetano Coll y Toste, Leyendas (SJ: Instituto de Cultura Puertorriqueña, 1971), pp. iii-iv.

22.4 Braschi, Wilfredo. "Cayetano Coll y Toste." In his Perfiles puertorriqueños (SJ: Biblioteca de Autores Puertorriqueños, 1978), pp. 91-92.

22.5 Cadilla Colón, Francisco M. "Don Cayetano Coll y Toste." In his Los ochocentistas (Barcelona: Rumbos, 1961), pp. 163-89.

22.6 Carreras, Carlos N. "Al lector." In Cayetano Coll y Toste, Leyendas puertorriqueñas (SJ: Puerto Rico Ilustrado, 1924), pp. i-v.

22.7 __________. "Al lector..." In Cayetano Coll y Toste, Tradiciones y leyendas puertorriqueñas (Barcelona: Maucci, 1928?), I, 5-8.

22.8 Coll, Edna. "Apuntes biográficos." In Cayetano Coll y Toste, Selección de leyendas puertorriqueñas; 19. ed. (M: Orión, 1970), pp. 7-26. Various other editions.

22.9 Cuchí Coll, Isabel. "Biografía del Dr. Cayetano Coll y Toste." In Cayetano Coll y Toste, Selección de leyendas puertorriqueñas (Barcelona: Rumbos, 1962), pp. v-viii.

22.10 Géigel Polanco, Vicente. "Cayetano Coll y Toste." In his Valores de Puerto Rico (NY: Arno Press, 1975), pp. 87-93. Orig. SJ: Eugenio María de Hostos, 1943.

22.11 Guzmán Rodríguez, Manuel. "Proemio." In Cayetano Coll y Toste, Tradiciones y leyendas puertorriqueñas (Barcelona: Maucci, 1928?), II, 5-8.

22.12 Hostos, Adolfo de. "La vida y obras de Cayetano Coll y Toste." In Cayetano Coll y Toste, Puertorriqueños ilustres;

primera selección (NY: Las Américas, 1952), pp. 9-18. Also in Cayetano Coll y Toste, Puertorriqueños ilustres; segunda recopilación (Barcelona: Rumbos, 1963), pp. ix-xvii. Also in Cayetano Coll y Toste, Puertorriqueños ilustres; segunda selección (Barcelona: Rumbos, 1966), pp. ix-xvii.

22.13 Huyke, Juan B. "Cayetano Coll y Toste." In his Los triunfadores (SJ: Negociado de Materiales, Imprenta y Transporte, 1927), II, 127-33.

22.14 Limón de Arce, José Ramón. "Cayetano Coll y Toste." In his Poetas arecibeños (Arecibo: Harry C. del Pozo, 1926), pp. 145-64. Followed by a selection of his poetry.

22.15 Morales Carrión, Arturo. "Don Cayetano Coll y Toste y el Boletín histórico." Asomante, 6, 3 (1950), 79-81. Also in his Ojeada al proceso histórico y otros ensayos (SJ: Cordillera, 1971), pp. 116-19. Also 1974.

22.16 Pedreira, Antonio S. "Listas de Coll y Toste y Paul G. Miller." AtPR, 3 (1939), 96-104.

22.17 Rosa-Nieves, Cesáreo. "Cayetano Coll y Toste (1850-1930)." In his Plumas estelares en las letras de Puerto Rico (SJ: Ediciones de la Torre, Universidad de Puerto Rico, 1967), I, 443-57.

23

COLL Y VIDAL, ANTONIO (1898-)

Critical Essays

23.1 "Antonio Coll y Vidal." In La ciudad y los poetas (Palencia de Castilla, Spain: Rocamador, 1965), pp. 11-22.

23.2 Camejo, Rafael W. "Antonio Coll Vidal." In his Florecían los rosales (Caracas: Hernández, 1952), pp. 171-80.

23.3 Diego, José de. "Prólogo." In Antonio Coll y Vidal, Trovas de amor (Bayamón: Tip. El Progreso, 1916), pp. ix-xi.

23.4 Diez de Andino, Juan. "Un periodista auténtico." In his Desmenuzando hechos (Barcelona: Rvmbos, 1957), pp. 61-63.

23.5 Nervo, Amado. "Prólogo." In Antonio Coll y Vidal, Mediodía (NY: Hispania Press, 1919), pp. 15-19.

23.6 Rosa-Nieves, Cesáreo. "Antonio Coll y Vidal (1898-)." In his Plumas estelares en las letras de Puerto Rico

(SJ: Ediciones de la Torre, Universidad de Puerto Rico, 1967), II, 331-40.

24

CORCHADO Y JUARBE, MANUEL (1840-1884)

Critical Monographs and Dissertations

24.1 Cadilla de Martínez, María. Alturas paralelas (ensayos biográficos sobre d. Rafael del Valle Rodríguez y d. Manuel M. Corchado y Juarbe). SJ, 1941.

24.2 Enamorado-Cuesta, José. Manuel María Corchado y Juarbe, auténtico liberal puertorriqueño. SJ: Puerto Rico Libre, 1955.

Critical Essays

24.3 Bonafoux y Quintero, Luis. "Corchado y Juarbe." In his Literatura (Madrid: M. Ginés Hernández, 1887), pp. 42-47.

24.4 Coll y Toste, Cayetano. "Puertorriqueños ilustres. Manuel Corchado." BHPR, 7 (1920), 65-68. Also as "Manuel Corchado." In his Puertorriqueños ilustres; segunda selección (Barcelona: Rumbos, 1966), pp. 227-32.

24.5 Figueroa, Sotero. "Manuel María Corchado y Juarbe (1840-1884)." In his Ensayo biográfico de los que han contribuído al progreso de Puerto Rico (Ponce: "El Vapor", 1888), pp. 319-34.

24.6 Fonfrías, Ernesto Juan. "Manuel Corchado y Juarbe (1840-1884)." In his Sementera: ensayos breves y biografías mínimas (SJ: Club de la Prensa, 1962), pp. 83-96.

24.7 Géigel Polanco, Vicente. "Manuel Corchado y Juarbe." In his Valores de Puerto Rico (NY: Arno Press, 1975), pp. 37-44. Orig. SJ: Eugenio María de Hostos, 1943.

24.8 __________. "Prólogo." In Manuel Corchado y Juarbe, Obras completas (SJ: Instituto de Cultura Puertorriqueña, 1975), I, 5-42.

24.9 Hostos, Adolfo de. "Manuel Corchado y Juarbe (1840-1884)." In his Hombres representativos de Puerto Rico (SJ, 1961), pp. 45-49.

24.10 Medina y González, Zenón. "D. Manuel Corchado y Juarbe." In his Pinceladas (SJ: V. de González, 1895), pp. 30-31.

24.11 Meléndez, Ramón. "Manuel Corchado y Juarbe: personalidad polifacética." RICP, No. 20 (1963), 1-3.

24.12 Neumann Gandía, Eduardo. "Manuel Corchado y Juarbe." In his Benefactores y hombres notables de Puerto-Rico (Ponce: "Listín Comercial", 1899), II, 253-62.

24.13 Paniagua Picazo, Antonio. "Nota sobre Manuel Corchado." Asomante, 6, 2 (1950), 71-73.

24.14 Quiñones, Samuel R. "Sentido de un centenario." In his Temas y letras; 3. ed. (SJ: Biblioteca de Autores Puertorriqueños, 1955), pp. 119-23. Also in Antología del pensamiento puertorriqueño (1900-1970) (Río Piedras?: Editorial Universitaria, Universidad de Puerto Rico, 1975), pp. 574-76.

24.15 Ruiz García, Zoilo. "Manuel Corchado y Juarbe." In his Nuestros hombres de antaño (Mayagüez: Mayagüez Printing Co., 1920), pp. 24-25.

25

CORRETJER, JUAN ANTONIO (1908-)

Critical Essays

25.1 Arrigoitia, Luis de. "Cuatro poetas puertorriqueños: José de Diego, Luis Lloréns Torres, Luis Palés Matos, Juan Antonio Corretjer." Caravelle, No. 18 (1972), 59-76. Also in Instituto Internacional de Literatura Iberoamericana, Literatura de la emancipación hispanoamericana y otros ensayos (Lima: Universidad de San Marcos, 1972), pp. 173-78.

25.2 González, José Emilio. "Yerba bruja, imagen de Borinquen IV." AyL, 2a época, No. 17 (1958), 24.

25.3 López, Julio César. "El sentido de la patria en un poemario de Juan Antonio Corretjer." In his Pasión de poesía (jornada crítica) (Barcelona: Rumbos, 1967), pp. 17-22. Orig. SJ, 1960; pp. 15-22.

25.4 Medina, Ramón Felipe. "Juan Antonio Corretjer: homenaje a la figura total." SinN, 5, 3 (1975), 49-61.

25.5 Vega, José Luis. "Prólogo: la poesía de Juan Antonio Corretjer." In Juan Antonio Corretjer, Obras completas (SJ: Instituto de Cultura Puertorriqueña, 1977), I, 15-43.

26

DÁVILA, JOSÉ ANTONIO (1898-1941)

Critical Monographs and Dissertations

26.1 Ramos Mimoso, Adriana. Vida y poesía en José Antonio Dávila. Madrid: Cultura Hispánica, 1958.

Critical Essays

26.2 Balseiro, José A. "Un lírico neorromántico: José Antonio Dávila." In his Expresión de Hispanoamérica; primera serie (SJ: Instituto de Cultura Puertorriqueña, 1960), pp. 245-58.

26.3 Braschi, Wilfredo. "José Antonio Dávila." In his Perfiles puertorriqueños (SJ: Sociedad de Autores Puertorriqueños, 1978), pp. 13-15.

26.4 Géigel Polanco, Vicente. "Nota al margen de la poesía de José Antonio Dávila." AtPR, 4, 2 (1940), 153-58. Also as "Al margen de la poesía de José Antonio Dávila." In his Valores de Puerto Rico (NY: Arno Press, 1975), pp. 157-64. Orig. SJ: Eugenio María de Hostos, 1943.

26.5 __________. "Prólogo." In José Antonio Dávila, Prosa: ensayos, artículos y cartas literarias (SJ: Sociedad de Autores Puertorriqueños, 1971), pp. 9-13.

26.6 González, José Emilio. "[Motivos de Tristán]." Asomante, 14, 2 (1958), 92-94.

26.7 Marchand, Julia C. "José A. Dávila." In Puerto Rico. Universidad. Colegio de Artes y Ciencias. Seminario de Estudios Hispánicos, La naturaleza en la poesía puertorriqueña del siglo XX (Río Piedras, 1942), pp. 51-65. Boletín de la Universidad de Puerto Rico, serie XIII, no. 2.

26.8 Ramos Mimoso, Adriana. "Prólogo." In José Antonio Dávila, Motivos de Tristán (1920-1934) (SJ: Venezuela, 1957), pp. 5-8.

26.9 Rodríguez Escudero, Néstor A. "Vendimia, de José Antonio Dávila." In his El mar en la literatura puertorriqueña y otros ensayos (Barcelona: Rumbos, 1967), pp. 159-65.

26.10 Rosa-Nieves, Cesáreo. "José Antonio Dávila." In his Plumas estelares en las letras de Puerto Rico (SJ: Ediciones de la Torre, Universidad de Puerto Rico, 1967), II, 421-27.

26.11 Torres-Morales, José A. "Prólogo." In José Antonio Dávila, Vendimia; poemas, 1917-1939; 4. ed. (Río Piedras: Cultural, 1967), pp. 9-18.

26.12 Vientós Gastón, Nilita. "Un libro de José Antonio Dávila [Motivos de Tristán]." In her Indice cultural (Río Piedras: Ediciones de la Universidad de Puerto Rico, 1962-71), II, 179-81.

27

DÁVILA, VIRGILIO (1869-1943)

Critical Monographs and Dissertations

27.1 Arroyo de Colón, María. Vida y obra de Virgilio Dávila. Hato Rey: Asociación de Maestros de Puerto Rico, 1963. Orig. an unpublished thesis, Universidad de Puerto Rico, 1946.

27.2 Fernández Juncos, Manuel. Aromas de terruño, nuevo libro de d. Virgilio Dávila (boceto crítico). SJ: Germán Díaz, 1916.

27.3 Orama Padilla, Carlos. Virgilio Dávila, su vida y su obra. SJ: Esther, 1945. 2. ed., SJ: La Cordillera, 1963.

Critical Essays

27.4 Arroyo de Colón, María. "Análisis de la crítica sobre Virgilio Dávila." RICP, No. 42 (1969), 30-37.

27.5 Belaval, Emilio S. "Visión de un pueblito de antes." AtPR, 4, 4 (1940), 296-305. Also as "Visión de un pueblito de antes en la poética de Virgilio." In Virgilio Dávila, Pueblito de Antes; 7. ed. (SJ: Cordillera, 1974), pp. 19-29.

27.6 Castro, Tomás de Jesús. "Virgilio Dávila." In his Esbozos críticos (SJ: Baldrich, 1945), pp. 82-84.

27.7 "Dos poetas enjuician la obra de Virgilio Dávila: carta de Luis Muñoz Rivera. Carta de José P. H. Hernández." RICP, No. 42 (1969), 38-39.

27.8 Gallego, Laura. "Evocación de Virgilio Dávila." RICP, No. 5 (1959), 30-32.

27.9 González García, Matías. "Prólogo." In Virgilio Dávila, Patria; 3. ed. (SJ: Cordillera, 1971), pp. 17-24. Orig. 1903.

27.10 Gutiérrez, Guillermo. "Carta jíbara a Virgilio Dávila." RICP; no. 42 (1969), 20-21.

27.11 Hernández Aquino, Luis. "La actualidad de Virgilio Dávila." RICP, No. 42 (1969), 2-11.

27.12 Huyke, Juan B. "Virgilio Dávila." In his Triunfadores (SJ: Negociado de Materiales, Imprenta y Transporte, 1927), II, 227-33.

27.13 López, Julio César. "Un paralelo modernista: imagen de un cura en Virgilio Dávila y en Herrera y Reissig." In his La patria en dos poetas y un paralelo modernista (Barcelona: Ariel, 1968), pp. 33-38. Also SJ, 1968.

27.14 Martínez López, Benjamín. "Apuntes sobre Virgilio Dávila." In Virgilio Dávila, Obras completas (SJ: Instituto de Cultura Puertorriqueña, 1964), pp. v-xxvi.

27.15 Matos Paoli, Francisco. "Virgilio Dávila (1869-1943)." Asomante, 2, 1 (1946), 55-62.

27.16 Meléndez Muñoz, Miguel "Don Virgilio, yo...y Rocinante." In his Obras completas (SJ: Instituto de Cultura Puertorriqueña, 1963), III, 44-47.

27.17 Orama Padilla, Carlos. "El Pueblo de Antes en tres etapas de la vida de Virgilio Dávila." RICP, No. 42 (1969), 22-28.

27.18 Pedreira, Antonio S. "Sobre Un libro para mis nietos." REH-PR, 2 (1928), 82.

27.19 Real, Romualdo. "Prólogo." In Virgilio Dávila, Viviendo y amando (SJ: Cordillera, 1975), pp. 19-31. Orig. 1912.

27.20 Rosa-Nieves, Cesáreo. "Nota." In Virgilio Dávila, Pueblito de Antes; 7. ed. (SJ: Cordillera, 1974), pp. 11-14.

27.21 __________. "Nota crítica." In Virgilio Dávila, Un libro para mis nietos; 3. ed. (SJ: Cordillera, 1971), pp. 11-14.

27.22 __________. "Patria, amor y jibarismo en tres poetas puertorriqueños (José de Diego, Luis Lloréns Torres y Virgilio Dávila)." In his Ensayos escogidos... (SJ: Academia de Artes y Ciencias de Puerto Rico, 1970?), pp. 141-59.

27.23 __________. "Viñeta biográfica." In Virgilio Dávila, Aromas del terruño; 5. ed. (SJ: Cordillera, 1966), pp. 1-7.

27.24 __________. "Viñeta biográfica [y] Nota crítica." In Virgilio Dávila, Patria; 3. ed. (SJ: Cordillera, 1971), pp. 9-14.

27.25 __________. "Viñeta biográfica [y] Nota crítica." In Virgilio Dávila, Viviendo y amando (SJ: Cordillera, 1975), pp. 9-16.

27.26 __________. "Virgilio Dávila (1869-1943)." In his Plumas estelares en las letras de Puerto Rico (SJ: Ediciones de la Torre, Universidad de Puerto Rico, 1967), II, 87-98.

27.27 Silva, Ana Margarita. "Virgilio Dávila--1871-1943." In her El jíbaro en la literatura puertorriqueña; 2. ed. corr. y aum. (SJ: Silva, 1957), pp. 132-50. Orig. 1945.

27.28 Soto Ramos, Julio. "Obras completas de Virgilio Dávila." In his Yo soy yo y mi verdad... (SJ: Cordillera, 1973), pp. 15-21.

28

DEGETAU GONZÁLEZ, FEDERICO (1862-1914)

Critical Monographs and Dissertations

28.1 Al escritor puertorriqueño F. Degetau y González autor de Juventud. Madrid: Agustín Avral, 1895.

28.2 Mergal, Angel M. Federico Degetau; un orientador de su pueblo. HY: Hispanic Institute in the United States, 1944.

Critical Essays

28.3 Coll y Toste, Cayetano. "Federico Degetau." In his Puertorriqueños ilustres; segunda selcción (Barcelona: Rumbos, 1966), pp. 363-70.

28.4 Fernández Juncos, Manuel. "Federico Degetau y González." In his Antología puertorriqueña (NY: Hinds, Hayden & Eldredge, 1913), pp. 293-97. Various other editions.

28.5 Ferrer, Rafael. "Federico Degetau González." In his Lienzos (SJ, 1965), pp. 75-77.

28.6 __________. "Federico Degetau González. Panegírico." RAnt, 2, 1 (1914), 95-96.

28.7 Hostos, Adolfo de. "Federico Degetau y González (1862-1914)." In his Hombres representativos de Puerto Rico (SJ, 1961), pp. 158-64.

28.8 Martín, José Luis. "Degetau escritor (estudio de El fondo del aljibe)." Asomante, 7, 3 (1951), 40-47. Also in his Arco y flecha... (SJ: Club de la Prensa, 1961), pp. 39-50.

28.9 Rosa-Nieves, Cesáreo. "Federico Degetau y González (1862-1914)." In his Plumas estelares en las letras de Puerto Rico (SJ: Ediciones de la Torre, Universidad de Puerto Rico, 1967), I, 389-401.

28.10 Sánchez, Bonifacio. "A modo de prólogo." In Federico Degetau González, Cuentos pedagógicos y literarios (SJ: Puerto Rico Ilustrado, 1925), pp. i-viii.

28.11 Tolosa Latour, Manuel de. "Un ratito de conversación (conato de prólogo)." In Federico Degetau González, El secreto de la domadora. El fondo del aljibe; 3. ed. (Madrid: E. Teodoro, 1886), pp. vii-xiv.

28.12 Zahonero, José. "Mi primera epístola: a Federico Degetau." In Federico Degetau González, El secreto de la domadora. El fondo del aljibe (Madrid: E. Teodoro, 1886), pp. 227-35.

29

DÍAZ ALFARO, ABELARDO MILTON (1919-)

Critical Monographs and Dissertations

29.1 Carletta, María. Terrazo de Abelardo Díaz Alfaro. Unpublished thesis, Universidad de Puerto Rico, 1965.

Critical Essays

29.2 Díaz Alfaro de Sosa, Dalila. "Prólogo [e introducciones]." In Abelardo Milton Díaz Alfaro, Mi isla soñada; 4. ed. (Hato Rey: Ramallo, 1977), pp. ix-xxii.

29.3 Guevara Castañeira, Josefina. "Terrazo, de Abelardo Díaz Alfaro." In her Del Yunque a los Andes (SJ: Club de la Prensa, 1959), pp. 113-16.

29.4 Iventosch, Herman. "El 'Josco' de Díaz Alfaro y 'El Hosco' de Juan de Peña." Asomante, 23, 3 (1967), 25-31.

29.5 Lluch Mora, Francisco. "Terrazo, libro de realidad puertorriqueña." In his Miradero... (SJ: Cordillera, 1966), pp. 55-60.

29.6 Meléndez, Concha. "Abelardo Díaz Alfaro y la expresión puertorriqueña." In her Figuración de Puerto Rico y otros estudios (SJ: Instituto de Cultura Puertorriqueña, 1958), pp.

61-64. Also in her Obras completas (SJ: Instituto de Cultura Puertorriqueña, 1970-72), II, 395-98. See item no. 29.9.

29.7 Orgaz, Manuel. "Cantando a Puerto Rico." CHA, No. 145 (1962), 252-57.

29.8 Picón Salas, Mariano. "Prólogo." In Abelardo Díaz Alfaro, Terraza; 11. ed. (Bilbao: Vasco-Americana, 1948), pp. 13-17. Various other editions.

29.9 Torres León, Armando. "Meléndez, Concha. 'Abelardo Díaz Alfaro y la expresión puertorriqueña'." In his Ensayos en torno a Puerto Rico (SJ: Departamento de Instrucción Pública, 1968), pp. 99-103. See item no. 29.6.

29.10 Waldman, Gloria Feiman. "El tema de Puerto Rico en Abelardo Díaz Alfaro, René Marqués y Pedro Juan Soto." RICP, No. 25 (1975), 16-22.

30

DÍAZ VALCÁRCEL, EMILIO (1929-)

Bibliographies

30.1 Dalmau de Sánchez, María Mercedes. "Bibliografía de Emilio Díaz Valcárcel." REH-PR, 3, 1-2 (1973), 81-89.

Critical Monographs and Dissertations

30.2 Casanova-Sánchez, Olga. "La novela puertorriqueña contemporánea: Pedro Juan Soto y Emilio Díaz Valcárcel." DAI, 38 (1977), 298A-99A.

Critical Essays

30.3 Acosta-Belén, Edna. "Encuentro con Emilio Díaz Valcárcel." Plural, No. 99 (1979), 7-13.

30.4 Beauchamp, José Juan. "Figuraciones en el mes de marzo y el boom." Penélope, 1, 3-4 (1973), 4-11.

30.5 Campos, Jorge. "Díaz Varcárcel: Puerto Rico y Corea [El asedio y otros cuentos]." Insula, No. 226 (1965), 11.

30.6 Carpio, Campio. "[Napalm]." USF, No. 80 (1970), 348-49.

30.7 Curutchet, Juan Carlos. "[Figuraciones en el mes de marzo]." CHA, No. 258 (1972), 202-203.

30.8 González, José Emilio. "[Figuraciones en el mes de marzo]." SinN, 3, 1 (1972), 106-108.

30.9 ________. "[Proceso en diciembre]." Asomante, 20, 4 (1964), 57-62.

30.10 Ibargoyen Islas, Saúl. "Otra versión del infierno [Harlem todos los días]." Plural, No. 86 (1978), 68-69.

30.11 Irizarry, Estelle. "El ingreso de Puerto Rico en 'la nueva narrativa' por el camino del lenguaje." In IV Congreso de la Nueva Narrativa Hispanoamericana, Memorias (Cali, Col.?, 1974), I, 41-44.

30.12 Maldonado-Denis, Manuel. "[Proceso en diciembre]." CAm, No. 27 (1964), 106-108.

30.13 Marra López, José R. "[Proceso en diciembre]." Insula, No. 206 (1964), 9.

30.14 Meléndez, Concha. "[El hombre que trabajó el lunes]." Puerto, No. 2 (1968), 104-105.

30.15 Menton, Seymour. "[El asedio y otros cuentos]." AyLM, 2, 2 (1959), 89-91.

30.16 Miller, John C. "The emigrant and New York City: a consideration of four Puerto Rican writers." MELUS, 5, 3 (1978), 82-99. Díaz Valcárcel inter alios.

30.17 Morán, Carlos Roberto. "Figuraciones en el mes de marzo de Emilio Díaz Valcárcel." SinN, 3, 3 (1973), 75-81.

30.18 Nolla Conde, Olga. "[Figuraciones en el mes de marzo]." Zona, 1, 1 (1972), 20.

30.19 Orthmann, Nora G., and Caridad L. Silva de Velázquez. "Entrevista con Emilio Díaz Varlcárcel." Hispamérica, Nos. 25-26 (1980), 61-67.

30.20 Panico, Marie Joan. "Conversación con Emilio Díaz Valcárcel." RB/BR, 7, 2 (1980), 165-74.

30.21 Pope, Randolph D. "Dos novelas álbum: Libro de Manuel de Cortázar y Figuraciones en el mes de marzo de Díaz Valcárcel." RB/BR, 1 (1974), 170-84.

30.22 Rodríguez-Seda, Asela. "En torno a Inventario de Díaz Valcárcel." RICP, No. 72 (1976), 4-6.

30.23 Torre, José R. de la. "Cuatro puertas a una fábula: sobre Figuraciones en el mes de marzo de Emilio Díaz Valcárcel." NNH, 4 (1974), 75-89. Also Penélope, Nos. 3-4 (1973), 12-23.

31

DIEGO, JOSÉ DE (1866-1918)

Bibliographies

31.1 Arce de Vázquez, Margot. "Obras de José de Diego. Bibliografía selecta." Asomante, 22, 4 (1966), 79-83.

Critical Monographs and Dissertations

31.2 Arce de Vázquez, Margot. La obra literaria de José de Diego. SJ: Instituto de Cultura Puertorriqueña, 1967.

31.3 Dalmau Canet, Sebastián. Biografía de José de Diego. Estudio sobre su personalidad como literato, político, tribuno y legislador. SJ: Cantero, Fernández, 1923.

31.4 Meléndez, Concha. José de Diego en mi memoria. SJ: Instituto de Cultura Puertorriqueña, 1966.

31.5 Sáenz, Mercedes, and Iris Yolanda Reyes Benítez. Acercamiento a Luis Palés Matos y José de Diego. Río Piedras: Edil, 1976. Pertinent items are listed separately.

31.6 Segarra Plumey, Rafael. La poesía de José de Diego. Unpublished thesis, Universidad de Puerto Rico, 1960.

31.7 Sterling, Phillip, and María Brau. The quiet rebels; four Puerto Rican leaders: José Celso Barbosa, Luis Muñoz Rivera, José de Diego, Luis Muñoz Marín. Garden City, NY: Doubleday, 1968.

31.8 Terreforte Arroyo, Juan P. José de Diego y su libro Pomarrosas. Aguadilla: El Criollo, 1905.

Critical Essays

31.9 Alegría, Ricardo E. "Muñoz Rivera y de Diego ante la invasión norteamericana." RICP, No. 54 (1972), 19-22. Also in Antología del pensamiento puertorriqueño (1900-1970) (Río Piedras?: Editorial Universitaria, Universidad de Puerto Rico, 1975), pp. 423-27.

31.10 Arce, Carlos de. "José de Diego. Caballero del idioma y de la raza." Prensa, 2a época, No. 5 (1959), 30.

31.11 Arce de Vázquez, Margot. "Aguadilla en los versos de José de Diego." RICP, No. 1 (1961), 1-7.

31.12 ________. "El dolor y la esperanza en José de Diego." RICP, No. 31 (1966), 28-42.

31.13 ________. "Ensayos jurídicos de José de Diego. Aspectos literarios." RCAPR, 31, 1 (1970), 127-41.

31.14 ________. "Introducción." In José de Diego, Antología poética (SJ: Ateneo Puertorriqueño, 1966), pp. 7-9.

31.15 ________. "José de Diego y la lengua." Asomante, 22, 3 (1966), 33-52.

31.16 ________. "Poemas de amor de José de Diego." RICP, No. 1 (1958), 5-7.

31.17 Arrigoitia, Luis de. "Cuatro poetas puertorriqueños: José de Diego, Luis Lloréns Torres, Luis Palés Matos, Juan Antonio Corretjer." Caravelle, No. 18 (1972), 59-76. Also in Instituto Internacional de Literatura Iberoamericana, La literatura de la emancipación hispanoamericana y otros ensayos (Lima: Universidad de San Marcos, 1972), pp. 173-78.

31.18 ________. "Margot Arce de Vázquez y su libro sobre José de Diego." RICP, No. 37 (1967), 40-49. See item no. 31.2.

31.19 Babín, María Teresa. "Dignidad de la piedra." Asomante, 22, 3 (1966), 81-85.

31.20 ________. "Genio y figura de José de Diego (1866-1918)." AyL, No. 10 (1957), 3-5. Also in her Jornadas literarias (temas de Puerto Rico) (Barcelona: Rvmbos, 1967), pp. 93-101.

31.21 Belaval, Emilio S. "Prólogo." In José de Diego, Nuevas campañas (SJ: Cordillera, 1966), pp. vii-xv.

31.22 Campos, Jorge. "Estampa barcelonesa de José de Diego." RICP, No. 19 (1963), 15-16.

31.23 Coll y Toste, Cayetano. "Puertorriqueños ilustres. José de Diego." BHPR, 13 (1926), 74-86.

31.24 Corretjer, Juan Antonio. "En torno a José de Diego." Indice, Nos. 25-26 (1931), 6.

31.25 Dalmau Canet, Sebastián. "José de Diego." In his Crepúsculos literarios (SJ: Boletín Mercantil, 1903), pp. 47-49.

31.26 ________. "José de Diego. Estudio sobre su personalidad como literato, político, tribuno y legislador." In his Próceres (SJ: Correo Dominical, 1929), pp. 231-99. Same as item no. 31.3.

31.27 Diego, Georgina de. "Unas líneas." In José de Diego, Cantos de pitirre (Palma de Mallorca, 1950), pp. 7-11.

31.28 Diez de Andino, Juan. "José de Diego (1867-1918)."

In his Voces de la farándula... (Barcelona: Rvmbos, 1959), pp. 187-90.

31.29 Ferrer Canales, José. "Huellas de José de Diego." RI, No. 44 (1957), 323-32. Also in Instituto Internacional de Literatura Iberoamericana, La literatura del Caribe y otros temas (M, 1961), pp. 313-21. Also in his Acentos cívicos... (Río Piedras: Edil, 1972), pp. 89-101. Orig. 1971.

31.30 __________. "José Martí y José de Diego." Asomante, 22, 3 (1966), 53-80.

31.31 Fonfrías, Ernesto Juan. "José de Diego y la primera Academia Puertorriqueña de la Lengua." In his El Instituto de Lexicografía Hispanoamericana "Augusto Malaret" y la Academia Puertorriqueña de la Lengua. Ensayos (SJ: Instituto de Lexicografía Hispanoamericana "Augusto Malaret", 1976), pp. 61-67.

31.32 Freire, Joaquín. "José de Diego, fundador de la Unión Antillana en Cuba." RICP, No. 31 (1966), 5-7.

31.33 Géigel Polanco, Vicente. "José de Diego, legislador." Asomante, 22, 4 (1966), 33-46.

31.34 __________. "José de Diego y el problema constitucional de Puerto Rico." Indice, Nos. 25-26 (1931), 5-8.

31.35 __________. "Luis Muñoz Rivera y José de Diego: dos orientadores de nuestro pueblo." In his Valores de Puerto Rico (NY: Arno Press, 1975), pp. 69-85. Orig. SJ: Eugenio María de Hostos, 1943.

31.36 González, José Emilio. "La patria poética en José de Diego." Asomante, 22, 4 (1966), 58-76.

31.37 __________. "'Ultima actio' de José de Diego." RICP, No. 31 (1966), 17-23.

31.38 Gracia, Gilberto Concepción de. "José Diego, apóstol de la independencia." In Antología del pensamiento puertorriqueño (1900-1970) (Río Piedras?: Editorial Universitaria, Universidad de Puerto Rico, 1975), pp. 393-405.

31.39 Hernández Aquino, Luis. "José Gautier Benítez y José de Diego: los dos grandes cantores de Puerto Rico." RICP, No. 31 (1966), 10-13.

31.40 Lluch Mora, Francisco. "Apuntes sobre el tratamiento de la naturaleza en la poesía de José de Diego." Horizontes, No. 26 (1970), 33-44.

31.41 Maldonado-Denis, Manuel. "De Diego y Albizu Campos." CA, No. 178 (1971), 177-91.

31.42 __________. "La idea de la independencia de Puerto Rico en el pensamiento de José de Diego." Asomante, 22, 4 (1966), 19-31.

31.43 Marés, Federico. "Recordando a José de Diego." RICP, No. 41 (1968), 17-23.

31.44 Meléndez, Concha. "Fusión de imágenes en un retrato." RICP, No. 31 (1966), 2-4.

31.45 ________. "José de Diego en mi memoria." Asomante, 22, 3 (1966), 8-18. Also in her Obras completas (SJ: Instituto de Cultura Puertorriqueña, 1970-72), II, 539-685.

31.46 ________. "José de Diego y la poesía." In Institución del día del poeta (SJ: Sociedad de Autores Puertorriqueños, 1965), pp. 39-48. Also RICP, No. 32 (1966), 43-46.

31.47 ________. "Jovillos y volantines. Homenaje a José de Diego." In her Signos de iberoamérica (M: Manuel León Sánchez, 1936), pp. 15-39.

31.48 ________. "Parábolas y siluetas heroicas de José de Diego." RICP, No. 10 (1961), 1-4.

31.49 ________. "Poemas de amor de José de Diego." RICP, No. 1 (1958), 5-7.

31.50 ________. "La poesía de José de Diego." Guajana, 2a época, No. 2 (1966), 3-4.

31.51 ________. "Prólogo." In José de Diego, Cantos de rebeldía (SJ: Cordillera, 1966), pp. vii-xii.

31.52 ________. "Prólogo: tiempo de Jovillos (1886-1890)." In José de Diego, Jovillos (coplas de estudiante) (SJ: Cordillera, 1971), pp. 7-12.

31.53 ________. "Prólogo: tiempo de las parábolas." In José de Diego, Cantos de pitirre (SJ: Cordillera, 1975), pp. 7-13. Also 1971.

31.54 ________. "Tiempo de Pomarrosas." In José de Diego, Pomarrosas (SJ: Cordillera, 1971), pp. 9-17.

31.55 ________. "Tiempos en la poesía de José de Diego." In José de Diego, Obras completas (SJ: Instituto de Cultura Puertorriqueña, 1970), I, v-xxi.

31.56 ________. "Tristeza final de los poemas de amor de José de Diego." RICP, No. 2 (1959), 19-21.

31.57 Miranda Archilla, Graciany. "Sermón." In José de Diego, Hojas y flores; 2. ed. (SJ: Casa Baldrich, n.d.), no pagination.

31.58 Pedrosa Izarra, Ciriaco. "Nuevas perspectivas en la obra de José de Diego: descubrimiento de poemas juveniles."

Horizontes, No. 28 (1971), 95-113.

31.59 Quiñones, Samuel R. "José de Diego." Indice, Nos. 25-26 (1931), 3-4.

31.60 Reichard Esteves, Herman. "La colaboración de José de Diego en el seminario Emilio Mario." RICP, No. 44 (1969), 19-24.

31.61 Ribera Chevremont, Evaristo. "Disquisiciones literarias. Entrevista con José de Diego." In Antología del pensamiento puertorriqueño (1900-1970) (Río Piedras?: Editorial Universitaria, Universidad de Puerto Rico, 1975), pp. 883-86. Orig. as "Entrevista con José de Diego." RICP, No. 31 (1966), 24-25.

31.62 Ripoll, Luis. "Unas palabras ineludibles." In José de Diego, Antología poética (Palma de Mallorca, 1977), pp. 5-10.

31.63 Rodríguez Morales, Luis M. "José de Diego." RICP, No. 31 (1966), 45-49.

31.64 __________. "El tema religioso en la poesía de José de Diego." In his Ensayos y conferencias (Barcelona: Rumbos, 1962), pp. 59-80.

31.65 Rosa-Nieves, Cesáreo. "José de Diego (seud. León Americano: 1866-1918)." In his Plumas estelares en las letras de Puerto Rico (SJ: Ediciones de la Torre, Universidad de Puerto Rico, 1967), II, 29-49.

31.66 __________. "Laura: mujer, sombra y mito." In his La lámpara del faro... (SJ: Club de la Prensa, 1957), pp. 135-41.

31.67 __________. "Patria, amor y jibarismo en tres poetas puertorriqueños (José de Diego, Luis Lloréns Torres y Virgilio Dávila)." In his Ensayos escogidos... (SJ: Academia de Artes y Ciencias de Puerto Rico, 1970?), pp. 141-59.

31.68 Ruiz García, Zoilo. "José de Diego Martínez." In his Nuestros hombres de antaño (Mayagüez: Mayagüez Printing Co., 1920), pp. 144-45.

31.69 Sáenz, Mercedes. "José de Diego: notas en torno a su vida y análisis de los poemas 'Juana', 'Puntadas' y 'Testaferro'." In Mercedes Sáenz, and Iris Yolanda Reyes Benítez, Acercamiento a Luis Palés Matos y José de Diego, q.v., pp. 51-70.

31.70 Samalea Iglesias, Luis. "Ultima actio." Asomante, 22, 4 (1966), 77-78.

31.71 Suárez Díaz, Ada. "El Instituto 'José de Diego'." Asomante, 22, 4 (1966), 47-57.

32

DIEGO PADRÓ, JOSÉ ISAAC DE (1899-1974)

Bibliographies

32.1 "Bibliografía mínima." SinN, 6, 3 (1976), 63-66.

Critical Monographs and Dissertations

32.2 Diego Padró, José Isaac de. Escaparate iluminado (autobiografía poética). Barcelona: Rumbos, 1959.

32.3 Rodríguez Torres, Carmelo. Estilo de En babia. Unpublsihed thesis, Universidad de Puerto Rico, 1969.

32.3 Soto, Pedro Juan. Vie et oeuvre de José Ignacio [sic] de Diego Padró, romancier portoricain. Unpublished doctoral dissertation, Université de Toulouse, 1976.

Critical Essays

32.4 Barradas, Efraín. "José I. de Diego Padró y Luis Palés Matos: recuerdo de una amistad polémica." SinN, 6, 3 (1976), 41-45.

32.5 Camejo, Rafael W. "J. I. de Diego Padró." In his Florecían los rosales (Caracas: Hernández, 1952), pp. 115-22.

32.6 Castro, Tomás de Jesús. "J. I. Diego Padró." In his Esbozos críticos (SJ: Baldirch, 1945), pp. 88-89.

32.7 Diez de Andino, Juan. "Ocho epístolas mostrencas." In his Desmenuzando hechos (Barcelona: Rvmbos, 1957), pp. 92-94.

32.8 Gómez Costa, Arturo. "J. I. de Diego Padró." In his Vendimias en prosa (Barcelona: Vosgos, 1976), pp. 51-58.

32.9 Laguerre, Enrique A. "Las Epístolas mostrencas de Diego Padró." In his Pulso de Puerto Rico, 1952-1954 (SJ: Biblioteca de Autores Puertorriqueños, 1956), pp. 253-65.

32.10 Martínez Plée, Manuel. "Epílogo." In José Isaac de Diego Padró, La última lámpara de los dioses (Madrid: Ariel, 1921), pp. 189-93. 2. ed., SJ: Biblioteca de Autores Puertorriqueños, 1950; pp. 233-39.

32.11 Matos Paoli, Francisco. "José I. de Diego Padró (1899-1974)." In Escritores contemporáneos de Puerto Rico (SJ: Sociedad de Escritores Puertorriqueños, 1978), pp. 7-15.

32.12 Pérez Losada, José. "Pórtico." In José Isaac de Diego Padró, La última lámpara de los dioses (Madrid: Ariel, 1921), pp. v-xi. 2. ed., SJ: Biblioteca de Autores Puertorriqueños, 1950; pp. 7-11.

32.13 Rodríguez Torres, Carmelo. "Las ideas de Pío Baroja y José I. de Diego Padró en torno a la novela." SinN, 6, 3 (1976), 18-40.

32.14 Rosa-Nieves, Cesáreo. "José Isaac de Diego Padró (1896-)." In his Plumas estelares en las letras de Puerto Rico (SJ: Ediciones de la Torre, Universidad de Puerto Rico, 1967), II, 319-30.

32.15 Soto, Pedro Juan et al. "J. I. de Diego Padró: coloquio sobre su vida y obra." SinN, 6, 3 (1976), 6-17.

32.16 Soto Ramos, Julio. "El tiempo jugó conmigo." In his Cumbre y remanso... (SJ: Cordillera, 1963), pp. 76-82.

33

ESTEVES, JOSÉ DE JESÚS (1882-1918)

Critical Monographs and Dissertations

33.1 Casalduc de Miranda, Ismael. José de Jesús Esteves: el poeta. Unpublished thesis, Universidad de Puerto Rico, 1939.

Critical Essays

33.2 "Juicios sobre la obra de José de Jesús Esteves." In José de Jesús Esteves, Poemas selectos (Santurce: Arce, 1954?), pp. 9-11.

33.3 López, Julio César. "El tema de la patria en José de Jesús Esteves." In his La patria en dos poetas y un paralelo modernista (Barcelona: Ariel, 1968), pp. 24-31. Also SJ, 1968.

33.4 Robles de Cardona, Mariana. "El poeta José de Jesús Esteves." Asomante, 3, 2 (1947), 75-85.

33.5 Rodríguez Escudero, Néstor A. "Apuntes sobre la poesía de José de Jesús Esteves." In his Ensayos escogidos... (Barcelona: Rvmbos, 1960-), I, 80-84.

33.6 Rosa-Nieves, Cesáreo. "José de Jesús Esteves (1882-1918)." In his Plumas estelares en las letras de Puerto Rico (SJ: Ediciones de la Torre, Universidad de Puerto Rico, 1967), II, 123-35.

34

FELICIANO MENDOZA, ESTER (1917-)

Bibliographies

34.1 Alamo de Torres, Daisy. Bibliografía de Ester Feliciano Mendoza (1935-1980); 2. ed. SJ: Sociedad de Bibliotecarios de Puerto Rico, 1980.

Critical Essays

34.2 Arce de Vázquez, Margot. "Carta prólogo." In Ester Feliciano Mendoza, Nanas (SJ: Junta Editorial, Universidad de Puerto Rico, 1945), pp. 7-10. 2. ed., 1970; pp. 9-10.

34.3 Diez de Andino, Juan. "Coquí." In his Voces de la farándula... (Barcelona: Rvmbos, 1959), pp. 108-10.

34.4 __________. "Voz de la tierra mía. Un libro que trazuma regionalismo." Rumbos, No. 112 (1957), 83-85. Also as "Un libro que trasuma regionalismo." In his Desmenuzando hechos (Barcelona: Rmbos, 1957), pp. 305-308.

34.5 Ferrer Canales, José. "Canto de Ester Feliciano." Orfeo, 4, 7 (1957), 31-34.

34.6 Freire de Matos, Isabel. "[Ronda del mar]." Mairena, No. 7 (1981), 101-104.

34.7 Gómez Tejera, Carmen. "La nueva educación; poesía de Ester Feliciano Mendoza." RAM, 2, 2 (1943), 44.

34.8 Guevara Castañeira, Josefina. "Coquí, de Ester Feliciano Mendoza." In her Del Yunque a los Andes (SJ: Club de la Prensa, 1959), pp. 217-20.

34.9 Laguerre, Enrique A. "Al margen de los libros de Ester Feliciano." Prensa, 2a época, No. 4 (1959), 26.

34.10 __________. "Esther [sic] Feliciano Mendoza." In his Pulso de Puerto Rico, 1952-1954 (SJ: Biblioteca de Autores Puertorriqueños, 1956), pp. 283-92.

34.11 Manrique Cabrera, Francisco. "Página poética: Ester Feliciano Mendoza, Nanas." RAM, 4, 7 (1945), 191-99.

34.12 Meléndez, Concha. "Introducción a Sinfonía de Puerto Rico." RICP, No. 29 (1965), 1-4.

35

FERNÁNDEZ JUNCOS, MANUEL (1912-)

Critical Monographs and Dissertations

35.1 Carrino, Frank Gaetano. "Manuel Fernández Juncos: pivotal force in the insular movement of Puerto Rico through El buscapié." DA, 17 (1957), 1335.

35.2 Conde, Pedro. La vida y los tiempos de don Manuel Fernández Juncos. Unpublished thesis, Universidad de Puerto Rico, 1932.

35.3 Mercado, J. Datos biográficos de don Manuel Fernández Juncos. Madrid: La Editora, 1913.

Critical Essays

35.4 Arias, Pedro G. "Don Manuel Fernández Juncos. Interpretación y significación de una vida asturiana." BIEA, No. 63 (1968), 217-27.

35.5 Dalmau Canet, Sebastián. "D. Manuel Fernández Juncos." In his Crepúsculos literarios (SJ: Boletín Mercantil, 1903), pp. 13-18.

35.6 ________. "Manuel Fernández Juncos." In his Próceres (SJ: Correo Dominical, 1929), pp. 303-59.

35.7 Huyke, Juan B. "Manuel Fernández Juncos." In his Triunfadores (SJ: Negociado de Materiales, Imprenta y Transporte, 1926), pp. 5-12.

35.8 López, Julio César. "Algunos temas en los cuadros costumbristas de Manuel Fernández Juncos." In his Temas y estilos en ocho escritores (SJ, 1957), pp. 103-11.

35.9 Malaret, Augusto. "Manuel Fernández Juncos." In his Medallas de oro; 4. ed. (M: Orión, 1952), pp. 11-34. Various other editions.

35.10 Meléndez, Concha. "Galería puertorriqueña de Manuel Fernández Juncos." In her Personas y libros (SJ: Cordillera, 1970), pp. 11-49. Also in her Obras completas (SJ: Instituto de Cultura Puertorriqueña, 1970-72), IV, 233-71. Also in Manuel Fernández Juncos, Galería puertorriqueña (SJ: Instituto de Cultura Puertorriqueña, 1958), pp. 11-41.

35.11 ________. "Un hombre fabuloso." ILit, 2, 3-4 (1970-71), 12-13, 15.

35.12 Padilla, José G. "A mi buen amigo, el señor don Manuel Fernández Juncos: Epístola I." RP, 1, 1 (1887), 389.

35.13 Pedreira, Antonio S. "Necrología." REH-PR, 1 (1928), 415.

35.14 Rosa-Nieves, Cesáreo. "Manuel Fernández Juncos (1846-1928)." In his Plumas estelares en las letras de Puerto Rico (SJ: Ediciones de la Torre, Universidad de Puerto Rico, 1967), I, 421-42.

35.15 Torres Morales, José Antonio. "Introducción." In Manuel Fernández Juncos, Antología de sus obras (M: Orión, 1960), pp. 7-16.

36

FRANCO OPPENHEIMER, FÉLIX (1912-)

Critical Monographs and Dissertations

36.1 González Torres, Rafael A. La obra poética de Félix Franco Oppenheimer: estudio temático-analítico-estilístico. Río Piedras: Universidad de Puerto Rico, 1979.

36.2 Hernández Sánchez, Jesús. Félix Franco Oppenheimer, poeta del dolor. Barcelona: Rumbos, 1964. Also as Félix Franco Oppenheimer; poeta del dolor (vida y obra-bibliografía-antología). SJ: Yaurel, 1964.

36.3 Río, Rosario Esther. Félix Franco Oppenheimer: vida y obra. Unpublished thesis, Colegio de Agricultura y Artes Mecánicas [de Mayagüez], 1971.

36.4 Rosa-Nieves, Cesáreo. Del contorno hacia el dintorno; notas sobre el libro de ensayos: Contornos de Félix Franco Oppenheimer. SJ: Yaurel, 1961.

Critical Essays

36.5 Arce de Vázquez, Margot. "Prólogo." In Félix Franco Oppenheimer, Antología poética, 1950-1972 (SJ: Instituto de Cultura Puertorriqueña, 1976), pp. vii-xxi.

36.6 Gómez Costa, Arturo. "Félix Franco Oppenheimer." In his Vendimias en prosa (Barcelona: Vosgos, 1976), pp. 69-78.

36.7 _________. "Félix Franco Oppenheimer en la nueva poesía de América." BAAC, 10, 3-4 (1974), 260-71.

36.8 González Torres, Rafael A. "Félix Franco Oppenheimer y su visión metafísica." La torre, Nos. 75-76 (1972), 224-43.

36.9 Martín, José Luis. "El hombre y su angustia: poemario de Félix Franco Oppenheimer." Asomante, 8, 1 (1952), 41-53. Also in his Arco y flecha... (SJ: Club de la Prensa, 1961), pp. 111-38.

36.10 Monterde, Francisco. "Prólogo." In Félix Franco Oppenheimer, Los lirios del testimonio (SJ: Yaurel, 1964), pp. 9-10.

36.11 Palés Matos, Luis. "Prólogo." In Félix Franco Oppenheimer, El hombre y su angustia (1945-1950); 3. ed. (SJ: Cordillera, 1973), pp. 11-15. 2. ed., 1960. Orig. SJ: Yaurel, 1950; pp. 9-13.

36.12 Pereda, Clemente. "Prólogo." In Félix Franco Oppenheimer, Estas cosas así fueron; poemas; 2. ed. (SJ: Club de la Prensa, 1970), pp. 9-20.

36.13 Ribera Chevremont, Evaristo. "Unas palabras." In Félix Franco Oppenheimer, Prosas sin clave (SJ: Yaurel, 1971), pp. 11-15.

36.14 Rosa, Samuel de la. "Entrevista con F. Franco Oppenheimer: trascendentalismo, nuevo humanismo entroncado en las esencias mismas de la vida." Pegaso, 1, 1 (1952), 3-5.

36.15 Rosa-Nieves, Cesáreo. "Del tiempo y su figura y el transcendentalismo de Franco Oppenheimer." In his La lámpara del faro... (SJ: Club de la Prensa, 1957-60), II, 103-12.

36.16 _________. "Félix Franco Oppenheimer (1912)." In Escritores contemporáneos de Puerto Rico (SJ: Sociedad de Autores Puertorriqueños, 1978), pp. 1-15.

36.17 _________. "El hombre y su angustia." In his La lámpara del faro... (SJ: Club de la Prensa, 1957-60), I, 111-15.

37

GAUTIER BENÍTEZ, JOSÉ (1848-1880)

Critical Monographs and Dissertations

37.1 Bonham Deily, Myron. José Gautier Benítez. Unpublished Ph.D. dissertation, Cornell University, 1931.

37.2 Curet de De Anda, Miriam. La poesía de José Gautier Benítez. SJ: Editorial Universitaria, Universidad de Puerto Rico, 1980. Orig. an unpublished thesis, Universidad de Puerto Rico, 1950; signed Miriam Curet Cuevas.

37.3 Fernández-Marcane, Leonardo. "José Gautier Benítez y el romanticismo en Puerto Rico." DAI, 35 (1974), 4514A.

37.4 Girón de Segura, Socorro. Facsímiles de José Gautier Benítez. Madrid, 1964,

37.5 ________. José Gautier Benítez, vida y época; obras inéditas. Palma de Mallorca: Mossén Alcover, 1961.

37.6 Velada literaria en honor de José Gautier Benítez. San Germán: J. Ramón González, 1880.

Critical Essays

37.7 Amy, Francisco J. "Gautier Benítez." In his Predicar en desierto (SJ: El Alba, 1907), pp. 236-37.

37.8 Babín, María Teresa. "Nuestro Gautier." AtPR, 2, 4 (1936), 248-54.

37.9 Balseiro, José A. "Gautier Benítez y el espíritu de su época." In his El vigía (Madrid: "Mundo Latino", 1925), I, 143-204. Also in Antología del pensamiento puertorriqueño (1900-1970) (Río Piedras: Editorial Universitaria, Universidad de Puerto Rico, 1975), II, 887-900.

37.10 ________. "Nuevas notas sobre Gautier Benítez." Hispania, 13 (1930), 485-96.

37.11 Bonafoux, Luis. "Gautier." In his Ultramarinos (Madrid: M. Tello, 1882), pp. 114-19.

37.12 Carreras, Carlos N. "Prólogo." In José Gautier Benítez, Poesías; 4. ed. (SJ, 1924), pp. i-vii.

37.13 Coll y Toste, Cayetano. "¿Dónde nació nuestro eximio poeta José Gautier Benítez?" BHPR, 4 (1917), 126-28.

37.14 ________. "José Gautier Benítez." In his Puertorriqueños ilustres; segunda selección (Barcelona: Rumbos, 1966), pp. 325-28.

37.15 ________. "El poeta Gautier Benítez." BHPR, 6 (1919), 158-61.

37.16 Collado Martell, Alfredo. "José Gautier Benítez, el Gustavo Adolfo Bécquer de la lírica puertorriqueña." In José Gautier Benítez, Poesías (SJ: Librería y Editorial Campos, 1955), pp. 37-49. Also 194?; pp. 23-34. Orig. 1929.

37.17 Cortina Gómez, Rodolfo. "José Gautier Benítez, poeta esencial." RC-R, 1, 2 (1973), 43-48.

37.18 Elzaburu, Manuel. "José Gautier Benítez." In José Gautier Benítez, Poesías (SJ: Librería y Editorial Campos, 1955), pp. 21-36. Also 194?; pp. 7-21. Also Madrid: Aguilar, 1929; pp. 5-21. Orig. in first edition, SJ: González, 1880.

37.19 Fernández Méndez, Eugenio. "José Gautier Benítez." AyL, 2a época, No. 16 (1958), 19.

37.20 Figueroa, Sotero. "José Gautier Benítez (1848-1880)." In his Ensayos biográficos... (Ponce: El Vapor, 1888), pp. 251-62.

37.21 Girón de Segura, Socorro. "Los amores de Gautier en su poesía." In José Gautier Benítez, Epístolas (Madrid, 1956), pp. 79-92. Various other critical apparati.

37.22 ________. "José Gautier Benítez (1851-1880)." In José Gautier Benítez, Poesías (SJ: Instituto de Cultura Puertorriqueña, 1967), pp. 5-11.

37.23 ________. "Nota al lector." In José Gautier Benítez, Obra completa (Palma de Mallorca: Mossén Alvar, 1960), pp. 9-11.

37.24 González, José Emilio. "Prólogo." In José Gautier Benítez, Vida y obra poética (SJ: Campos, 1968), pp. 19-27. Various other editions.

37.25 ________. "Visión de Gautier." In José Gautier Benítez, Poesías (SJ: Librería y Editorial Campos, 1955), pp. 7-16.

37.26 Hernández Aquino, Luis. "El arco y la flecha de José Gautier Benítez." In Institución del día del poeta (SJ: Sociedad de Autores Puertorriqueños, 1965), pp. 15-29. Orig. RICP, No. 23 (1964), 1-6.

37.27 ________. "Dos cantores de Puerto Rico. Vidarte y Gautier." AyL, 2a época, No. 17 (1958), 3-6.

37.28 ________. "José Gautier Benítez y José de Diego: los dos grandes cantores de Puerto Rico." RICP, No. 31 (1966), 10-13.

37.29 __________. "Los precursores de Gautier Benítez." *RICP*, No. 22 (1964), 42-50.

37.30 Hostos, Adolfo de. "José Gautier Benítez (1851-1880)." In his *Hombres representativos de Puerto Rico* (SJ, 1961), pp. 106-15.

37.31 Malaret, Augusto. "José Gautier Benítez." In his *Medallas de oro* (SJ: Biblioteca de Autores Puertorriqueños, 1938), pp. 105-37. 3. ed., SJ, 1942; pp. 111-45. 4. ed., M: Orión, 1952; pp. 145-88. Signed 1911.

37.32 Matos Bernier, Félix. "José Gautier Benítez." In his *Pedazos de roca* (Ponce: "La Libertad", 1894), pp. 183-88.

37.33 Medina y González, Zenón. "José Gautier Benítez." In his *Pinceladas* (SJ: V. de González, 1895), pp. 40-43.

37.34 Pedreira, Antonio S. "El héroe galopante." In his *Aclaraciones y crítica* (Río Piedras: Phi Eta Mu, Universidad de Puerto Rico, 1941), pp. 227-32. Also Río Piedras: Edil, 1969.

37.35 Rosa-Nieves, Cesáreo. "Boceto crítico para un estudio de la poesía de Gautier Benítez." In José Gautier Benítez, *Vida y obra poética* (SJ: Campos, 1968), pp. 5-18. Various other editions.

37.36 __________. "José Gautier Benítez." *RICP*, No. 32 (1966), 1-6.

37.37 __________. "José Gautier Benítez (1848-1880)." In his *Ensayos escogidos...* (SJ: Academia de Artes y Ciencias de Puerto Rico, 1970?), pp. 53-65.

37.38 __________. "José Gautier Benítez (1848-1880)." In his *Plumas estelares en las letras de Puerto Rico* (SJ: Ediciones de la Torre, Universidad de Puerto Rico, 1967), I, 137-51.

37.39 __________. "Nuevos aproches en torno a José Rodolfo Gautier Benítez." In his *La lámpara del faro...* (SJ: Club de la Prensa, 1957), pp. 143-56. Orig. *Anales*, No. 5 (1954), 68-71.

37.40 Siaca Rivera, Manuel. "José Gautier Benítez." *Asomante*, 1, 4 (1945), 79-92.

37.41 Tejera, Diego V. "El poeta." *RP*, 6, 6 (1892), 16-20.

38

GONZÁLEZ, JOSÉ LUIS (1926-)

Bibliographies

38.1 Ruscadella Bercedóniz, Isabel. "Bibliografía de José Luis González." TC, No. 12 (1979), 115-27.

Critical Monographs and Dissertations

38.2 Díaz Quiñones, Arcadio. Conversación con José Luis González. Río Piedras: Huracán, 1976. Same as item no. 38.11.

Critical Essays

38.3 "Aproximación a Balada de otro tiempo de J. L. González." TC, No. 12 (1979), 92-114.

38.4 Avellaneda, Andrés O. "Para leer a José Luis González: un repaso de su segunda salida." CHA, No. 308 (1976), 156-69.

38.5 __________. "Qué sabe usted de la narrativa puertorriqueña o Relato de la segunda salida de José Luis González." Contémpora, 1 (1974), 10-12.

38.6 Cadilla, Carmen Alicia. "Puertorriqueñidad del cuento de José Luis González." In José Luis González, En la sombra (SJ: Venezuela, 1943), pp. 5-7.

38.7 Castro Pareda, Rafael. "El tema del amor en Balada de otro tiempo." El cóndor, 5, 1 (1980), 22-33.

38.8 Córdova Infante, Julia. "[5 cuentos de sangre]." Asomante, 2, 1 (1946), 84-85.

38.9 Délano, Luis Enrique. "José Luis González, escritor y combatiente." In José Luis González, Paisá--un relato de la emigración (M: Fondo de Cultura Popular, 1950), pp. 9-14.

38.10 Díaz Quiñones, Arcadio. "[Balada de otro tiempo]." SinN, 9, 2 (1978), 92-95.

38.11 __________. "Conversación con José Luis González." SinN, 6, 4 (1976), 73-81. Same as item no. 38.2.

38.12 __________. "José Luis González, Premio Villaurrutia [Balada de otro tiempo]." Plural, No. 90 (1979), 62-63.

38.13 "Entrevista a José Luis González." Reintegro, 1, 3 (1981), 18-20.

38.14 Ferré, Rosario. "[Mambrú se fue a la guerra]." Zona, 1, 3 (1973), 20.

38.15 González, José Luis. "El arte del cuento." In José Luis González, and Lizandro Chávez Alfaro, La expresión literaria (Xalapa, Méx.: Universidad Veracruzana, 1978?), pp. 5-35. No. 2 in the series, La expresión literaria.

38.16 ________. "El escritor en el exilio." Insula, Nos. 356-57 (1976), 13. Also in his El país de cuatro pisos y otros ensayos (Río Piedras: Huracán, 1980), pp. 105-13.

38.17 Ibargoyen Islas, Saúl. "Tiempos de nuestro tiempo [Balada de otro tiempo]." Plural, No. 85 (1978), 67-69.

38.18 Laguerre, Enrique A. "Presentación de José Luis González." In his Polos en la cultura iberoamericana (Boston: Florentia, 1977), pp. 115-17.

38.19 Lizalde, Eduardo. "[En este lado]." IMex, 5, 11 (1955), 142-43.

38.20 Marqués, René. "José Luis González." In his Cuentos puertorriqueños; 3. ed. (Río Piedras: Cultural, 1971), pp. 77-86. Orig. 1959.

38.21 Matos Paoli, Francisco. "José Luis González: cuentista del hombre común." In José Luis González, 5 cuentos de sangre (SJ, 1945), pp. 5-11.

38.22 Orthmann, Nora G., and Caridad L. Silva de Velázquez. "José Luis González: observaciones sobre su obra y su generación." SinN, 10, 2 (1979), 29-38.

38.23 Pitol, Sergio. "[Paisá]." IMex, 6, 13-14 (1955), 63-65.

38.24 Rama, Angel. "José Luis González o la cortina del silencio sobre Puerto Rico." In José Luis González, En Nueva York y otras desgracias (M: Siglo XXI, 1973), pp. 1-5.

38.25 Rodríguez-Seda, Asela. "[Mambrú se fue a la guerra]." RC-R, 2, 2 (1974), 54-57.

38.26 Soto, Pedro Juan. "José Luis González, ese desconocido." In José Luis González, Veinte cuentos y Paisá (Río Piedras: Cultural, 1973), pp. 9-21.

38.27 Sotomayor, Aurea María. "Apuntes de un cronista: La llegada." Reintegro, 1, 3 (1981), 28-29.

38.28 Torres Santiago, José Manuel. "Respuesta a una carta abierta de José Luis González." Guajana, 4a época, No. 2 (1974), no pagination.

38.29 Vázquez, Margarita, and Daisy Caraballo. "José Luis González." In La gran enciclopedia de Puerto Rico (Madrid" Ediciones R, 1976), IV, 114-21.

38.30 Vientós Gastón, Nilita. "José Luis González en 'New World writing'." In her Indice cultural (Río Piedras: Ediciones de la Universidad de Puerto Rico, 1962-71), III, 23-24.

38.31 __________. "Paisá: una novela de José Luis González." In her Indice cultural (Río Piedras: Ediciones de la Universidad de Puerto Rico, 1962-71), I, 79-81.

39

GONZÁLEZ GARCÍA, MATÍAS (1866-1938)

Critical Monographs and Dissertations

39.1 Cuevas de Marcano, Concepción. Matías González García: vida y obra. SJ: Coquí, 1966. Orig. an unpublished thesis, Universidad de Puerto Rico, 1962.

Critical Essays

39.2 "Confesiones de Matías González para Indice." Indice, No. 7 (1929), 100.

39.3 Dávila, Virgilio. "Prólogo." In Matías González García, Cosas de antaño y cosas de ogaño... (Caguas: R. Morel Campos, 1918-22), II, i-v.

39.4 Fernández Juncos, Manuel. "Prólogo." In Matías González García, Cosas de antaño y cosas de ogaño... (Caguas: R. Morel Campos, 1918-22), I, i-iii.

39.5 Gómez Tejera, Carmen. "Las novelas de Matías González García." Indice, No. 7 (1929), 101.

39.6 Martínez Capó, Juan. "Introducción." In Matías González García, Cuentos; primera selección (SJ: Rumbos, 1960), pp. 5-23.

39.7 "Matías González García: apuntación biográfica." Indice, No. 7 (1929), 99.

39.8 "Opiniones." Indice, No. 7 (1929), 103.

39.9 Pedreira, Antonio S. "Apreciación del cuentista." Indice, No. 7 (1929), 102.

39.10 Rosa-Nieves, Cesáreo. "Matías González García, el costumbrista." In his Ensayos escogidos... (SJ: Academia de Artes y Ciencias de Puerto Rico, 1970?), pp. 117-19.

39.11 ________. "Matías González García (1866-1938)." In his Plumas estelares en las letras de Puerto Rico (SJ: Ediciones de la Torre, Universidad de Puerto Rico, 1967), I, 593-614.

40

HERNÁNDEZ, JOSÉ P. H. (1892-1922)

Critical Monographs and Dissertations

40.1 Siaca Rivera, Manuel. José P. H. Hernández: vida y obra. SJ: Coquí, 1965.

Critical Essays

40.2 Arana, Felipe N. "José P. H. Hernández." Prensa, 2a época, No. 4 (1959), 9.

40.3 Camejo, Rafael W. "José P. H. Hernández." In his Florecían los rosales (Caracas: Hernández, 1952), pp. 67-74.

40.4 Carreras, Carlos N. "José P. H. Hernández." In his Hombres y mujeres de Puerto Rico (M: Orión, 1957), pp. 241-56. Various subsequent editions.

40.5 ________. "Prólogo." In José P. H. Hernández, Cantos de la sierra (SJ: Biblioteca Puerto Rico Ilustrado, 1925), pp. i-iii.

40.6 Colón, Emilio M. "[Prólogo]." In José P. H. Hernández, Poesías (SJ: Coquí, 1965), I, no pagination.

40.7 Dalta, Luis. "En el pórtico." In José P. H. Hernández, Coplas de la vereda (SJ: Standard Printing Work, 1918?), pp. 3-6.

40.8 González, José Emilio. "P. H. Hernández, Antología, 1956." Asomante, 14, 2 (1958), 88-90.

40.9 Lloréns, Washington. "José P. H. Hernández." In his Críticas profanas (SJ: Progreso, 1936), pp. 61-66.

40.10 Matos Paoli, Francisco. "José P. H. Hernández (1892-1922)." Asomante, 2, 4 (1946), 70-81.

40.11 Porras Cruz, Jorge Luis. "Nueva ojeada a la poesía de José P. H. Hernández." AtPR, 4, 3 (1940), 241-48. Also

RICP, No. 24 (1964), 28-30. Also in his Estudios y artículos (Río Piedras: Editorial Universitaria, Universidad de Puerto Rico, 1974), pp. 45-53.

40.12 Rafael, Juan Vicente. "Prólogo." In José P. H. Hernández, El último combate (elegías) (SJ: "La Democracia", 1921), pp. 3-5.

40.13 Rosa-Nieves, Cesáreo. "José P. H. Hernández (1892-1922)." In his Plumas estelares en las letras de Puerto Rico (SJ: Ediciones de la Torre, Universidad de Puerto Rico, 1967), II. 409-20.

40.14 Siaca Rivera, Manuel. "Introducción." In José P. H. Hernández, Antología (SJ: Ateneo Puertorriqueño, 1956), pp. i-iv.

40.15 _________. "José P. H. Hernández." In Puerto Rico. Universidad. Seminario de Estudios Hispánicos, La naturaleza en la poesía puertorriqueña del siglo XX (Río Piedras, 1942), pp. 34-50. Boletín de la Universidad de Puerto Rico, serie XIII, no. 2.

40.16 _________. "Vida y obra de José P. H. Hernández." In José P. H. Hernández, Obra poética (SJ: Instituto de Cultura Puertorriqueña, 1966), pp. 9-125.

40.17 Vientós Gastón, Nilita. "Una antología de P. H. Hernández." In her Indice cultural (Río Piedras: Ediciones de la Universidad de Puerto Rico, 1962-71), II, 171-73.

41

HERNÁNDEZ AQUINO, LUIS (1907-)

Critical Essays

41.1 Arce de Vázquez, Margot. "La poesía de Luis Hernández Aquino." In Luis Hernández Aquino, Voz en el tiempo... (SJ: Biblioteca de Autores Puertorriqueños, 1952), pp. i-xlvii.

41.2 Castro, Tomás de Jesús. "Luis Hernández Aquino." In his Esbozos críticos (SJ: Baldrich, 1945), pp. 85-87.

41.3 Dávila, José Antonio. "A Luis Hernández Aquino." In his Prosa: ensayos, artículos y cartas literarias (SJ: Sociedad de Autores Puertorriqueños, 1971), pp. 261-62.

41.4 Figueria, Gastón. "Prólogo." In Luis Hernández Aquino, Isla para la angustia (SJ: Insula, Casa Baldrich, 1943), pp. 5-7.

41.5 González, José Emilio. "Luis Hernández Aquino: jornada hacia su poesía." In Luis Hernández Aquino, Antología poética (Río Piedras: Universidad de Puerto Rico, 1974), pp. 7-35.

41.6 Jiménez Malaret, René. "Niebla lírica." In his Puntos de vista (SJ: Betances, 1961), pp. 17-21.

41.7 López, Julio César. "Luis Hernández Aquino y su visión de España." In his Pasión y poesía (jornada crítica) (Barcelona: Rumbos, 1967), pp. 23-31.

41.8 "Luis Hernández Aquino." In La ciudad de los poetas (Palencia de Castilla, Spain: Rocamador, 1965), pp. 63-66.

41.9 Matos Paoli, Francisco. "El paisaje en la poesía de Hernández Aquino." In Luis Hernández Aquino, Isla para la angustia (SJ: Insula, Casa Baldrich, 1943), pp. 8-10.

41.10 Meléndez, Concha. "La isla ignorada de Hernández Aquino." In her Figuraciones de Puerto Rico y otros ensayos (SJ: Instituto de Cultura Puertorriqueña, 1958), pp. 77-79. Also in her Obras completas (SJ: Instituto de Cultura Puertorriqueña, 1970-72), II, 415-18.

41.11 Moreno Jiménez, Domingo. "Luis Hernández Aquino a la luz del integralismo." DíaE, 1, 2 (1941), 7-9.

41.12 Soto Ramos, Julio. "Fe de erratas de la antología Nueva poesía de Puerto Rico de Angel Valbuena Briones y L. Hernández Aquino." In his Una pica en Flandes (SJ: Club de la Prensa, 1959), pp. 115-38.

41.13 ________. "Nuestra aventura literaria." In his Yo soy yo y mi verdad... (SJ: Cordillera, 1973), pp. 71-98.

41.14 Villaronga, Luis. "Luis Hernández Aquino, poeta magno." In Luis Hernández Aquino, Poemas de la vida breve (SJ: Venezuela, 1940), pp. 9-15.

41.15 Vizcarrondo, Carmelina. "El subjetivismo en la poesía de Luis Hernández Aquino." In Luis Hernández Aquino, Poemas de la vida breve (SJ: Venezuela, 1940), pp. 19-21.

42

HOSTOS, EUGENIO MARÍA DE (1839-1903)

Bibliographies

42.1 "Bibliografía de Eugenio María de Hostos." BBIA, 2 (1939), 8-9.

42.2 "Complemento biográfico y bibliografía." In Comisión Pro Celebración del Centenario del Natalicio de Eugenio María de Hostos, América y Hostos..., q.v., pp. 341-91.

42.3 Hostos, Adolfo de. Indice hemero-bibliográfico de Eugenio María de Hostos (incluye material inédito, inconografía y hostiana), 1863-1940. SJ: Comisión Pro Celebración del Centenario del Natalicio de Hostos, 1940.

42.4 Rosenbaum, Sidonia C. "Eugenio María de Hostos: bibliografía." RHM, 5 (1939), 319-23.

Critical Monographs and Dissertations

42.5 Alonso, Luis Ricardo. "Hostos y Martí: novelistas." DAI, 36 (1975), 1546A.

42.6 Arán, Pedro. Biografía de Hostos. NY, 1952.

42.7 Arismendi Robióu, J. Leyendo y recordano. Santiago, República Dominicana: "El Diario", 1951.

42.8 Balsiero, José A. Eugenio María de Hostos: Hispanic American public servant. Coral Gables, FL: University of Miami Hispanic-American Studies, 1949.

42.9 Benítez, Justo Pastor. Bajo el alero asunceño. Rio de Janeiro: Ministério de Educação e Cultura, Serviço de Documentação, 1955.

42.10 Blanco-Fombona, Rufino. Hostos. Montevideo: Claudio García, 1945. Followed by the text of Hostos's Hamlet.

42.11 Boletines de la Comisión Pro Celebración del Natalicio de Hostos. SJ, 1938-39. 11 nos.

42.12 Borda de Sainz, Jo Ann Marie. "Eugenio María de Hostos: his philosophy." DAI, 38 (1978), 6152A.

42.13 Bosch, Juan. Hostos el sembrador. La Habana: Trópico, 1939.

42.14 __________. Mujeres en la vida de Hostos. SJ: Asociación de Mujeres Graduadas de la Unviersidad de Puerto Rico, 1938. 2. e.d, 1939.

42.15 Carreras, Carlos N. Hostos, apóstol de la libertad. Madrid: Juan Bravo, 1950. 2. ed., SJ: Cordillera, 1971.

42.16 Caso, Antonio. La filosofía moral de Hostos. M: Ateneo de la Juventud, 1910. Same as item no. 42.86.

42.17 Cestero, Tulio Manuel Eugenio María de Hostos, hombre representativo de América. BA: Academia Nacional de la Historia, 1940. Same as item no. 42.88.

42.18 Comisión Pro Celebración del Centenario del Natalicio de Eugenio María de Hostos. América y Hostos. La Habana: La Habana Cultural, 1939. Pertinent items are listed separately.

42.19 Díaz Laparra, Marco. Eugenio María de Hostos y fray Matías de Córdova: dos panoramas biográficos. Guatemala: Ministerio de Educación Pública, 1950. Also Guatemala: "José de Pineda Ibarra", 1967.

42.20 Esténger, Rafael. Hostos; biografía para niños. La Habana: Alfa, 1942.

42.21 __________. Sociología americana. La Habana: Molina, 1939. Same as item no. 42.106.

42.22 Eugenio María de Hostos: biografía y bibliografía. Santo Domingo: Oiga, 1904.

42.23 Eugenio María de Hostos (1839-1903); vida y obra, bibliografía-antología. NY: Hispanic Institute in the United States, 1940. Same as RHM, 5 (1939) listings.

42.24 Ferrer, José. Hostos, ciudadano de América. SJ: Cantero Fernández, 1936. See item no. 42.112.

42.25 Guernelli, Adelaida L. "Eugenio María de Hostos: ensayista y crítico literario." DA, 28 (1968), 4630A.

42.26 Henríquez Ureña, Camila. Ideas pedagógicas de Hostos. Santo Domingo: Revista de Educación, 1932. 2. ed., Santo Domingo: Secretaría de Educación, 1974.

42.27 Hostos, Adolfo de. Tras las huellas de Hostos. Río Piedras: Universidad de Puerto Rico, 1966.

42.28 Hostos, Bayoán L. de. Eugenio María de Hostos, íntimo. Santo Domingo: Montalvo, 1929.

42.29 Hostos, Eugenio Carlos de. Eugenio M. de Hostos. Biografía y bibliografía. Santo Domingo: Oiga, 1904.

42.30 __________. Eugenio María de Hostos, peregrino del ideal. Paris: Ediciones Literarias y Artísticas, 1954.

42.31 __________. Eugenio María de Hostos, promoter of Pan

Americanism; a collection of writings and a bibliography... Madrid, 1954? Pertinent items are listed separately.

42.32 __________. Hostos, hispanoamericanista. Madrid: Bravo, 1952? Pertinent items are listed separately.

42.33 La influencia de Hostos en la cultura dominicana; respuestas a la encuesta de El Caribe. Ciudad Trujillo: Editora del Caribe, 1956.

42.34 Lepervanche Parparcén, René de. Hostos (introducción al estudio "Hostos, sus ideas constitucionales"). Caracas: Bolívar, 1941.

42.35 Lugo Guernelli, Adelaida. Eugenio María de Hostos: ensayista y crítico literario. SJ: Instituto de Cultura Puertorriqueña, 1970. Orig. an unpublished dissertation, Hostos, crítico literario. Universidad de Puerto Rico, 1956.

42.36 Magdaleno, Mauricio. Hostos y Albizu Campos. SJ: Puerto Rico Libre, 1939.

42.37 O'Neill de Milán, Luis. Eugenio María de Hostos. SJ: Imprenta del Gobierno Insular, 1950.

42.38 Parrish, Robert T. A study of the personality and thought of Eugenio María de Hostos. Unpublished Ph.D. dissertation, University of Wisconsin, 1940.

42.39 Pedreira, Antonio S. Hostos, ciudadano de América. Madrid: Espasa-Calpe, 1931. Also SJ: Instituto de Cultura Puertorriqueña, 1965. Also SJ: Edil, 1968. See item no. 42.221.

42.40 Ramírez Santibáñez, José. Estudio crítico-biográfico sobre Eugenio María de Hostos. Mayagüez, 1912.

42.41 Rodríguez Demorizi, Emilio. Camino de Hostos. Ciudad Trujillo: Montalvo, 1939.

42.42 __________. Hostos en Santo Domingo. Ciudad Trujillo: García, 1939.

42.43 __________. Luperón y Hostos. Ciudad Trujillo: Montalvo, 1939.

42.44 Roig de Leuchsenring, Emilio. Hostos, apóstol de la independencia y libertad de Cuba y Puerto Rico. La Habana: Municipio de La Habana, Administración del Alcalde, 1939.

42.45 __________. Hostos y Cuba. La Habana: Municipio de La Habana, 1939.

42.46 Romeu y Fernández, Raquel. Eugenio María de Hostos, antillanista y ensayista. Madrid: Facultad de Filosofía y Letras, Seminario de Estudios Americanistas, 1959.

42.47 Sisler, Robert Frank. "Eugenio M. de Hostos: a comparative study of the educational and political contributions." DA, 24 (1963), 1346.

42.48 Tejeda, Francisco Elías de. Las doctrinas políticas de Eugenio María de Hostos. Madrid: Cultura Hispánica, 1949.

42.49 Trujillo, Rafael Leonidas, hijo. Encuesta acerca de Hostos, iniciada por el diario El Caribe. Ciudad Trujillo, 1957.

42.50 Velasco Ibarra, J. M. El derecho constitucional en Eugenio María de Hostos. Quito: Escuela Tipográfica Salesiana, 1928.

42.51 Waltzer, Hildreth Naomi. "The inner pilgrimmage of Eugenio María de Hostos as seen through Bayoán." DAI, 37 (1977), 5866A-67A.

Critical Essays

42.52 Alba, Pedro de. "Dos hombres de ayer." CAm, No. 101 (1958), 193-208. Also as "Hostos y Enrique Federico Amiel, dos hombre de ayer." AyL, 2a época, No. 25 (1959), 9-14.

42.53 __________. "Eugenio María de Hostos and his ideas of social morality." BUP, 73, 2 (1939), 85-95. Also in Eugenio Carlos de Hostos, Eugenio María de Hostos, promoter of Pan Americanism..., q.v., pp. 101-24.

42.54 __________. "La moral social de Eugenio María de Hostos." BUP, 73, 2 (1939), 63-75. Also in Comisión Pro Celebración del Centenario del Natalicio de Eugenio María de Hostos, América y Hostos, q.v., pp. 189-20C.

42.55 __________. "La peregrinación heroica de Eugenio María de Hostos." In Eugenio María de Hostos, Hostos (antología) (M: Secretaría de Educación Pbulica, 1944), pp. vii-xxix. Also in Eugenio Carlos de Hostos, Hostos hispanoamericanista, q.v., pp. 95-119.

42.56 Alfaro, Rogelio E. "A sketch of Hostos' life." In Eugenio Carlos de Hostos, Eugenio María de Hostos, promoter of Pan Americanism..., q.v., pp. 59-63.

42.57 Aloy, Miguel Angel. "Eugenio María de Hostos, maestro de América." In Eugenio María de Hostos, Hostos, peregrino del ideal, q.v., pp. 15-32.

42.58 Alpizar, Sergio P. "Hostos: rememoración y mensaje." In Eugenio Carlos de Hostos, Hostos, peregrino del ideal, q.v., pp. 391-402.

42.59 Amador, Fernán Félix de. "Hostos y el sentido solidario de Latino América." RAMG, 1, 1 (1938), 44-45. Also in Eugenio Carlos de Hostos, Hostos, hispanoamericanista, q.v., pp. 363-66.

42.60 Andreu de Aguilar, Isabel. "Eugenio María de Hostos, mantenedor de los derechos de la mujer." RAMG, 1, 3 (1938), 26-28.

42.61 Arce de Vázquez, Margot. "Hostos, patriota ejemplar." RAMG, 1, 2 (1938), 3. Also in Eugenio Carlos de Hostos, Hostos, hispanoamericanista, q.v., pp. 53-58.

42.62 Arévalo Martínez, Rafael. "Hostos." RHon, No. 85 (1940), 11-12, 22.

42.63 Arismendi Robiou, J. "Recuerdos del maestro." In Eugenio Carlos de Hostos, Hostos, peregrino del ideal, q.v., pp. 303-15. Orig. in his Leyendo y recordando (Santiago, República Dominicana: El Diario, 1951), pp. 4-11, 15-19, 21-27, 29, 31-33, 47, 49.

42.64 Arroyo, Anita. "Hostos y Martí, universales." RICP, No. 24 (1964), 4-11.

42.65 Astol, Eugenio. "Hostos y la liga de patriotas." In Eugenio Carlos de Hostos, Hostos, peregrino del ideal, q.v., pp. 271-83.

42.66 Asturias, Miguel Angel. "Influencia de Hostos en la generación de 1920." In Eugenio Carlos de Hostos, Hostos, peregrino del ideal, q.v., pp. 236-38.

42.67 Babín, María Teresa. "El pensamiento de Hostos (1839-1903)." RICP, No. 59 (1973), 17-22.

42.68 Balseiro, José A. "Crítica y estilo literarios en Eugenio María de Hostos." In Comisión Pro Celebración del Centenario del Natalicio de Eugenio María de Hostos, América y Hostos, q.v., pp. 53-63. Orig. RI, No. 1 (1939), 17-27. Also in his El vigía (SJ: Biblioteca de Autores Puertorriqueños, 1942), III, 79-96.

42.69 __________. "Eugenio María de Hostos: servidor público de América." In his Expresión de Hispanoamérica; primera serie (SJ: Instituto de Cultura Puertorriqueña, 1960), pp. 101-19. 2. ed., rev., Madrid: Gredos, 1970; pp. 112-33. Also as "Eugenio María de Hostos, a public servant of the Americas." In his The Americas look at each other (Coral Gables, FL: University of Miami Press, 1969), pp. 104-24. Also as "Eugenio María de Hostos: Hispanic America [sic] public servant." In Eugenio Carlos de Hostos, Eugenio María de Hostos, promoter of Pan Americanism..., q.v., pp. 21-43.

42.70 __________. "La significación del Centenario en Conmemoración de Eugenio María de Hostos." In Eugenio Carlos de Hostos, Hostos, peregrino del ideal, q.v., pp. 239-46.

42.71 Barbagelata, Hugo D. "Eugenio María de Hostos." In Eugenio Carlos de Hostos, Hostos, peregrino del ideal, q.v., pp. 165-79.

42.72 Barrera, Isaac J. "Hombre de América." In Eugenio Carlos de Hostos, Hostos, peregrino del ideal, q.v., pp. 227-29.

42.73 Belaval, Emilio S. "Eugenio María de Hostos y la utopía americana." BAAC, 3, 1 (1967), 5-8.

42.74 Blanco-Fombona, Rufino. "Eugenio María de Hostos." IA, 7, 6 (1924), 534-39. Also in Spanish, RevFi, 19 (1924), 203-209.

42.75 __________. "Eugenio María de Hostos." In his Grandes escritores de América, siglo XIX (Madrid: Renacimiento, 1917), pp. 173-221. Also CCont, 2, 4 (1914), 400-27. Also as "Eugenio María de Hostos (1839-1903)." In Comisión Pro Celebración del Natalicio de Eugenio María de Hostos, América y Hostos, q.v., pp. 97-129. Also in Eugenio María de Hostos, Moral social (Madrid: América, 1917), pp. vii-lvii.

42.76 Bosch, Juan. "Hostos y la revolución cubana." BUP, 73, 1 (1939), 10-15.

42.77 __________. "Mujeres en la vida de Hostos." In Eugenio Carlos de Hostos, Hostos, hispanoamericanista, q.v., pp. 165-203. Same as item no. 42.14.

42.78 Bouchard, Paul. "Eugenio María de Hostos et son oeuvre, 1938-1903: pages choisies, traduites par Maurice Lebel." Culture, 31 (1970), 65-71.

42.79 Brañas, César. "Coloquio con Eugenio María de Hostos después de la alabanza." In Eugenio Carlos de Hostos, Hostos, peregrino del ideal, q.v., pp. 222-26.

42.80 Brightman, Edgard Sheffield. "América y Hostos." In Eugenio Carlos de Hostos, Eugenio María de Hostos, promoter of Pan Americanism..., q.v., pp. 84-86.

42.81 __________. "Eugenio María de Hostos, philosopher of personality." In Eugenio Carlos de Hostos, Eugenio María de Hostos, promoter of Pan Americanism..., q.v., pp. 15-18. Also as "Eugenio María de Hostos, filósofo de la personalidad." ULH, No. 33 (1939), 57-61. Also Luminar, 3, 2 (1939), 204-208.

42.82 __________. "El Fichte de la América española." ND, 20, 3 (1939), 8-9.

42.83 Capó, José María. "Eugenio María Hostos o la armonía." Educación, 12, 6 (1962), 97-123.

42.84 Carvalho, E. de. "Eugenio María de Hostos." In his Príncipes del espíritu americano (Madrid: América, 1930), pp. 239-41.

42.85 Caso, Antonio. "The centenary of Eugenio María de Hostos." BUP, 73 (1939), 26. Also in Eugenio Carlos de Hostos, Eugenio María de Hostos, promoter of Pan Americanism..., q.v., pp. 77-78.

42.86 __________. "La filosofía moral de Eugenio María de Hostos." In Comisión Pro Celebración del Natalicio de Eugenio María de Hostos, América y Hostos, q.v., pp. 209-22. Orig. in Conferencias del Ateneo de la Juventud (M: Lacaud, 1910), pp. 11-31. Also Ateneo, No. 13 (1911), 15-24.

42.87 "Centenario del sabio maestro e ilustre antillano Eugenio María de Hostos." Clío, 7 (1939), entire issue.

42.88 Cestero, Tulio Manuel. "Eugenio María de Hostos, hombre representativo de América." BANH, 13 (1940), 339-65. Same as item no. 42.17.

42.89 __________. "Eugenio María de Hostos, sociólogo portorriqueño." BIS, No. 2 (1943), 177-95.

42.90 __________. "Introducción." In Eugenio Carlos de Hostos, Hostos, hispanoamericanista, q.v., pp. 13-45. Same as item no. 42.17.

42.91 Coll y Toste, Cayetano. "Eugenio María de Hostos." In his Puertorriqueños ilustres; segunda selección (Barcelona: Rumbos, 1966), pp. 218-22.

42.92 __________. "Puertorriqueños ilustres. Hostos (1839-1903)." BHPR, 5 (1918), 260-62.

42.93 Córdoba, Diego. "Odisea y actualidad de Hostos." RNC, Nos 87-88 (1951), 199-225.

42.94 Crawford, William Rex. "Eugenio María de Hostos y Bonilla." In his A century of Latin American thought (Cambridge, MA: Harvard University Press, 1944), pp. 236-46. Also in Eugenio Carlos de Hostos, Hostos, hispanoamericanista, q.v., pp. 343-54. Also in Eugenio Carlos de Hostos, Eugenio María de Hostos, promoter of Pan Americanism..., q.v., pp. 125-37.

42.95 Cruz Monclova, Lidio. "Ensayo sobre Romeo y Julieta." In Eugenio Carlos de Hostos, Hostos, peregrino del ideal, q.v., pp. 201-10.

42.96 __________. "Prólogo." In Eugenio María de Hostos, Romeo y Julieta (Río Piedras: Caguas, 1939), pp. 11-25.

42.97 Daireaux, Max. "Actualité de E. M. de Hostos." In Eugenio Carlos de Hostos, Eugenio María de Hostos, promoter

<u>of Pan Americanism...</u>, q.v., pp. 166-71. Also as "Actualidad de Eugenio María de Hostos." In <u>Eugenio Carlos de Hostos, hispanoamericanista</u>, q.v., pp. 335-41.

42.98 Dalmau Canet, Sebastián. "Para honrar a de Hostos." In his <u>Crepúsculos literarios</u> (SJ: Boletín Mercantil, 1903), pp. 67-69.

42.99 Daubón, José A. "Eugenio María de Hostos." In his <u>Cosas de Puerto Rico; segunda serie</u> (SJ: Tipografía la Correspondencia, 1905), pagination unknown.

42.100 Dávila, José Antonio. "Don Eugenio María de Hostos." <u>Educación</u>, 10, 2 (1961), 31-44.

42.101 __________. "Un ensayo hostiano [<u>Romeo y Julieta</u>]." In his <u>Prosa: ensayos, artículos y cartas literarias</u> (SJ: Sociedad de Autores Puertorriqueños, 1971), pp. 145-47.

42.102 Despradel y Batista, Guido. "Las proyectadas granjas agrícolas del señor Hostos." In Eugenio Carlos de Hostos, <u>Hostos, peregrino del ideal</u>, q.v., pp. 336-41. Also <u>Clío</u>, 7 (1939), 60-62.

42.103 Enjuto y Ferrán, Federico. "Hostos en su visión del siglo XX." <u>CA</u>, No. 21 (1945), 134-40.

42.104 Espina, Concha. "Eugenio María de Hostos." In Eugenio Carlos de Hostos, <u>Hostos, hispanoamericanista</u>, q.v., pp. 49-52.

42.105 "Esquema biográfico de Eugenio María de Hostos." In Eugenio Carlos de Hostos, <u>Hostos, peregrino del ideal</u>, q.v., pp. 405-54.

42.106 Estênger, Rafael. "Sociopatía americana (comentarios a Hostos)." <u>RBC</u>, 43, 3 (1939), 442-52. Also in Eugenio Carlos de Hostos, <u>Hostos, hispanoamericanista</u>, q.v., pp. 293-305. Same as item no. 42.21.

42.107 Estrade, Paul. "Hostos en <u>La república cubana</u> (donde yace su texto inédito: 'Cuba, desde Chile')." <u>SinN</u>, 3, 4 (1973), 30-36.

42.108 "Eugenio María de Hostos; noticia biográfica." In Comisión Pro Celebración del Centenario del Natalicio de Eugenio María de Hostos, <u>América y Hostos</u>, q.v., pp. 4-33.

42.109 Fernández Méndez, Eugenio. "El pensamiento social de Eugenio María de Hostos." <u>RICP</u>, No. 23 (1964), 43-49.

42.110 Fernos Isern, Antonio. "Eugenio María de Hostos." <u>BAAC</u>, 2, 2 (1966), 351-55.

42.111 Ferrer Canales, José. "Una faceta de Hostos." In Instituto Internacional de Literatura Iberoamericana, <u>XVII</u>

Congreso (Madrid: Cultura Hispánica del Centro Iberoamericano de Cooperación, 1978), III, 1459-67.

42.112 _________. "Hostos, ciudadano de América." In his Marginalia (SJ?: Venezuela?, 1939), pp. 79-100.

42.113 _________. "Hostos humano." CA, No. 27 (1946), 169-79.

42.114 _________. "Hostos y Giner de los Ríos (cincuentenario de Giner)." Asomante, 21, 4 (1965), 7-28.

42.115 _________. "Luis A. Ferré cita a Hostos." In his Acentos cívicos... (Río Piedras: Edil, 1972), pp. 313-19.

42.116 Fiallo, Viriato A. "El intuicionismo filosófico." Clío, 7 (1939), 62-64. Also in Eugenio Carlos de Hostos, Hostos, peregrino del ideal, q.v., pp. 158-62. Also as "Der philosophische Institutionismus des Denkers Eugenio María de Hostos." IAR, 4 (1939), 317-18.

42.117 Figueroa, Sotero. "Eugenio María de Hostos." In Eugenio Carlos de Hostos, Hostos, peregrino del ideal, q.v., pp. 377-86.

42.118 Florit, Eugenio. "Hostos, el sembrador apasionado." RHM, 31 (1965), 127-32.

42.119 Forgione, José D. "Noticia biobiliográfica." In Eugenio María de Hostos, Páginas escogidas (BA: Estrada, 1952), pp. vii-lxiv.

42.120 Fránquiz Ventura, José Antonio. "A commemorative edition of de Hostos' complete works." In Eugenio Carlos de Hostos, Eugenio María de Hostos, promoter of Pan Americanism ..., q.v., pp. 147-53.

42.121 _________. "Esencia ideológica de Hostos." In Comisión Pro Celebración del Centenario del Natalicio de Eugenio María de Hostos, América y Hostos, q.v., pp. 305-25. Orig. Luminar, No. 2 (1939), 180-203.

42.122 _________. "La visión de Kant y el ensueño de Hostos." In Eugenio Carlos de Hostos, Hostos, peregrino del ideal, q.v., pp. 77-97.

42.123 Frantz, Harry W. "Eugenio María de Hostos, Puerto Rican 'Don Quixote of liberty', finds a faithful biographer." In Eugenio Carlos de Hostos, Eugenio María de Hostos, promoter of Pan Americanism..., q.v., pp. 64-68. See item no. 42.39.

42.124 Fromm, Hilde. "Eugenio María de Hostos: ein Leben für Ibero-Amerika." IAA, 14, 1 (1940), 68-75.

42.125 Galdames, Luis. "Hostos: semblanza de una nueva vida." Nosotros, 2a época, No. 34 (1939), 16-29. Also in Eugenio Carlos de Hostos, Hostos, hispanoamericanista. q.v., pp. 147-63.

42.126 Gallagher, Basil. "The Don Quixote of liberty." In Eugenio Carlos de Hostos, Eugenio María de Hostos, promoter of Pan Americanism..., q.v., pp. 86-94.

42.127 García-Girón, Edmundo. "Hostos versus Beerbohm Tree: plagiarism?" BHS, 33 (1957), 46-49.

42.128 García Godoy, Federico. "Hostos." In Eugenio Carlos de Hostos, Hostos, peregrino del ideal, q.v., pp. 163-64.

42.129 Géigel Polanco, Vicente. "Eugenio María de Hostos." In his Valores de Puerto Rico (NY: Arno Press, 1975), pp. 61-65. Orig. SJ: Eugenio María de Hostos, 1943.

42.130 __________. "Hostos en el destino de Puerto Rico." RICP, No. 25 (1964), 32-37.

42.131 __________. "Hostos, realidad actuante en nuestro mundo moral." AtPR, 3 (1939), 3-21. Also REduc, No. 52 (1939), 46-58.

42.132 __________. "Puerto Rico en el Centenario de Hostos." In his El despertar de un pueblo (SJ: Biblioteca de Autores Puertorriqueños, 1942), pp. 63-103.

42.133 __________. "La vida de Hostos, su mayor legado." In Eugenio Carlos de Hostos, Hostos, peregrino del ideal, q.v., pp. 256-70.

42.134 Gómez, Máximo. "Eugenio María de Hostos." In Comisión Pro Celebración del Natalicio de Eugenio María de Hostos, América y Hostos, q.v., pp. 35-38.

42.135 González, José Emilio. "Eugenio María de Hostos y la reforma de la enseñanza." RICP, No. 29 (1965), 8-17.

42.136 __________. "Hostos y la crítica social." RCS, 15, 4 (1971), 499-511.

42.137 __________. "Meditación sobre la vida de Eugenio María de Hostos." RICP, No. 6 (1960), 6-10.

42.138 González, José Luis. "Tres fundadores de la literatura puertorriqueña: Hostos, Brau, Zeno Gandía." Humanismo, Nos. 48-49 (1958), 96-115.

42.139 González, Manuel Pedro. "Tres autores americanos." Atenea, No. 106 (1934), 180-83. Hostos inter alios.

42.140 Guerra Mondragón, Benjamín. "Hostos crítico." Idearium, 1, 2 (1917), 49-53.

42.141 Henríquez y Carvajal, Francisco. "[Essais]." Clío, 4 (1936), 150-51.

42.142 __________. "Eugenio María de Hostos." In Eugenio Carlos de Hostos, Hostos, hispanoamericanista, q.v., pp. 67-74.

42.143 __________. "Hostos en Santo Domingo." In Eugenio Carlos de Hostos, Hostos, peregrino del ideal, q.v., pp. 285-89.

42.144 __________. "La palabra del maestro." Clío, 7 (1939), 45-47.

42.145 Henríquez García, E. "Hostos a través de su vida y de mis recuerdos." In Eugenio Carlos de Hostos, Eugenio M. Hostos..., q.v., pp. 353-75.

42.146 __________. "La muerte de Hostos." In Comisión Pro Celebración del Natalicio de Eugenio María de Hostos, América y Hostos, q.v., pp. 335-40.

42.147 __________. "Nostalgias antillanas de Eugenio María de Hostos." In Eugenio Carlos de Hostos, Hostos, peregrino del ideal, q.v., pp. 316-35. Also Lyceum, No. 36 (1935), 5-22.

42.148 Henríquez Ureña, Camila. "Ideas pedagógicas de Hostos." RIP, No. 1 (1928), 47-60. Also RFLC, 39 (1929), 10-84, 142-202. Also in Comisión Pro Celebración del Natalicio de Eugenio María de Hostos, América y Hostos, q.v., pp. 229-303.

42.149 __________. "La peregrinación de Eugenio María Hostos." CAm, No. 82 (1974), 6-17.

42.150 Henríquez Ureña, Max. "Actividad e influencia de Hostos en Santo Domingo." In Eugenio Carlos de Hostos, Hostos, hispanoamericanista, q.v., pp. 75-83.

42.151 Henríquez Ureña, Pedro. "Ciudadano de América." In his Ensayos en busca de nuestra expresión (BA: Raigal, 1952), pp. 109-14. Also in Eugenio María de Hostos, Moral social (BA: Losada, 1939), pp. 7-13.

42.152 __________. "La concepción sociológica de Hostos." In his Ensayos críticos (La Habana: Esteban Fernández, 1905), pp. 81-98.

42.153 __________. "Préface." In Eugenio María de Hostos, Essais (Paris: Institut International de Coopération Intellectuelle, 1936), pp. 7-13.

42.154 __________. "Prólogo." In Eugenio María de Hostos, Antología (Madrid: Juan Bravo, 1952), pp. 13-21.

42.155 __________. "La sociología de Hostos." In his Horas de estudio (Paris: Sociedad de Ediciones Literarias y Artísticas, 1910), pp. 75-88. Also in Comisión Pro Celebración del Natalicio de Eugenio María de Hostos, América y Hostos, q.v., pp. 147-55.

42.156 Hernández de León, Federico. "Hamlet tras el diáfano espíritu de Hostos." In Eugenio Carlos de Hostos, Hostos, peregrino del ideal, q.v., pp. 218-21.

42.157 Hernández de Norman, Isabel. "Eugenio María de Hostos (1839-1903)." In her La novela criolla en las Antillas (NY: Plus Ultra, 1977), pp. 55-70.

42.158 ________. "Eugenio María de Hostos (1839-1903)." In her La novela romántica en las Antillas (NY: Ateneo Puertorriqueño de Nueva York, 1969), pp. 55-70.

42.159 Herrera, Felipe. "El espíritu de Hostos en la integración americana." Centro, No. 1 (1965), 7-11.

42.160 Hostos, Adolfo de. "El americanismo de Hostos." RAMG, 3, 2 (1941), 14-17. Also in Eugenio Carlos de Hostos, Hostos, hispanoamericanista, q.v., pp. 367-76.

42.161 ________. "Apuntes para la historia de las ideas en América. El 'culto de la conciencia' de Hostos." RHI, No. 1 (1959), 265-72.

42.162 ________. "Eugenio María de Hostos (1839-1903)." In his Hombres representativos de Puerto Rico (SJ, 1961), pp. 35-45.

42.163 ________. "Hostos como educador." In Eugenio Carlos de Hostos, Hostos, peregrino del ideal, q.v., pp. 98-144. Also in his Al servicio de Clío (SJ: Negociado de Materiales, Imprenta y Transportes, 1942), pp. 135-88.

42.164 Hostos, Bayoán de. "Hostos anecdótico." RAMG, 1, 2 (1938), 9-11.

42.165 Hostos, Eugenio Carlos de. "Hostos juzgado por los norteamericanos." In Comisión Pro Celebración del Centenario del Natalicio de Eugenio María de Hostos, América y Hostos, q.v., pp. 65-77.

42.166 ________. "Hostos y Puerto Rico." Educación, 10, 2 (1961), 45-51.

42.167 ________. "Noticia biográfica." In Eugenio María de Hostos, Lecciones de derecho constitucional (Paris: Paul Ollendorff, 1908), pp. vii-xvi. Also in his Eugenio M. Hostos, q.v., pp. 5-26. Also in his América y Hostos, q.v., pp. 9-33.

42.168 Hunt, A. F., Jr. "Eugenio María de Hostos on constitutional science." In Eugenio Carlos de Hostos, Eugenio María de Hostos, promoter of Pan Americanism..., q.v., pp. 164-65.

42.169 Iduarte, Andrés. "Rebeldía y disciplina en Hostos." RHM, 5 (1939), 289-300. Also in Eugenio Carlos de Hostos, Hostos, hispanoamericanista, q.v., pp. 121-40.

42.170 Lagmanovich, David. "La crítica literaria en Hostos." SinN, 3, 4 (1973), 23-29.

42.171 Laguerre, Enrique A. "Hostos y Martí." In his Polos en la cultura iberoamericana (Boston: Florentia, 1977), pp. 137-47.

42.172 Landa, Gabriel. "Eugenio María de Hostos y Cuba." In Eugenio Carlos de Hostos, Hostos, peregrino del ideal, q.v., pp. 343-49.

42.173 Lebel, Maurice. "Eugenio María de Hostos (1839-1903) et le XXe siècle." ESec, 43 (1964), 141-46.

42.174 Ledesma Morales, M. "Eugenio María de Hostos." ND, 8, 9 (1927), 6.

42.175 Lee de Muñoz Marín, Muna. "Eugenio María de Hostos: after one hundred years." BA, 14 (1940), 124-28.

42.176 ________. "Eugenio María de Hostos. His international significance as an educator." BA, 14 (1940), 122-24. Also in Eugenio Carlos de Hostos, Eugenio María de Hostos, promoter of Pan Americanism..., q.v., pp. 45-55. Also as "Eugenio María de Hostos, su significación internacional como educador." Isla, No. 3 (1939), 7-9.

42.177 Lloréns, Washington. "Hamlet visto por Hostos y Goethe." BAAC, 3, 1 (1967), 107-14.

42.178 Lluch Mora, Francisco. "Breves consideraciones en torno a La peregrinación de Bayoán de Eugenio María de Hostos." In his Miradero: ensayos de crítica literaria (SJ: Cordillera, 1966), pp. 11-19.

42.179 ________. "Breves consideraciones en torno al ensayo Hamlet, de Eugenio María de Hostos." In his Miradero: ensayos de crítica literaria (SJ: Cordillera, 1966), pp. 21-33.

42.180 ________. "Consideraciones en torno a algunas páginas del Diario de Eugenio María de Hostos." In his Miradero: ensayos de crítica literaria (SJ: Cordillera, 1966), pp. 25-35.

42.181 Lugo, Américo. "Los escritos literarios de Hostos." In Eugenio Carlos de Hostos, Hostos, peregrino del ideal, q.v., pp. 180-200.

42.182 Magdaleno, Mauricio. "Hostos, acontecimientos de América." In Comisión Pro Celebración del Centenario del Natalicio de Eugenio María de Hostos, América y Hostos, q.v., pp. 223-27. Orig. RAm, 35, 3 (1939), 33-34. Also as "Hostos, a milestone in the life of America." In Eugenio Carlos de Hostos, Eugenio María de Hostos, promoter of Pan Americanism..., q.v., pp. 139-45. Also RHon, No. 45 (1938), 3-4.

42.183 __________. "Hostos, el patriota de Puerto Rico." Claridad, No. 335 (1939), no pagination. Also RHon, No. 79 (1939), 5-6, 22.

42.184 Maldonado-Denis, Manuel. "Hostos, el antillano." CAm, No. 75 (1972), 19-30. Also RICP, No. 56 (1972), 10-18. Also CA, No. 184 (1972), 92-107.

42.185 __________. "Introducción al pensamiento social de Eugenio María de Hostos." In Eugenio María de Hostos, América: la lucha por la libertad (M: Siglo XXI, 1980), pp. 13-47. Also CAm, No. 124 (1981), 51-66.

42.186 Manrique Cabrera, Francisco. "Hostos: vivir peregrinante en confesión." SinN, 3, 4 (1973), 5-22.

42.187 __________. "Semblanza de una semblanza." RICP, No. 70 (1976), 10-16.

42.188 Martín, José Luis. "Hostos, escritor." RICP, No. 50 (1971), 16-20.

42.189 Martínez Estrada, Ezequiel. "Hostos, Sarmiento y Martí, educadores." PLit, 2, 3 (1964), 23.

42.190 Martínez y Cordero, Eladio. "Eugenio M. Hostos y la república de Cuba." In Eugenio Carlos de Hostos, Hostos, peregrino del ideal, q.v., pp. 387-90.

42.191 Massuh, Víctor. "Hostos y el positivismo hispanoamericano." CA, No. 54 (1950), 167-90.

42.192 __________. "Hostos y la filosofía." In Eugenio Carlos de Hostos, Hostos, peregrino del ideal, q.v., pp. 53-75.

42.193 Matos Bernier, Félix. "Eugenio María de Hostos." In his Muertos y vivos (SJ: El País, 1905), pp. 171-76.

42.194 __________. "Sociología (Eugenio M. Hostos)." In his Isla de arte (SJ: La Primavera, 1907), pp. 197-206.

42.195 Mead, Robert G. "Montalvo, Hostos y el ensayo americano." In his Perspectivas interamericanas (NY: Las Américas, 1967), pp. 89-102. Orig. Hispania, 36 (1956), 56-62.

42.196 Mejía, F. A. "Hostos ante la historia dominicana y de América." Clío, 7 (1939), 47-57.

42.197 Mejía Nieto, Arturo. "Hostos, un precursor americano." Nosotros, 2a época, No. 34 (1939), 30-34. Also RABN, 18 (1939), 116-19. Also ND, 33, 1 (1953), 72-75.

42.198 Meléndez, Concha. "Hostos y la naturaleza de América." In Comisión Pro Celebración del Centenario del Natalicio de Eugenio María de Hostos, América y Hostos, q.v., pp. 79-95.

Also in her Asomante (SJ: Cordillera, 1970), pp. 25-42. Also in her Obras completas (SJ: Instituto de Cultura Puertorriquela, 1970-72), II, 25-42. Also RHM, 5 (1939), 309-19. Also in in her Asomante (SJ: Universidad de Puerto Rico, 1943), pp. 15-32.

42.199 __________. "Hostos y Santo Domingo: construcción del hombre nuevo." Educación, 14, 14 (1965), 49-57. Also RICP, No. 19 (1963), 1-5. Also in her Palabras para oyentes (SJ: Cordillera, 1971), pp. 173-85. Also in her Obras completas (SJ: Instituto de Cultura Puertorriqueña, 1970-72), III, 609-21.

42.200 __________. "Juan Bosch ante Hostos." In Juan Bosch, Mujeres en la vida de Hostos, q.v., pp. 7-9. Also in her Asomante (SJ: Cordillera, 1970), pp. 43-45. Also in her Obras completas (SJ: Instituto de Cultura Puertorriqueña, 1970-72), II, 43-45.

42.201 Méndez, José Luis. "Hostos vs. la literatura." Reintegro, 1, 1 (1980), 20-22.

42.202 Méndez Ballester, Manuel. "Apuntes sobre la filosofía educativa de Eugenio María de Hostos." JDE, 1, 6 (1938), 45-48. Also as "Notes on the educational philosophy of Eugenio María de Hostos." JDE, 1, 6 (1938), 13-17.

42.203 Méndez Santos, Carlos. "Eugenio María Hostos." Horizontes, No. 22 (1968), 5-16.

42.204 Miranda, Wenceslao. "Hostos: su personalidad y actualidad de la Moral social." In his Ensayos (Lugo: Celta, 1972), pp. 117-32.

42.205 Mistral, Gabriela. "Cómo ve Gabriela Mistral a Hostos." In Comisión Pro Celebración del Centenario del Natalicio de Eugenio María de Hostos, América y Hostos, q.v., pp. 39-45.

42.206 Montenegro, Ernesto. "O humanismo de Eugenio María de Hostos." In Eugenio Carlos de Hostos, Eugenio María de Hostos, promoter of Pan Americanism..., q.v., pp. 172-78.

42.207 Mora, Gabriela. "El Diario de Hostos: labor de un intimista." BR/RB, 2 (1975), 86-98. Also as "Hostos intimista: introducción a su diario." ALHisp, Nos. 2-3 (1973-74), 311-62.

42.208 Mora, José Antonio. "Hostos y la visión del Caribe." Américas, 20, 1 (1968), 1-2. Also as "Hostos' Caribbean vision." Americas [English edition], 19, 12 (1967), 1-2.

42.209 Moral, Agustín. "Proyección americana de Hostos." LyP, 6, 18 (1966), 21-23.

42.210 Morales, Angel Luis. "Eugenio María de Hostos: apuntes sobre su obra literaria." Asomante, 2, 2 (1946), 66-92.

42.211 ________. "Juicio de Hostos sobre Ruiz Belvis y Betances." Asomante, 1, 3 (1945), 80-91.

42.212 Mota, Fabio A. "El ideario de Hostos." In Eugenio Carlos de Hostos, Hostos, peregrino del ideal, q.v., pp. 145-57.

42.213 Negroni, H. A. "Hostos y su pensamiento militar." Asomante, 24, 4 (1968), 21-35. Also JIAS, 11 (1969), 272-85.

42.214 Orrego Luco, Augusto. "Chile en su exposición de septiembre [memoria de don Eugenio María de Hostos]." RSant, 3 (1873), 316-35.

42.215 Ortuzar Errazuriz, Gabriela, and Paul Estrada. "Una página de Hostos." SinN, 5, 3 (1975), 47-48.

42.216 Padilla de Sanz, Trinidad. "Cómo conocí a de Hostos." RICP, No. 33 (1966), 1-2.

42.217 Padín, José. "Eugenio María de Hostos, revolucionario." RHM, 5 (1939), 301-306. Also RICP, No. 27 (1965), 18-22. Also in Eugenio Carlos de Hostos, Hostos, peregrino del ideal, q.v., pp. 247-55.

42.218 Paniagua Serracante, José. "Hostos: ubicación filosófica en América." AyL, 2a época, No. 25 (1959), 3-17.

42.219 Pattee, Richard. "El sentido americanista en Hostos." RHM, 5 (1939), 306-309. Also in Eugenio Carlos de Hostos, Hostos, hispanoamericanista, q.v., pp. 355-61.

42.220 Pedreira, Antonio S. "Biografía mínima de Eugenio María de Hostos." RAMG, 1, 2 (1938), 4-8.

42.221 ________. "Hostos, ciudadando de América." In his Obras completas (SJ: Instituto de Cultura Puertorriqueña, 1970), II, 553-718. Same as item no. 42.39.

42.222 ________. "Hostos político." In Comisión Pro Celebración del Centenario del Natalicio de Eugenio María de Hostos, América y Hostos, q.v., pp. 157-88.

42.223 ________. "Hostos y Martí." Hostos, No. 1 (1928), pagination unknown. Also RBC, 26, 2 (1930), 249-53.

42.224 ________. "El maestro Eugenio María de Hostos." ULH, No. 22 (1939), 5-37.

42.225 ________. "El pensamiento político de Hostos." RI, No. 2 (1939), 297-305.

42.226 ________. "Prólogo." In Eugenio María de Hostos, Hamlet (Río Piedras: Sociedad E. M. de Hostos, Universidad de Puerto Rico, 1929), pp. 5-15.

42.227 Pérez Ruiz, José Antonio. "Positivismo en Hostos." _Asomante_, 26, 1 (1973), 19-23.

42.228 Posada, Adolfo. "El libro de Hostos sobre _Derecho constitucional_." In Comisión Pro Celebración del Centenario del Natalicio de Eugenio María de Hostos, _América y Hostos_, q.v., pp. 327-35.

42.229 Rabassa, Gregory. "Cuba en la vida y en la obra de Eugenio María de Hostos." _ND_, 37, 1 (1957), 26-31.

42.230 Ramos, Samuel. "La personalidad de Hostos." _LetrasM_, 2, 2 (1939), 1-2.

42.231 Reyes Ramos, América, and Jorge María Ruscadella Bercedóniz. "El ideal de la Confederación de las Grandes Antillas Españolas, en Eugenio María de Hostos y José Martí." _RICP_, No. 58 (1973), 39-55.

42.232 Rivera, Guillermo. "El ensayo de Hostos sobre Plácido." _Hispania_, 22 (1939), 145-52.

42.233 Robles de Cardona, Mariana. "Hostos el educador, el polígrafo, el moralista." _Río Piedras_, Nos. 3-4 (1973-74), 127-45.

42.234 Rodríguez Demorizi, Emilio. "Hostos y Meriño." In Eugenio Carlos de Hostos, _Hostos, peregrino del ideal_, q.v., pp. 300-302. Also _Clío_, No. 34 (1939), pagination unknown.

42.235 __________. "El padre Bellini y Eugenio María de Hostos." In Eugenio Carlos de Hostos, _Hostos, hispanoamericanista_, q.v., pp. 85-93.

42.236 Roig de Leuchsenring, Emilio. "Hostos y Martí, dos ideologías antillanas concordantes." _RBC_, 43 (1939), 5-19.

42.237 Román Rivas, Angel M. "Eugenio María de Hostos y Bonilla: el tema del deber en dos vicencias; la patria y la familia." _BAAC_, 12, 3 (1976), 39-49.

42.238 Rosa, Edelmira G. de. "_La peregrinación de Bayoán_: introducción al tema antillano." _Educación_, 14, 14 (1965), 59-78.

42.239 Rosa-Nieves, Cesáreo. "Eugenio María de Hostos (1839-1903)." In his _Plumas estelares en las letras de Puerto Rico_ (SJ: Ediciones de la Torre, Universidad de Puerto Rico, 1967), I, 207-26.

42.240 __________. "Eugenio María de Hostos: un krausista de América." _BAAC_, 3, 1 (1967), 167-72.

42.241 __________. "El pensamiento estético en la obra de Hostos." _RICP_, No. 14 (1962), 14-17.

42.242 ________. "Romería política de Eugenio María de Hostos." RICP, No. 15 (1962), 38-40.

42.243 ________. "Tres inquietudes insignes en la vida de Eugenio María Hostos (1839-1903)." In his Ensayos escogidos... (SJ: Academia de Artes y Ciencias de Puerto Rico, 1970), pp. 93-108.

42.244 Rowe, Leo S. "Hostos en la Unión Panamericana." Claridad, No. 336 (1939), no pagination. Also in Eugenio Carlos de Hostos, Hostos, hispanoamericanista, q.v., pp. 59-62. Also as "Hostos in the Pan American Union." BUP, 63 (1939), 61-62. Also in Eugenio Carlos de Hostos, Eugenio María de Hostos, promoter of Pan Americanism..., q.v., pp. 79-81.

42.245 Sáez, Antonia. "Teatro infantil de Hostos." RAMG, 1, 2 (1938), 12.

42.246 Sánchez Fernández, Luis Amador. "Eugenio María de Hostos." In his Cuatro estudios: Hostos, Martí, Rodó, Blanco-Fombona (São Paulo: Universidade de São Paulo, Faculdade de Filosofia, Ciências e Letras, 1958), pp. 11-34.

42.247 Sánchez Hidalgo, Efraín. "Hostos, educador." Pedagogía, 12, 1 (1964), 65-84.

42.248 Santos Vargas, Leonidas. "La filosofía educativa de Eugenio María de Hostos." El cóndor, 2, 2 (1977), 48-57.

42.249 Santovenia, Emeterio S. "Aguilera y Hostos." Carteles, No. 46 (1938), 13-14.

42.250 ________. "Hostos, precursor de Martí." Carteles, No. 44 (1938), 15.

42.251 ________. "Hostos y la revolución cubana." Carteles, No. 45 (1938), 50.

42.252 Schroenrich, Otto. "Hostos." In his Santo Domingo: a country with a future (NY: Macmillan, 1918), pp. 198-99. Also in Eugenio Carlos de Hostos, Eugenio María de Hostos, promoter of Pan Americanism..., q.v., pp. 69-70.

42.253 Sharp Shepard, Isabel. "Eugenio María de Hostos." BUP, 59 (1925), 565-68.

42.254 Silva, Víctor Domingo. "Un ilustre antillano prócer de Chile." In Eugenio Carlos de Hostos, Hostos, hispanoamericanista, q.v., pp. 327-33.

42.255 Soler, Ricaurte. "Premisas para una interpretación del pensamiento filosófico de Hostos." In his Estudios sobre historia de las ideas en América (Panamá: Imprenta Nacional, 1906?), pp. 101-17.

42.256 Suárez Murias, Marguerite. "Los iniciadores de la novela en Puerto Rico." Asomante, 18, 3 (1962), 43-48.

42.257 Susto, Juan Antonio. Eugenio María de Hostos y Bonilla (1839-1903)." Lotería, 2a época, No. 67 (1961), 76-79.

42.258 Tejeda, Francisco Elías de. "Las doctrinas políticas de Eugenio María de Hostos." In Eugenio Carlos de Hostos, Hostos, hispanoamericanista, q.v., pp. 207-91.

42.259 Tió, Aurelio. "Plebiscito, patriotismo y bilingüismo." BAAC, 3, 2 (1967), 161-66.

42.260 Toro Cuebas, Emilio del. "Discurso." In Comisión Pro Celebración del Centenario del Natalicio de Eugenio María Hostos, América y Hostos, q.v., pp. 45-51.

42.261 ________. "Hostos en el capitolio de Puerto Rico." In Eugenio Carlos de Hostos, Hostos, hispanoamericanista, q.v., pp. 63-66.

42.262 Torres, Carlos Arturo. "Hostos; conferencia leída en el paraninfo de la Universidad de Caracas para la Asociación de Estudiantes de Venezuela." In his Estudios de crítica moderna (Madrid: América, n.d.), pp. 181-205. Also as "Hostos." In his Discursos (Bogotá: Ministerio de Educación de Colombia, 1946), pp. 91-112. Also in his Discursos (Caracas: El Cojo, 1911), pp. 111-43. Also in Comisión Pro Celebración del Centenario del Natalicio de Eugenio María de Hostos, América y Hostos, q.v., pp. 131-45.

42.263 Torres, José Antonio. "Hostos y la literatura infantil." Asomante, 10, 4 (1954), 76-80.

42.264 ________. "El trágico desconocimiento de Hostos de Puerto Rico." AyL, 2a época, No. 25 (1959), 6-7.

42.265 Trelles Govín, Carlos M. "Un gran amigo de Cuba: Eugenio M. de Hostos." CyA, 7, 9 (1903), 259-62.

42.266 Troncoso Sánchez, Pedro. "Hostos y nosotros." Clío, No. 34 (1939), 35-38. Also in Eugenio Carlos de Hostos, Hostos, peregrino del ideal, q.v., pp. 290-99.

42.267 Valldejuli Rodríguez, Juan. "Don Eugenio María de Hostos, político y patriota." BAAC, 3, 1 (1967), 145-56.

42.268 Vela, David. "Eugenio María de Hostos, voz americana." In Eugenio Carlos de Hostos, Hostos, peregrino del ideal, q.v., pp. 230-35.

42.269 Velasco Ibarra, J. M. "El derecho constitucional en Eugenio María de Hostos." In Eugenio Carlos de Hostos, Hostos, hispanoamericanista..., q.v., pp. 307-25.

42.270 Verdugo, Iber H. "Naturaleza y función de lo literario en Hostos." RevH, No. 3 (1960), 113-20.

42.271 Vidrine, Sylvia. "Hostos as seen by an American

schoolgirl." In Eugenio Carlos de Hostos, Eugenio María de Hostos, promoter of Pan Americanism..., q.v., pp. 71-74.

42.272 Vientós Gastón, Nilita. "Hostos y Martí." In her Indice cultural (Río Piedras: Ediciones de la Universidad de Puerto Rico, 1962-71), I, 245-47.

42.273 Villaronga, Luis. "Hostos, personaje hamletiano." In Eugenio Carlos de Hostos, Hostos, peregrino del ideal, q.v., pp. 211-17.

42.275 Vitier, Medardo. "Ensayos de Hostos." In his Del ensayo americano (M: Fondo de Cultura Económica, 1945), pp. 95-116.

42.276 Winship, Blanton. "The centennary of Eugenio María de Hostos." In Eugenio Carlos de Hostos, Eugenio María de Hostos, promoter of Pan Americanism..., q.v., pp. 82-83.

42.277 Zamudio Z., J. "Desconocimiento y magnitud de Hostos, 1838-1939." Ateneo, No. 93 (1939), 221-33.

43

JOGLAR CACHO, MANUEL (1898-)

Critical Monographs and Dissertations

43.1 Babín, María Teresa. El monólogo lírico de Joglar Cacho. SJ: Venezuela, 1961. Same as item no. 43.3.

43.2 Ross, Waldo. Meditación sobre los Soliloquios de Lázaro. SJ, 1961.

Critical Essays

43.3 Babín, María Teresa. "El monólogo lírico de Joglar Cacho." Asomante, 17, 3 (1961), 55-63. Also in her Jornadas literarias... (Barcelona: Rvmbos, 1967), pp. 156-67. Same as item no. 43.1.

43.4 __________. "Transmutación poética de las influencias 'locales' en la lírica de Luis Palés Matos, Evaristo Ribera Chevremont y Manuel Joglar Cacho." In Instituto Internacional de Literatura Iberoamericana, Literatura iberoamericana: influjos locales (M, 1965), pp. 27-33.

43.5 Fonfrías, Ernesto Juan. "Letras puertorriqueñas: Manuel Joglar Cacho." In his Sementera; ensayos breves y biografías mínimas (SJ: Club de la Prensa, 1962), pp. 19-25.

43.6 Géigel Polanco, Vicente. "Manuel Joglar Cacho (1898)." In Escritores contemporáneos de Puerto Rico (SJ: Sociedad de Autores Puertorriqueños, 1978), pp. 109-14.

43.7 Lluch Mora, Francisco. "En torno a Faena íntima de Manuel Joglar Cacho." In his Miradero (SJ: Cordillera, 1966), pp. 133-42. Also as "Anotaciones marginales en torno a Faena íntima de M. Joglar Cacho." In Manuel Joglar Cacho, Faena íntima (SJ: Venezuela, 1955), pp. 7-17.

43.8 Martínez, Luis. "Presencia de Dios en la poesía de Joglar Cacho." Horizontes, No. 28 (1971), 115-34.

43.9 Miranda, Luis Antonio. "Palabras liminares." In Manuel Joglar Cacho, Góndolas de nácar (SJ: Harry C. del Pozo, 1925), pp. 9-13.

43.10 Onís, Federico de. "Introduction." In Manuel Joglar Cacho, Soliloquios of Lazarus (Soliloquios de Lázaro) (SJ: Juan Ponce de León, 1963), pp. 9-17.

43.11 Ramírez de Arellano, Diana. "Introducción a la poesía de Manuel Joglar Cacho." ILit, 3a época, Nos. 2-3 (1969), 14.

43.12 Rosa-Nieves, Cesáreo. "Manuel Joglar Cacho (1898-)." In his Plumas estelares en las letras de Puerto Rico (SJ: Ediciones de la Torre, Universidad de Puerto Rico, 1967), II. 361-70.

43.13 Ruscadella Bercedóniz, Jorge María. "Prólogo: el asedio de la inmortalidad en Donde cae y no cae la noche de Manuel Joglar Cacho." In Manuel Joglar Cacho, Donde cae y no cae la noche (Manatí, 1978), pp. 7-25.

44

LAGO, JESÚS MARÍA (1873-1929)

Critical Monographs and Dissertations

44.1 Suria de Crespo, Carmen Delia. Jesus María Lago: vida y obra. Unpublished thesis, Universidad de Puerto Rico, 1957.

Critical Essays

44.2 Hernández Paralitici, Pedro A. "Jesús María Lago: apuntes sobre su vida y su obra." BAPH, 4, 13 (1975), 23-39.

44.3 Morales, Angel Luis. "Prólogo." In Jesús María Lago, Antología (SJ: Ateneo Puertorriqueño, 1959), pp. 5-15.

44.4 Quiñones, Samuel R. "Jesús María Lago: --apreciación del poeta." Indice, No. 17 (1930), 269.

44.5 Rosa-Nieves, Cesáreo. "Jesús María Lago Quiñones (1873-1929)." In his Plumas estelares en las letras de Puerto Rico (SJ: Ediciones de la Torre, Universidad de Puerto Rico, 1967), II, 73-86.

45

LAGUERRE, ENRIQUE A.

Critical Monographs and Dissertations

45.1 Beauchamp, José Juan. Imagen del puertorriqueño en la novela (en Alejandro Tapia y Rivera, Manuel Zeno Gandía y Enrique A. Laguerre). Río Piedras: Editorial Universitaria, Universidad de Puerto Rico, 1976.

45.2 Colón, José M. La naturaleza en Manuel Zeno Gandía y Enrique Laguerre. Unpublished thesis, Universidad de Puerto Rico, 1949.

45.3 García Cabrera, Manuel. Laguerre y sus polos de la cultura iberoamericana. SJ: Biblioteca de Autores Puertorriqueños, 1978.

45.4 Morfi, Angelina. Enrique A. Laguerre y su obra: La resaca, cumbre de su arte de novelar. SJ: Instituto de Cultura Puertorriqueña, 1964. Orig. an unpublished thesis, Análisis estilístico de La resaca de Enrique A. Laguerre. Universidad de Puerto Rico, 1963.

45.5 Rosa-Nieves, Cesáreo. Cañas al sol en La llamarada (novela de Enrique A. Laguerre). Humacao: Tipografía Comercial, 1938.

45.6 Umpierre-Herrera, Luz María. "Un compromiso en la literatura: corrientes ideológicas en tres novelistas puertorriqueños: Manuel Zeno Gandía, Enrique A. Laguerre y Pedro Juan Soto." DAI, 39 (1979), 5539A.

45.7 Zayas Micheli, Luis Osvaldo. Lo universal en Enrique Laguerre. Río Piedras: Edil, 1974.

Critical Essays

45.8 Arriví, Francisco. "Entrada por las raíces; ensayo sobre la novela La ceiba en el tiesto..." In his Entrada por las raíces... (SJ: Serie La Entraña, 1964), pp. 137-57.

45.9 Campos, Jorge. "Amor a la tierra y crítica social: una novela de Enrique A. Laguerre [Cauce sin río]." Insula, No. 190 (1962), 11.

45.10 Castro, Tomás de Jesús. "Enrique A. Laguerre." In his Esbozos críticos (SJ: Baldrich, 1945), pp. 71-76.

45.11 Cherubini, Arnaldo. "La narrativa sociale di Enrique Laguerre." Ausonia, 31, 5-6 (1976), 70-78.

45.12 Cruz López, David. "La lengua del jíbaro en las novelas de Enrique A. Laguerre." Educación, No. 15 (1965), 62-89.

45.13 Díaz Márquez, Luis. "La novela de Enrique A. Laguerre y sus vínculos generacionales." Horizontes, No. 38 (1976), 5-16.

45.14 "Enrique Laguerre." In Enrique A. Laguerre, Obras completas (SJ: Instituto de Cultura Puertorriqueña, 1962), I, 7-10. Various other editions.

45.15 Gómez del Pardo, Carlos. "La preocupación por Puerto Rico en las novelas de Enrique A. Laguerre." RICP, No. 24 (1964), 34-39.

45.16 González, José Emilio. "Cauce sin río de Enrique Laguerre." Asomante, 19, 2 (1963), 63-66.

45.17 ________. "[La ceiba en el tiesto]." Asomante, 12, 4 (1956), 105-10.

45.18 ________. "[El laberinto]." Asomante, 16, 4 (1960), 70-76.

45.19 González, José Luis. "[Los dedos de la mano]." Asomante, 8, 3 (1952), 93-94.

45.20 Grismer, Raymond Leonard, and César Arroyo. "Enrique A. Laguerre." In their Vida y obras de autores puertorriqueños (La Habana: "Alfa", 1941-), I, 15-17.

45.21 Guevara Castañeira, Josefina. "Tres obras de Enrique A. Laguerre: La resaca, La ceiba en el tiesto, Pulso de Puerto Rico." In her Del Yunque a los Andes (SJ: Club de la Prensa, 1959), pp. 135-54.

45.22 Henrández Aquino, Luis. "Solar Montoya." InsulaSJ, 1, 5 (1942), 12-16.

45.23 Lloréns, Washington. "La llamarada--Enrique Laguerre." In his Críticas profanas (SJ: Progreso, 1936), pp. 15-19.

45.34 Macías de Cartaya, Graziella. "Valor lírico del paisaje puertorriqueño en las novelas de Enrique Laguerre." Horizontes, No. 38 (1976), 45-62.

45.35 Marcilese, Mario. "Enrique A. Laguerre." RICP, No. 35 (1967), 27-32.

45.36 Martín, José Luis. "Sobre una novela de Laguerre: Los dedos de la mano." In his Arco y flecha... (SJ: Club de la Prensa, 1961), pp. 161-65.

45.37 Martínez Nadal, Ernesto. "Consideraciones sobre la novela Cauce sin río de Enrique A. Laguerre." RICP, No. 22 (1964), 11-14.

45.38 Meléndez, Concha. "El llamado de la montaña (apuntes sobre la novela de Enrique A. Laguerre)." In her Signos de Iberoamérica (M: Manuel León Sánchez, 1936), pp. 119-24. Also in her Obras completas (SJ: Instituto de Cultura Puertorriqueña, 1970-72), I, 397-404.

45.39 __________. "Prólogo." In Enrique A. Laguerre, Obras completas (SJ: Instituto de Cultura Puertorriqueña, 1962), I, 11-15.

45.40 __________. "Prólogo [a Solar Montoya]." In Enrique A. Laguerre, Obras completas (SJ: Instituto de Cultura Puertorriqueña, 1962), I, 245-47.

45.41 __________. "La resaca." In her Figuraciones de Puerto Rico y otros estudios (SJ: Instituto de Cultura Puertorriqueña, 1958), pp. 73-76. Also in her Obras completas (SJ: Instituto de Cultura Puertorriqueña, 1970-72), II, 409-14. Orig. Asomante, 6, 1 (1950), 84-86.

45.42 __________. "Solar Montaya, novela de Enrique A. Laguerre." In her Asomante (SJ: Universidad de Puerto Rico, 1943), pp. 53-56. Also in her Obras completas (SJ: Instituto de Cultura Puertorriqueña, 1970-72), II, 53-56.

45.43 __________. "Visita a la Capilla Alfonsina y El fuego y su aire." SinN, 2, 2 (1971), 5-12. Also in her Literatura de ficción en Puerto Rico (SJ: Cordillera, 1971), pp. 185-95.

45.44 Morfi, Angelina. "Enrique A. Laguerre (1906)." In Escritores contemporáneos de Puerto Rico (SJ: Sociedad de Autores Puertorriqueños, 1978), pp. 17-29.

45.45 __________. "La resentida de Enrique A. Laguerre." In her Temas del teatro (Santo Domingo: Caribe, 1969), pp. 101-106.

45.46 __________. "Valor y significación de la novela de Enrique A. Laguerre." *RICP*, No. 26 (1965), 24-28.

45.47 Pedreira, Antonio S. "*La llamarada*: gran novela puertorriqueña." In his *Aclaraciones y crítica* (Río Piedras: Phi Eta Mu, Universidad de Puerto Rico, 1941), pp. 209-14. Also Río Piedras: Edil, 1969. Also in his *Obras completas* (SJ: Instituto de Cultura Puertorriqueña, 1970), I, 605-609.

45.48 __________. "Prólogo." In Enrique A. Laguerre, *La llamarada*; 18. ed. (Río Piedras: Cultural, 1971), pp. i-xii. Various other editions. Orig. as "Prólogo a la segunda edición." In Enrique A. Laguerre, *Obras completas* (SJ: Instituto de Cultura Puertorriqueña, 1962), I, 19-25.

45.49 Picó, Rafael. "El hombre y el medio en dos obras puertorriqueñas." *CaribeSJ*, 1, 1 (1941), 33-35, 43.

45.50 Rivera Malvé, Lydia. "Los cuentos de Enrique Laguerre." In Puerto Rico. Universidad. Facultad de Humanidades. Seminario de Estudios Hispánicos, *El cuento puertorriqueño en el siglo XX* (Río Piedras: Editorial Universitaria, Universidad de Puerto Rico, 1963), pp. 7-42.

45.51 Rodríguez Escudero, Néstor A. "Nota sobre *La resaca*, una novela de Laguerre." In his *Ensayos escogidos (sobre autores de Europa y América)* (Barcelona: Rvmbos, 1960-). pp. 65-70.

45.52 Romero García, Luz Virginia. "Análisis estructural de la obra *Los amos benévolos* de Enrique A. Laguerre." *RICP*, No. 74 (1977), 3-8.

45.53 Rosa-Nieves, Cesáreo. "Enrique A. Laguerre, novelista puertorriqueño." *Prensa*, 2a época, Nol 5 (1995), 9. Also in his *La lámpara del faro...* (SJ: Club de la Prensa, 1957-60), II, 147-55.

45.54 Sánchez-Villar, Isabel. "Los títulos en la novelística laguerriana." *RICP*, No. 37 (1967), 8-10.

45.55 Sola Márquez, María. "Puerto Rico entre amos y guaracha: novelas de Enrique Laguerre y Luis Rafael Sánchez." *SinN*, 10, 2 (1979), 84-97.

45.56 Vientós Gastón, Nilita. "Enrique A. Laguerre, *La llamarada*." *AtPR*, 1, 4 (1935), 310-12.

45.57 __________. "Una novela de Laguerre: *La ceiba en el tiesto*." In her *Indice cultural* (Río Piedras: Ediciones de la Universidad de Puerto Rico, 1962-71), I, 239-42.

45.58 Zayas Micheli, Luis Osvaldo. "La estructura mítica de *La resaca*." *Horizontes*, No. 38 (1976), 27-44.

45.59 __________. "*El fuego y su aire*, síntesis del novelar de Enrique Laguerre." *ALHisp*, No. 1 (1972), 251-80.

45.60 __________. "El pensamiento mítico en Los amos benévolos." Horizontes, No. 38 (1976), 63-66.

46

LAIR, CLARA (1895-1973)

Critical Monographs and Dissertations

46.1 Cuchí Coll, Isabel. Dos poetisas de América: Clara Lair y Julia de Burgos. SJ: Departamento de Instrucción, 1965. Also Barcelona: Manuel Pareja, 1970.

Critical Essays

46.2 Braschi, Wilfredo. "Clara Lair." In his Perfiles puertorriqueños (SJ: Biblioteca de Autores Puertorriqueños, 1978), pp. 31-34.

46.3 __________. "Clara Lair en el recuerdo." RICP, No. 60 (1973), 2-3.

46.4 Dávila, José Antonio. "Clara Lair y Carmelina Vizcarrondo." In his Prosa: ensayos, artículos y cartas literarias (SJ: Sociedad de Autores Puertorriqueños, 1971), pp. 155-57.

46.5 Diez de Andino, Juan. "Una poetisa de América." In his Voces de la farándula... (Barcelona: Rvmbos, 1959), pp. 104-107.

46.6 García Méndez, Miguel A. "Pórtico." In Clara Lair, Arras de cristal... (SJ: Biblioteca de Autores Puertorriqueños, 1937), pp. 709. Various subsequent editions.

46.7 Neggers, Gladys. "Clara Lair y Julia de Burgos: reminiscencias de Evaristo Rivera Chevremont y Jorge Font Saldaña." RevI, 4 (1974), 258-63.

46.8 Ramírez de Arellano, Diana. "Clara Lair (1895-1973)." In Escritores contemporáneos de Puerto Rico (SJ: Sociedad de Autores Puertorriqueños, 1978), pp. 131-43.

46.9 __________. "Tributo a la poesía de Clara Lair." RICP, No. 34 (1967), 51-55. Also RICP, No. 60 (1973), 5-9.

46.10 Rosa-Nieves, Cesáreo. "Clara Lair (seud. of Mercedes Negrón de Muñoz, 1895?-)." In his Plumas estelares en las *letras de Puerto Rico* (SJ: Ediciones de la Torre, Universidad de Puerto Rico, 1967), II, 429-41.

46.11 Tió, Salvador. "Duelo por Clara Lair." *RICP*, No. 60 (1973), 4.

47

LLORÉNS TORRES, LUIS (1876-1944)

Bibliographies

47.1 Alegría, Félix L. "Luis Lloréns Torres: bibliografía." *RHM*, 19 (1953), 85-87.

47.2 Carballo de Abreu, Daisy. "La prosa de Luis Lloréns Torres." *REH-PR*, 1, 3-4 (1971), 81-91.

Critical Monographs and Dissertations

47.3 Cabrera de Ibarra, Palmira. *Luis Lloréns Torres ante el paisaje*. Unpublished thesis, Universidad de Puerto Rico, 1947.

47.4 Corretjer, Juan Antonio. *Lloréns: juicio histórico*. NY, 1945.

47.5 Duffy, Kenneth J. *Luis Lloréns Torres, poet of Puerto Rico*. Unpublished Ph.D. dissertation, University of Pittsburgh, 1941.

47.6 Hadjopoulos, Theresa Ortiz de. *Luis Lloréns Torres: a study of his poetry*. NY: Plus Ultra, 1977.

47.7 Lloréns, Washington. *Los grandes amores del poeta Luis Lloréns Torres*. SJ: Campos, 1959.

47.8 Marrero, Carmen. *Luis Lloréns Torres (1876-1944). Vida y obra. Bibliografía. Antología*. NY: Hispanic Institute in the United States, 1953. 2. ed., SJ: Cordillera, 1968.

47.9 Ortiz de Lugo, Nilda Sofía. *Vida y obra de Luis Lloréns Torres*. SJ: Instituto de Cultura Puertorriqueña, Orig. unpublished Ph.D. dissertation, Universidad de Puerto Rico, 1966.

47.10 Sosa de Ramírez, Hilda. *América en la poesía de Luis Lloréns Torres*. Unpublished thesis, Unviersidad de Puerto Rico, 1967.

Critical Essays

47.11 Abril, Mariano. "Prólogo." In Luis Lloréns Torres, Amorosas (Ponce: La Democracia, 1900), pp. i-viii.

47.12 Arce, Carlos de. "Introducción." In Luis Lloréns Torres, Al pie de la Alhambra (SJ: Cordillera, 1968), pp. 7-25.

47.13 ________. "Introducción." In Luis Lloréns Torres, Alturas de América; 3. ed. (SJ: Cordillera, 1970), pp. 7-25.

47.14 ________. "Introducción." In Luis Lloréns Torres, El grito de Lares... (SJ: Cordillera, 1967), pp. 7-25. Various other editions.

47.15 ________. "Introducción." In Luis Lloréns Torres, Sonetos sinfónicos (SJ: Cordillera, 1968), pp. 7-25.

47.16 ________. "Introducción." In Luis Lloréns Torres, Voces de la campana mayor (SJ: Cordillera, 1968), pp. --25.

47.17 Arce de Vázquez, Margot. "Las décimas de Lloréns Torres." Asomante, 21, 1 (1965), 37-46.

47.18 ________. "La realidad puertorriqueña en la poesía de Lloréns Torres." In her Impresiones (notas puertorriqueñas) (SJ: Yaurel, 1950), pp. 81-87. Orig. RAMG, 5, 3 (1944), 5-10.

47.19 Arrigoitia, Luis de. "Cuatro poetas puertorriqueños: José de Diego, Luis Lloréns Torres, Luis Palés Matos, Juan Antonio Corretjer." Caravelle, No. 18 (1972), 59-76. Also as "Cuatro poetas puertorriqueños." In Instituto Internacional de Literatura Iberoamericana, La literatura de la emancipación hispanoamericana y otros ensayos (Lima: Universidad de San Marcos, 1972), pp. 173-78.

47.20 Babín, María Teresa. "Introducción [a La prosa del poeta Luis Lloréns Torres (1867-1944)]." In Luis Lloréns Torres, Obras completas (SJ: Instituto de Cultura Puertorriqueña, 1967-69), II, vii-xxxiii.

47.21 Belaval, Emilio S. "El estilo poético de Luis Lloréns Torres." BAAC, 3, 3 (1967), 483-93.

47.22 Braschi, Wilfredo. "Luis Lloréns Torres." In his Perfiles puertorriqueños (SJ: Biblioteca de Autores Puertorriqueños, 1978), pp. 9-11.

47.23 ________. "Presencia de Luis Lloréns Torres." BAAC, 12, 4 (1976), 1-4.

47.24 Cabrera, J. F. "El paisaje y la tierra en Luis Lloréns Torres." AyL, 2a época, No. 18 (1958), 7-10.

47.25 Cabrera de Ibarra, Palmira. "Añoranza y tiempo en la poesía de Luis Lloréns Torres." RICP, No. 7 (1960), 19-23.

47.26 Chocano, José Santos. "Prólogo." In Luis Lloréns Torres, Puerto Rico lírico y otros poemas (SJ: Antillana, 1920), pp. ix-xvi.

47.27 Corretjer, Juan Antonio. "Fragmentos de un ensayo crítico-biográfico, Lloréns." AyL, 2a época, No. 18 (1958), 3-5.

47.28 ________. "Lloréns: aproximación al bohío." RICP, No. 27 (1965), 5-7.

47.29 Cortón, Antonio. "Carta-prólogo [a América]." In Luis Lloréns Torres, América; estudios históricos y filológicos sobre Puerto Rico; 2. ed. (SJ: Cordillera, 1967), pp. 15-26. Orig. Madrid: V. Suárez, 1898. Also in Luis Lloréns Torres, Obras completas (SJ: Instituto de Cultura Puertorriqueña, 1967-69), II, 7-17.

47.30 Cuchí Coll, Isabel. "Luis Lloréns Torres." In her Oro nativo (SJ, 1936), pp. 93-108.

47.31 Cuevas, Carmen Leila. "Luis Lloréns Torres, hombre de palpitar eterno." BAAC, 12, 4 (1976), 17-20.

47.32 Díaz Quiñones, Arcadio. "La isla afortunada: sueños liberadores y utópicos de Luis Lloréns Torres." SinN, 6, 1 (1975), 5-19; 6, 2 (1975), 5-32.

47.33 Duffy, Kenneth J. "Lloréns Torres y el criollismo literario." EstudiosD, 1, 2 (1952), 9-22.

47.34 Franco Oppenheimer, Félix. "¿Existe una poesía genuinamente puertorriqueña?" BAAC, 12, 4 (1976), 11-15. Also in his Contornos... (SJ: Yaurel, 1960), pp. 87-90.

47.35 Géigel Polanco, Vicente. "Luis Lloréns Torres." In his Valores de Puerto Rico (SJ: Eugenio María de Hostos, 1943), pp. 135-38. Also NY: Arno Press, 1975.

47.36 Guevara Castañeira, Josefina. "Luis Loréns Torres, el poeta y el hombre." In her Del Yunque a los Andes (SJ: Club de la Prensa, 1959), pp. 13-27.

47.37 Gutiérrez Ortiz, Víctor. "Prologue/prólogo." In Luis Lloréns Torres, Patriotic thrills. Vibraciones patrióticas (SJ: El Compás, 1918), pp. i-iii.

47.38 Huyke, Juan B. "Luis Lloréns Torres." In his Triunfadores (SJ: Negociado de Materiales, Imprenta y Transporte, 1927), II, 53-59.

47.39 Jordán Sarria, Ramiro. "Presentación." In Luis Lloréns Torres, Artículos de revistas y periódicos (SJ: Cordillera, 1971), pp. vii-xi.

47.40 Labarthe, Pedro Juan. "Luis Lloréns Torres, poeta de las tierras antillanas." RAm, 24 (1936), 375.

47.41 ________. "Mi homenaje a Lloréns Torres." RAm, 41 (1944), 129-30.

47.42 Laguerre, Enrique A. "Apuntes sobre Lloréns Torres." In his Polos en la cultura iberoamericana (Boston: Florentia, 1977), pp. 89-92.

47.43 Lloréns, Washington. "Los grandes amores del poeta Luis Lloréns Torres." BAAC, 3, 3 (1967), 581-615. Shorter versions appeared in BAAC, 12, 4 (1976), 41-55; and Prensa, 2a época, No. 8 (1959), 7-9.

47.44 ________. "Voces de la campana mayor--Luis Lloréns Torres." In his Críticas profanas (SJ: Progreso, 1936), pp. 55-61.

47.45 McLaughlin, Agnes V. "Una comparación entre la poesía de Luis Lloréns Torres y la de Walt Whitman: temas, técnicas y estilo." Horizontes, Nos. 31-32 (1973), 73-93.

47.46 Marrero, Carmen. "América en la poesía de Lloréns Torres." RevI, 4 (1974), 308-21.

47.47 ________. "Facetas poéticas de Luis Lloréns Torres." BAAC, 12, 4 (1976), 21-39.

47.48 ________. "Luis Lloréns Torres: vida y obra." RHM, 19 (1953), 1-84.

47.49 ________. "Paisaje y naturaleza en Luis Lloréns Torres." RICP, No. 19 (1963), 39-42.

47.50 ________. "Poética y estética de Luis Lloréns Torres." BAAC, 3, 3 (1967), 571-78.

47.51 ________. "Prólogo." In Luis Lloréns Torres, Obras completas (SJ: Instituto de Cultura Puertorriqueña, 1967-69), I, v-cxxiv.

47.52 Muñoz Rivera, Luis. "El Grito de Lares: prólogo." In Luis Lloréns Torres, El grito de Lares (Aguadilla: Libertad, 1927), pp. 9-12. Also as "Prólogo." In Luis Lloréns Torres, El grito de Lares... (SJ: Cordillera, 1967), pp. 29-32. Orig. Aguadilla: Libertad, 1916.

47.53 Navarro Tomás, Tomás. "El verso en Velas épicas de Luis Lloréns Torres." REH-PR, 1-4 (1972), 185-90.

47.54 Negroni, Héctor Andrés. "El gallo en la poesía de Luis Lloréns Torres." RICP, No. 44 (1969), 27-32.

47.55 Nieto Peña, Roque. "Prólogo." In Luis Lloréns Torres, Versos del camino (SJ: Romero, 1943), pp. 5-6.

47.56 Pareja, Miguel María de. "Juicios sobre Al pie de La Alhambra publicados por la prensa española en 1899." BAAC, 12, 4 (1976), 79-83.

47.57 Pedreira, Antonio S., and Concha Meléndez. "Luis Lloréns Torres, el poeta de Puerto Rico." RABA, No. 115 (1933), 83-107. Also RBC, 31 (1933), 330-52. Also RAMG, 5, 3 (1944), 25-42.

47.58 "Proyecto de un monumento a Luis Lloréns Torres." BAPH, 4, 16 (1976), 221-25.

47.59 Roig, Pablo. "Prólogo." In Luis Lloréns Torres, Mosaicos (Mayagüez: Mayagüez Printing Co., 1922), pp. 11-13.

47.60 Rosa-Nieves, Cesáreo. "Luis Lloréns Torres (seud. Luis de Puertorrico: 1876-1944)." In his Plumas estelares en las letras de Puerto Rico (SJ: Ediciones de la Torre, Universidad de Puerto Rico, 1967), pp. 51-71.

47.61 ________. "Luis Lloréns Torres, poeta representativo de nuestra puertorriqueñidad (seud. Luis de Puertorrico, 1876-1944)." BAAC, 3, 3 (1967), 547-69.

47.62 ________. "El pancalismo de Luis Lloréns Torres." RICP, No. 9 (1960), 5-8.

47.63 ________. "Patria, amor y jibarismo en tres poetas puertorriqueños (José de Diego, Luis Lloréns Torres y Virgilio Dávila)." In his Ensayos escogidos... (SJ: Academia de Artes y Ciencias de Puerto Rico, 1970?), pp. 141-59.

47.64 Santos Silva, Loreina. "El euforismo en Luis Lloréns Torres: introducción a los rasgos de vanguardia en su poesía." Atenea, 9, 3-4 (1972), 117-30.

47.65 ________. "El grito de Lares de Luis Lloréns Torres y Mariana o el alba de René Marqués." La gotera, 3, 2 (1972), 19; 3, 3 (1972), 13-15.

47.66 Tió, Aurelio. "Proyecto de un monumento a Luis Lloréns Torres." BAAC, 3, 3 (1967), 541-45.

47.67 Tirado Verrier, Rafael, and José Fernández Bremón. "Juicios sobre América, publicados en la prensa española en 1899." BAAC, 12, 4 (1976), 85-93.

47.68 Toledo Alamo, Domingo. "Luis Lloréns Torres, abogado-poeta." RAMG, 5, 3 (1944), 43-46.

47.69 Valldejuli Rodríguez, Juan. "Luis Lloréns Torres." BAAC, 12, 4 (1976), 5-9.

48

LLUCH MORA, FRANCISCO (1924-)

Critical Essays

48.1 Babín, María Teresa. "Francisco Lluch Mora (1924)." In Escritores contemporáneos de Puerto Rico (SJ: Sociedad de Autores Puertorriqueños, 1978), pp. 59-65.

48.2 Figueroa Chapel, Ramón. "Francisco Lluch Mora: descenso a la esperanza." RevL, No. 8 (1970), 574-83.

48.3 Franco Oppenheimer, Félix. "Francisco Lluch Mora, Del barro a Dios..." In his Contornos... (SJ: Yaurel, 1960), pp. 155-66.

48.4 Guevara Castañeira, Josefina. "Apuntes sobre la poesía de Lluch Mora." In her Del Yunque a los Andes (SJ: Club de la Prensa, 1959), pp. 63-70.

48.5 Martín, José Luis. "Poesía del deseo translúcido (acercamiento impresionista a Del asedio y la clasura, libro de versos de Francisco Lluch Mora)." In his Arco y flecha... (SJ: Club de la Prensa, 1961), pp. 139-46. Orig. Pegaso, 1, 1 (1952), 15-16.

48.6 Zapata Acosta, Ramón. "La poesía de Francisco Lluch Mora." In Congreso de Poesía Puertorriqueña, Crítica y antología de la poesía puertorriqueña... (SJ: Instituto de Cultura Puertorriqueña, 1958), pp. 77-86.

48.7 ________. "Presencia de la muerte en la poesía de Francisco Lluch Mora." RHM, 34 (1968), 810-15.

49

LÓPEZ LÓPEZ, JOAQUÍN (1900-1942)

Critical Monographs and Dissertations

49.1 Martínez Masdeu, Edgar. Joaquín López López: su vida y su obra. SJ: Coquí, 1972. Orig. an unpublished thesis, Universidad de Puerto Rico, 1965.

Critical Essays

49.2 Castro, Tomás de Jesús. "Joaquín López López." In his Esbozos críticos (SJ: Baldrich, 1945), pp. 69-70.

49.3 Franco Oppenheimer, Félix. "La poesía de Joaquín López López." In his Contornos... (SJ: Yaurel, 1960), pp. 79-85. Orig. 1948.

49.4 Franquiz, José A. "Sentido de la metáfora. A propósito de la poesía de Joaquín López López." CaribeSJ, 1, 4 (1942), 10-12.

49.5 Grismer, Raymond Leonard, and César Arroyo. "Joaquín López López." In their Vida y obras de autores puertorriqueños (La Habana: "Alfa", 1941-), I, 54-55. Also Ann Arbor: University Microfilms, 1976. Also 1978. Only vol. I ever published.

49.6 Laguerre, Enrique A. "Prólogo." In Joaquín López López, Romancero de la luna (SJ: Biblioteca de Autores Puertorriqueños, 1939), pp. 9-16.

49.7 Lloréns, Washington. "A plena lumbre de Joaquín López López." In his Críticas profanas (SJ: Progreso, 1936), pp. 32-36.

49.8 Pedreira, Antonio S. "A pleno prólogo." In Joaquín López López, A plena lumbre (SJ: "Florente", 1934), pp. 7-15.

49.9 Rosa-Nieves, Cesáreo. "Boceto para un estudio de la poesía de Joaquín López López." In his La lámpara del faro... (SJ: Club de la Prensa, 1957-60), I, 103-109.

49.10 Vizcarrondo, Carmelina. "Proemio." In Joaquín López López, Antología (SJ: Ateneo Puertorriqueño, 1960), pp. 5-10.

50

LÓPEZ SURIA, VIOLETA (1926-)

Critical Essays

50.1 Arrigoitia, Luis de. "La poesía amorosa de Violeta López Suria." In Violeta López Suria, Amorosamente (M: Areyto, 1961), pp. v-xxiv.

50.2 Arroyo, Anita. "La voz de violeta de Violeta López Suria." RICP, No. 49 (1970), 1-6.

50.3 González, José Emilio. "[Me va la vida]." Asomante, 22, 1 (1966), 78-80.

50.4 __________. "Nuevas perspectivas sobre la poesía de Violeta López Suria." La torre, Nos. 73-74 (1971), 107-40.

50.5 ________. "Violeta López Suria, Diluvio." AyL, 2a época, No. 25 (1959), 19.

50.6 López, Julio César. "Un poemario de Violeta Suria, Hubo unos pinos claros." In his Temas y estilos en ocho escritores (SJ, 1967), pp. 71-78.

50.7 Martínez Capó, Juan. "Esquema temático de la poesía de Violeta López Suria." In Violeta López Suria, Antología poética (Río Piedras: Editorial Universitaria, Universidad de Puerto Rico, 1970), pp. v-xv.

51

LUGO, SAMUEL (1905-)

Critical Essays

51.1 Arce de Vázquez, Margot. "Yumbra." In Samuel Lugo, Yumbra (SJ: Venezuela, 1943), pp. 7-13.

51.2 Gómez Costa, Arturo. "Samuel Lugo." In his Vendimias de prosa (Barcelona: Vosgos, 1976), pp. 98-103.

51.3 Laguerre, Enrique A. "La poesía de Samuel Lugo." In his Pulso de Puerto Rico, 1952-1954 (SJ: Biblioteca de Autores Puertorriqueños, 1956), pp. 266-73.

51.4 Pedreira, Antonio S. "Donde caen las claridades." In his Aclaraciones y críticas (SJ: Phi Eta Mu, 1941), pp. 165-70. Also Río Piedras: Edil, 1969. Also in his Obras completas (SJ: Instituto de Cultura Puertorriqueña, 1970), I, 573-77.

51.5 Ribera Chevremont, Evaristo. "Prólogo." In Samuel Lugo, Donde caen las claridades (SJ: "Florente", 1934), pp. vii-xii.

52

MALARET, AUGUSTO (1878-1967)

Critical Monographs adn Dissertations

52.1 Fonfrías, Ernesto Juan. El Instituto de Lexicografía Hispanoamericana "Augusto Malaret" y la Academia Puertorriqueña de la Lengua; ensayos. SJ: Instituto de Lexicografía Hispanoamericana "Augusto Malaret", 1976.

52.2 La obra de Malaret; opiniones fragmentarias. NY, 1960. Orig. SJ: Tipografía San Juan, 1937.

Critical Essays

52.3 Alfonso, Luis. "Nota preliminar." In Augusto Malaret, Diccionario de americanismos; 3. ed. (BA: Emecé, 1946), pp. 9-24.

52.4 "Augusto Malaret, lexicógrafo de América." BAAC, 3, 1 (1967), 129-30.

52.3 Babín, María Teresa. "Augusto Malaret. Vocabulario de Puerto Rico." La torre, No. 14 (1956), 200-203.

52.4 _________. "Personalidad de don Augusto Malaret." BAAC, 3, 2 (1967), 213-27. Also in her Jornadas críticas (temas de Puerto Rico) (Barcelona: Rvmbos, 1967), pp. 302-15. Also RICP, No. 35 (1967), 14-18.

52.5 Barret, L. L. "Semántica americana (notas)." HR, 14 (1946), 84-85.

52.6 Belaval, Emilio S. "Augusto Malaret." BAAC, 3, 2 (1967), 205-12.

52.7 Dávila, José Antonio. "A Augusto Malaret." In his Prosa: ensayos, artículos y cartas literarias (SJ: Sociedad de Autores Puertorriqueños, 1971), pp. 263-64.

52.8 Fernández Juncos, Manuel. "Prólogo." In Augusto Malaret, Diccionario de provincialismos de Puerto Rico (SJ: Cantero Fernández, 1917), pp. 5-12.

52.9 González de Rosa, Edelmira. "Plática con don Augusto Malaret." Educación, No. 13 (1964), 149-52.

52.10 Guzmán Rodríguez, Manuel. "Medallas de oro." In Augusto Malaret, Medallas de oro; 3. ed. (SJ, 1942), pp. i-vi.

52.11 Kany, C. E. "[Lexicón de fauna y flora]." RIB, 12 (1962), 315-17.

52.13 "Opiniones sobre la obra de Malaret." BAAC, 3, 2 (1967), 241-58.

52.14 Rosa-Nieves, Cesáreo. "Augusto Malaret Yordán (1878-1967)." In his Plumas estelares en las letras de Puerto Rico (SJ: Ediciones de la Torre, Universidad de Puerto Rico, 1967), II, 215-24.

52.15 Tió, Aurelio. "Un grande en las humanidades." BAAC, 3, 2 (1967), 229-39.

53

MANRIQUE CABRERA, FRANCISCO (1908-)

Critical Monographs and Dissertations

53.1 Fránquiz Ventura, José Antonio. Los tiempos poéticos de Manrique Cabrera y la metafísica del tiempo en su poesía. M: Luminar, 1944.

53.2 González, José Emilio. Poesía y lengua en la obra de Francisco Manrique Cabrera. Río Piedras: Cultural, 1976.

53.3 Zayas Micheli, Luis Osvaldo. Francisco Manrique Cabrera y la generación del treinta. Unpublished thesis, Universidad de Puerto Rico, 1969.

Critical Essays

53.4 Arce de Vázquez, Margot. "Memoria de Francisco Manrique Cabrera." SinN, 9, 2 (1978), 9-10.

53.5 Arrigoitia, Luis de. "Cronista del devenir puertorriqueño (historia y periodismo)." SinN, 9, 2 (1978), 19-22.

53.6 Babín, María Teresa. "[Poemas de mi tierra tierra]." Brújula, 2, 7-8 (1936), 271.

53.7 "Biografías breves. Francisco Manrique Cabrera." La voz, 2, 2 (1957), 8.

53.8 Castro, Tomás de Jesús. F. Manrique Cabrera." In his Esbozos críticos (SJ: Baldrich, 1945), pp. 19-23.

53.9 Dávila, José Antonio. "Poemas de mi tierra tierra de Francisco Manrique Cabrera." In his Prosa: ensayos, artículos y cartas literarias (SJ: Sociedad de Autores Puertorriqueños, 1971), pp. 171-74.

53.10 Ferré, Rosario. "El maestro." SinN, 9, 2 (1978), 24-25.

53.11 Ferrer Canales, José. "Poemas de tierra [Poemas de mi tierra tierra]." Ambito, 1, 6 (1937), 15-16.

53.12 González, José Emilio. "El hombre de letras." SinN, 9, 2 (1978), 13-18.

53.13 Laguerre, Enrique A. "Francisco M. Cabrera: adelantado de nuestra cultura." In his Polos en la cultura iberoamericana (Boston: Florentia, 1977), pp. 99-104.

53.14 López-Baralt, Luce. "El maestro." SinN, 9, 2 (1978), 25-26.

53.15 Mari Bras, Juan. "Obra política." SinN, 9, 2 (1978), 22-24.

53.16 Nolla, Olga. "El maestro." SinN, 9, 2 (1978), 26-27.

53.17 Pasarell, Emilio J. "Historia de la literatura puertorriqueña." In his Ensayos y artículos (SJ: Cordillera, 1968), pp. 185-88.

53.18 Soto Ramos, Julio. "La historia empieza mañana: ansiedades y presencias de Cabrera." In his Una pica en Flandes... (SJ: Club de la Prensa, 1959), pp. 97-114.

53.19 Vientós Gastón, Nilita. "Una historia de la literatura puertorriqueña." In her Indice cultural (Río Piedras: Ediciones de la Universidad de Puerto Rico, 1962-71), II, 85-87.

53.20 Zayas Micheli, Luis Osvaldo. "Estructuras míticas en la obra de F. M. Cabrera." Horizontes, No. 41 (1977), 5-25.

53.21 ________. "Manrique Cabrera y la generación del treinta." SinN, 9, 2 (1978), 10-13.

54

MARÍN, FRANCISCO GONZALO (1863-1897)

Critical Monographs and Dissertations

54.1 Braschi, Juan. Biografía de Francisco Gonzalo Marín. Arecibo: El Machete, 1909.

54.2 Esteves, José de Jesús. Breve estudio biográfico del

arecibeño F. Gonzalo Marín. Manatí: Mantí Print Co., 1913.

54.3 Figueroa de Cifredo, Patria. Francisco Gonzalo Marín: héroe y poeta (1863-1897). SJ: Instituto de Cultura Puertorriqueña, 1967. Same as item no. 54.13.

54.4 Limón de Arce, José. Biografía de Francisco Gonzalo Marín. Arecibo: Correo del Norte, 1910.

Critical Essays

54.5 Babín, María Teresa. "Vida y poesía de Pachín Marín." In Francisco Gonzalo Marín, Antología (SJ: Ateneo Puertorriqueño, 1958), pp. 5-11. Also as "Vida y poesía de Pachín Marín (1863-1897)." In her Jornadas literarias... (Barcelona: Rvmbos, 1967), pp. 85-92.

54.6 Cadilla Colón, Francisco M. "Francisco Gonzalo Marín." In his Los ochocentistas (Barcelona: Rumbos, 1961), pp. 191-211.

54.7 Coll y Toste, Cayetano. "Francisco Gonzalo Marín (1863-1897)." In his Puertorriqueños ilustres; segunda selección (Barcelona: Rumbos, 1966), pp. 353-62.

54.8 ________. "Pachín Marín." ILit, Nos. 2-3 (1969), 61-63. Also RICP, No. 17 (1962), 47-50.

54.9 Fernández Juncos, Manuel. "Francisco Gonzalo Marín." In his Antología puertorriqueña (NY: Hinds, Hayden & Eldredge, 1913), pp. 219-21. Various other editions.

54.10 Ferrer Canales, José. "Francisco Gonzalo Marín (Pachín)." In his Acentos cívicos... (Río Piedras: Edil, 1972), pp. 157-66.

54.11 Figueroa, Sotero. "Francisco Gonzalo Marín (Pachín)." In Plumas amigas (SJ: Cantero, Fernández, 1912), pp. 294-97.

54.12 Figueroa de Cifredo, Patria. "Datos biográficos y glosas." In Francisco Gonzalo Marín, Cinco narraciones (SJ, 1972), pp. 17-24.

54.13 ________. "Francisco Gonzalo Marín, héroe y poeta." RICP, No. 21 (1963), 40-45. Same as item no. 54.3

54.14 Malaret, Augusto. "Francisco Gonzalo Marín." In his Medallas de oro; 4. ed. (M: Orión, 1952), pp. 189-209. 2. ed., SJ: Biblioteca de Autores Puertorriqueños, 1938; pp. 139-54. 3. ed., SJ, 1942; pp. 147-63. Orig. SJ: Biblioteca de Autores Puertorriqueños, 1928.

54.15 ________. "Francisco Gonzalo Marín." BAAC, 3, 2 (1967), 259-76.

54.16 Morales, Arturo. "Documentos de nuestra historia." RICP, No. 18 (1963), 51-52.

54.17 Quintana, Jorge. "La expulsión de Venezuela de Francisco Gonzalo Marín." RICP, No. 37 (1967), 27-32.

54.18 Rosa-Nieves, Cesáreo. "Francisco Gonzalo Marín (1863-1897; Pachín)." In his Plumas estelares en las letras de Puerto Rico (SJ: Ediciones de la Torre, Universidad de Puerto Rico, 1967), I, 227-48.

54.19 ________. "Prólogo." In Francisco Gonzalo Marín, Cinco narraciones (SJ, 1972), pp. 11-15.

54.20 Rosabal Rosales, José. "Nuestro homenaje." In Francisco Gonzalo Marín, En la arena; 2. ed. (Manzanillo, Cuba?, 1944?), pp. 3-6.

54.21 Tirado, Modesto A. "Poeta y patriota. Bohemio y mártir." In Francisco Gonzalo Marín, En la arena; 2. ed. (Manzanillo, Cuba?, 1944?), pp. 7-10.

55

MARQUÉS, RENÉ (1919-1979)

Bibliographies

55.1 Rodríguez Ramos, Esther. "Aproximación a una bibliografía: René Marqués." SinN, 10, 3 (1979), 121-48.

Critical Monographs and Dissertations

55.2 Espinosa Torres, Victoria. El teatro de René Marqués y la escenificación de su obra: Los soles truncos. Unpubloshed doctoral dissertation, Universidad Nacional Autónoma de México, 1969.

55.3 Flores, Ronald Charles. "The specter of assimilation: the evolution of the theme of nationalism in the theater of René Marqués." DAI, 35 (1975), 7302A.

55.4 López Cruz, Hilda. Obra de René Marqués. Unpublished dissertation, Università di Firenze, 1974.

55.5 McLeod, Ralph D. "The theater of René Marqués: a search for identity in life and in literature." DAI, 36 (1976), 6730A.

55.6 Martin, Eleanor J. René Marqués. NY: Twayne, 1979.

55.6a ________. "The society in the drama of René Marqués." DAI, 33 (1973), 6366A.

55.7 Pilditch, Charles R. René Marqués: a study of his fiction. NY: Plus Ultra Educational Publishers, 1976. Orig. as A study of René Marqués from 1948 to 1952. Unpublished Ph.D. dissertation, Rutgers University, 1966.

55.8 Rodríguez Ramos, Esther. Los cuentos de René Marqués. Hato Rey: Editorial Universitaria, Universidad de Puerto Rico, 1975.

55.9 Shaffer, James Edward. "The jíbaro dialect of Puerto Rico as exemplified in selections of La carreta by René Marqués." DAI, 32 (1972), 3982A.

55.10 Soler-Tossas, José. "Estudios y análisis de cuatro obras teatrales de René Marqués." DAI, 33 (1973), 6885A-86A.

55.11 Zalacaín, Daniel. "Marqués, Díaz, Gambaro: temas y técnicas absurdistas en el teatro hispanoamericano." DAI, 38 (1977), 820A.

Critical Essays

55.12 Aguirre, Angel M. "René Marqués and the struggle of the Puerto Rican theatre." RevI, 2 (1973), 536-48.

55.13 Andreu Iglesias, César. "El hombre en La carreta." AyL, 2, 7 (1954), 16.

55.14 Arce de Vázquez, Margot. "Los soles truncos: comedia trágica de René Marqués." SinN, 10, 3 (1979), 58-70.

55.15 Arriví, Francisco et al. "La casa sin reloj." In his Entrada por las raíces (SJ: Serie La Entraña, 1964), pp. 183-87.

55.16 Babín, María Teresa. "Apuntes sobre La carreta." Asomante, 9, 4 (1953), 63-79. Also Asomante, 20, 4 (1964), 7-20. Also as "La carreta." In her Jornadas literarias (temas de Puerto Rico) (Barcelona: Rumbos, 1967), pp. 173-97.

55.17 ________. "La carreta en el tiempo." SinN, 10, 3 (1979), 45-57.

55.18 ________. "Prólogo." In René Marqués, La carreta; 12. ed. (Río Piedras: Cultural, 1963), pp. v-xxxi.

55.19 Barradas, Efraín. "El machismo existencialista de René Marqués." SinN, 8, 3 (1977), 69-81.

55.20 Barreda-Tomás, Pedro M. "Lo universal, lo nacional y lo personal en el teatro de René Marqués (1919)." In Instituto

Internacional de Literatura Iberoamericana, El teatro en Iberoamérica (M, 1966), pp. 135-47.

55.21 Barrera, Ernesto M. "La volutad rebelde en Carnaval afuera, carnaval adentro de René Marqués." LATR, 8, 1 (1974), 11-19.

55.22 Bockus Aponte, Barbara. "Translator's introduction." In René Marqués, The docile Puerto Rican (essays) (Philadelphia: Temple University Press, 1976), pp. xi-xvi.

55.23 Bonmar, Jorge Luis. "Juan Bobo y René Marqués." AyL, 2a época, No. 1 (1957), 17-18.

55.24 Bravo-Elizondo, Pedro. "La muerte no entrará en palacio: tragedia de la traición." In his Teatro hispanoamericano de crítica social (Madrid: Playor, 1975), pp. 82-94.

55.25 Carmona, Neli Jo. "Análisis del cuento 'Purificación en la calle de Cristo'." El cóndor, 2, 2 (1977), 40-45.

55.26 __________. "René Marqués: cuentista de la promoción del cuarenta." El cóndor, 1, 1 (1976), 15-21.

55.27 Colón, Eliseo R. "René Marqués (1919-1979)." RI, Nos. 110-11 (1980), 237-40.

55.28 Dauster, Frank. "New plays of René Marqués." Hispania, 43 (1960), 451-52.

55.29 __________. "René Marqués y el tiempo culpable." In his Ensayos sobre teatro hispanoamericano (M: SepSetentas, 1975), pp. 102-26.

55.30 __________. "The theater of René Marqués." Symposium, 18 (1964), 35-45.

55.31 Dellepiane, Angela B. "Un cuento con claves de René Marqués." In René Marqués, Ese mosaico fresco sobre aquel mosaico antiguo (Río Piedras: Cultural, 1975), pp. 69-81. Orig. as "Leyendo un cuento con claves de René Marqués." SinN, 2, 3 (1972), 24-30.

55.32 Díaz de Concepción, Abigaíl. "La carreta (comentarios de un psicólogo social)." RCS, 9, 1 (1965), 77-81.

55.33 Díaz Quiñones, Arcadio. "El arte del cuento en René Marqués." In Puerto Rico. Universidad. Facultad de Humanidades. Seminario de Estudios Hispánicos, El cuento puertorriqueño en el siglo XX (Río Piedras: Editorial Universitaria, Universidad de Puerto Rico, 1963), pp. 73-105.

55.34 __________. "Los desastres de la guerra: para leer a René Marqués." SinN, 10, 3 (1979), 15-44.

55.35 Diez de Andino, Juan. "Otro día nuestro." In his Desmenuzando hechos (Barcelona: Rvmbos, 1957), pp. 1-9-71.

55.36 Domenech, Ricardo. "[Un niño azul para esa sombra]." CHA, Nos. 128-29 (1960), 259-63.

55.37 ________. "[Teatro]." Insula, Nos. 164-65 (1960), 14-15.

55.38 Espinosa, Victoria. "La trascendencia dramática de René Marqués." RICP, Nos. 76-77 (1977), 61-69.

55.39 Fraser, Howard M. "Theatricality in The fanlights and Payment as pledged." TAH, No. 19 (1977), 6-8.

55.40 Gautier, Luis A. "René Marqués 1919-1979." LATR, 12, 2 (1979), 60.

55.41 Gómez Lance, Betty Rita. "Los cuentos de René Marqués." RBUS, 90, 2 (1965), 89-108.

55.42 Guevara Castañeira, Josefina. "Otro día nuestro, de René Marqués." In her Del Yunque a los Andes (SJ: Club de la Prensa, 1959), pp. 193-201.

55.43 Hinostrosa, Rodolfo. "[En una ciudad llamada San Juan]." CAm, No. 24 (1964), 107-108.

55.44 Holzapfel, Tamara. "The theater of René Marqués: in search of identity and form." In Dramatists in revolt: the new Latin American theater (Austin: University of Texas Press, 1976), pp. 746-66.

55.45 Hortas, Carlos R. "René Marqués' La mirada: a closer look." LALR, No. 16 (1980), 196-212.

55.46 Jaimes-Freyre, Mireya. "Otro día nuestro de René Marqués." AyL, 2a época, No. 2 (1957), 17-19.

55.47 Jones, Willis Knapp. "Three great Latin American dramatists: Eichelbaum, Usigli, and Marqués." Specialia, No. 1 (1969), 43-49.

55.48 Lacomba, José M. "Introducción: corte transversal de la obra cuentística de René Marqués: 1955-1975." In his Inmersos en el silencio (Río Piedras: Antillana, 1976), pp. 9-24.

55.49 ________. "Premios y honores importantes obtenidos por René Marqués." SinN, 10, 3 (1979), 119-20.

55.50 Laguerre, Enrique A. "[Otro día nuestro]." Asomante, 11, 3 (1955), 67-70.

55.51 ________. "Teatro experimental en el Ateneo [La carreta]." In his Pulso de Puerto Rico, 1952-1954 (SJ: Biblioteca de Autores Puertorriqueños, 1956), pp. 305-14.

55.52 Lugo, Eunice. "La víspera del hombre. A novel by René Marqués." In Studies in honor of M. G. Bernadette... (NY: Las Américas, 1965), pp. 245-70.

55.53 Maldonado-Denis, Manuel. "[En una ciudad llamada San Juan]." Asomante, 19, 1 (1963), 68-70.

55.54 __________. "Reflexiones en torno a un mito: la 'docilidad' del puertorriqueño." CAm, No. 123 (1980), 131-35.

55.55 Marqués, René. "La leyenda hebrea de Abrahán, Sara e Isaac [Sacrificio en el Monte Moriah]." In his Ensayos; 2. ed. rev. y aum. (Río Piedras: Antillana, 1972), pp. 271-306.

55.56 Martin, Eleanor J. "Caligula and La muerte no entrará en palacio: a study in characterization." LATR, 9, 2 (1976), 21-30.

55.57 __________. "Carnaval afuera, carnaval adentro: síntesis del pensamiento social de René Marqués." RC-R, 2, 1 (1974), 39-49.

55.58 Marzán, Julio. "A moralist in spite of himself." Review, No. 19 (1976), 88-90.

55.59 Meléndez, Concha. "Cuentos de René Marqués." In her Obras completas (SJ: Instituto de Cultura Puertorriqueña, 1970-72), II, 399-407. Orig. in her Figuración de Puerto Rico y otros estudios (SJ: Instituto de Cultura Puertorriqueña, 1958), pp. 65-72.

55.60 __________. "Isla personificada en un cuento de René Marqués." In René Marqués, Ese mosaico fresco sobre aquel mosaico antiguo (Río Piedras: Cultural, 1975), pp. 51-63. Orig. SinN, 2, 3 (1972), 17-23.

55.61 __________. "[La víspera del hombre]." Asomante, 16, 2 (1960), 102-107. Also in her Literatura de ficción en Puerto Rico, cuento y novela (SJ: Cordillera, 1971), pp. 135-43. Also in her Obras completas (SJ: Instituto de Cultura Puertorriqueña, 1970-72), IV, 561-69.

55.62 Montes Huidobro, Matías. "Significantes de la teatralidad Marqués: Carnaval afuera, carnaval adentro." BR/RB, 7, 1 (1980), 39-52.

55.63 Morfi, Angelina. "El apartamiento: nueva ruta en el teatro de René Marqués." In her Temas del teatro (Santo Domingo: Caribe, 1969), pp. 107-12.

55.64 __________. "Biografía mínima." SinN, 10, 3 (1979), 115-18.

55.65 Murad, Timothy. "René Marqués' Juan Bobo y la dama de Occidente: folklore as pantomime and the arts of cultural affirmation." RC-R, 7, 4 (1979), 36-47.

55.66 Nieves-Colón, Mirna. "Símbolos y mitos en La víspera del hombre." Romanica, 11 (1974), 34-39.

55.67 Pasarell, Emilio J. "El apartamiento de René Marqués." In his Ensayos y artículos (SJ: Cordillera, 1968), pp. 151-54.

55.68 Pilditch, Charles. "La escena puertorriqueña [Los soles truncos]." Asomante, 17, 2 (1961), 51-58.

55.69 __________. "La muerte no entrará en palacio: una obra en busca de un estreno." SinN, 10, 3 (1979), 71-82.

55.70 __________. "Recent fiction by René Marqués." Chasqui, 6, 1 (1976), 77-79.

55.71 Portela, Francisco V. "Una entrevista con René Marqués: nuestro colaborador habla de teatro y literatura puertorriqueña." AyL, 2a época, No. 8 (1957), 3-5.

55.72 Restrepo Fernández, Iván. "[En una ciudad llamada San Juan]." AyL, 4, 1 (1961), 89-90.

55.73 Riccio, Robert A. "Studies in Puerto Rican drama: Los soles truncos." Atenea, 1, 4 (1964), 21-25.

55.74 Rosado, Josué. "La docilidad puertorriqueña. René Marqués: su concepto del hombre puertorriqueño actual." SinN, 10, 3 (1979), 98-114.

55.75 Salgado, María A. "El cepillo de dientes and El apartamiento: two opposing views of alienated man." RomN, 17 (1977), 247-54.

55.76 Sánchez, Luis Rafael. "Las divinas palabras de René Marqués." SinN, 10, 3 (1979), 11-14.

55.77 Santos Silva, Loreina. "El grito de Lares de Luis Lloréns Torres y Mariana o el alba de René Marqués." La gotera, 3, 2 (1972), 19; 3, 3 (1972), 13-15.

55.78 __________. "Reflexiones sobre Los soles truncos." Ceiba, 2, 3(1973), 63-67.

55.79 Saz, Agustín del. "La tierra y la frustración del emigrante. La carreta de René Marqués." In his Teatro social hispanoamericano (Barcelona: Labor, 1967), pp. 107-11.

55.80 Shaw, Donald L. "René Marqués, La muerte no entrará en palacio: an analysis." LATR, 2, 1 (1968), 31-38.

55.81 Siemens, William L. "Assault on the schizoid wasteland: René Marqués, El apartamiento." LATR, 7, 2 (1974), 17-23.

55.82 Sola, María. "René Marqués ¿escritor marginado?" SinN, 10, 3 (1979), 83-97.

55.83 Valenzuela, Víctor M. "A Puerto Rican play: The ox-cart by René Marqués." In his Contemporary Latin American writers (NY: Las Américas, 1971), pp. 47-55.

55.84 Vázquez Alamo, Francisco. "Análisis prologal. Dos dramas de amor, poder y desamor: David y Jonatán y Tito de Berenice." In René Marqués, David y Jonatán, Tito y Berenice (Río Piedras: Antillana, 1970), pp. 7-13.

55.85 __________. "Breve análisis crítico: Carnaval afuera, carnaval adentro." In René Marqués, Carnaval afuera, carnaval adentro (Río Piedras: Antillana, 1971), pp. 11-19.

55.86 __________. "Notas prologales. Dos obras neoconvencionales o del 'absurdo' de René Marqués: La casa sin reloj y El apartamiento." In René Marqués, Teatro III (Río Piedras: Cultural, 1971), pp. 7-10.

55.87 __________. "[Prólogo]." In René Marqués, Teatro II (Río Piedras: Cultural, 1971), pp. 7-12.

55.88 __________. "El teatro de René Marqués." In René Marqués, Sacrificio en el Monte Moriah (Barcelona: Antillana, 1969), pp. 9-20.

55.89 Vidal, Hernán. "La muerte no entrará en palacio: universalismo y muerte al padre terrible." ExTL, 2 (1973), 9-15.

55.90 Vientós Gastón, Nilita. "René Marqués (1919-1979)." SinN, 10, 3 (1979), 9-10.

55.91 Waldman, Gloria Feiman. "El tema de Puerto Rico en Abelardo Díaz Alfaro, René Marqués y Pedro Juan Soto." RICP, No. 69 (1975), 16-22.

55.92 Zalacaín, Daniel. "René Marqués, del absurdo a la realidad." LATR, 12, 1 (1978), 33-37.

55.93 __________. "El tiempo, tema fundamental en la obra de René Marqués." KRQ, 27 (1980), 485-93.

55.94 Zayas, Dean Manuel. "La carreta en La carreta, de René Marqués." Prometeo, 1, 3 (1963), 30.

55.95 Zayas Micheli, Luis Osvaldo. "La víspera del hombre, novela de René Marqués (valoración artística)." Horizontes, No. 15 (1964), 19-24.

56

MARRERO, CARMEN (1907-)

Critical Essays

56.1 Dávila, José Antonio. "Fémina de Carmen Marrero." In his Prosa: ensayos, artículos y cartas literarias (SJ: Sociedad de Autores Puertorriqueños, 1971), pp. 197-200.

56.2 Grismer, Raymond Leonard, and César Arroyo. "Carmen Marrero." In their Vida y obras de autores puertorriqueños (La Habana: "Alfa", 1941-), I, 66-67. Also Ann Arbor: University Microfilms, 1976. Also 1978. Only vol. I ever published.

56.3 Meléndez, Concha. "Toque de lo alcanzado [Sonetos de la verdad]." In her Poetas hispanoamericanos diversos (SJ: Cordillera, 1971), pp. 197-207. Also in her Obras completas (SJ: Instituto de Cultura Puertorriqueña, 1970-72), IV, 203-13. Orig. in Carmen Marrero, Sonetos de la verdad (NY: Las Américas, 1964), pp. ix-xxi.

56.4 Sáez, Antonia. "Prólogo." In Carmen Marrero, Tierra y folklore (SJ: Cordillera, 1967), pp. 9-13.

56.5 Soto Ramos, Julio. "Sonetos de la verdad." In his Yo soy yo y mi verdad... (SJ: Cordillera, 1973), pp. 65-69.

57

MATIENZO CINTRÓN, ROSENDO (1855-1913)

Critical Monographs and Dissertations

57.1 Díaz Soler, Luis M. Rosendo Matienzo Cintrón; orientador y guardián de una cultura. Río Piedras: Universidad de Puerto Rico, Instituto de Literatura Puertorriqueña, 1960.

57.2 Medina González, Adolfo. Rosendo Matienzo Cintrón: estudio biográfico. Mayagüez: National Printing Co., 1914.

Critical Essays

57.3 Carreras, Carlos N. "Rosendo Matienzo Cintrón." In his Hombres y mujeres de Puerto Rico (M: Orión, 1957), pp. 85-94. Various subsequent editions.

57.4 Coll y Toste, Cayetano. "El gesto del patriota." BHPR, 6 (1919), 162-64.

57.5 ________. "Rosendo Matienzo Cintrón." In his Puertorriqueños ilustres; segunda selección (Barcelona: Rumbos, 1966), pp. 345-48.

57.6 Fonfrías, Ernesto Juan. "Rosendo Matienzo Cintrón, espiritista." In his Tintillo bravo del quehacer puertorriqueño (SJ: Club de la Prensa, 1968), pp. 167-83.

57.7 Lloréns Torres, Luis. "Rosendo Matienzo Cintrón: su inmortal creación Pancho Ibero como tipo representativo de Hispano-América." RAnt, 1, 1 (1914), 53-55. Also as "Matienzo. Su inmortal creación del 'Pancho Ibero' como tipo representativo de Hispano-América." RICP, No. 49 (1970), 46-47.

57.8 Morales Carrión, Arturo. "Perfil de Matienzo Cintrón." In his Ojeada al proceso histórico y otros ensayos (SJ: Cordillera, 1971), pp. 77-94. Also 1974.

57.9 Rosa-Nieves, Cesáreo. "Rosendo Matienzo Cintrón (1855-1913)." In his Plumas estelares en las letras de Puerto Rico (SJ: Ediciones de la Torre, Universidad de Puerto Rico, 1967), I, 513-25.

58

MATOS BERNIER, FÉLIX (1869-1937)

Critical Monographs and Dissertations

58.1 Díaz de Olano, Carmen Rosa. Felix Matos Bernier, su vida y su obra. SJ: Biblioteca de Autores Puertorriqueños, 1956, c1955. Orig. an unpublished thesis, Universidad de Puerto Rico, 1940.

Critical Essays

58.2 Abril, Mariano. "Cantos rodados (libro de Matos Bernier)." In his Sensaciones de un cronista (SJ: La Democracia, 1903), pp. 69-73.

58.3 Dalmau Canet, Sebastián. "Félix Matos Bernier." In his Crepúsculos literarios (SJ: Boletín Mercantil, 1903), pp. 35-41.

58.4 Rosa-Nieves, Cesáreo. "Félix Matos Bernier (1869-1937; seud. Fray Justo)." In his Plumas estelares en las letras de

Puerto Rico (SJ: Ediciones de la Torre, Universidad de Puerto Rico, 1967), I, 497-511.

58.5 Soto Ramos, Julio. "Félix Matos Bernier." In his Yo soy yo y mi verdad... (SJ: Cordillera, 1973), pp. 205-12.

59

MATOS PAOLI, FRANCISCO (1915-)

Critical Monographs and Dissertations

59.1 González Torres, Rafael A. La búsqueda de lo absoluto; la poesía de Francisco Matos Paoli. SJ: Biblioteca de Autores Puertorriqueños, 1978.

Critical Essays

59.2 Arce de Vázquez, Margot. "Prólogo." In Francisco Matos Paoli, Criatura del rocío (SJ: Ateneo Puertorriqueño, 1958), pp. 7-8.

59.3 Cartaña, Luis. "Prólogo." In Francisco Matos Paoli, Antología minuto; 2. ed. (Mayagüez, 1978), pp. 5-9.

59.4 Dávila, José Antonio. "Cardo labriego de Francisco Matos Paoli." In his Prosa: ensayos, artículos y cartas literarias (SJ: Sociedad de Autores Puertorriqueños, 1971), pp. 185-89.

59.5 "Francisco Matos Paoli." In La ciudad de los poetas (Palencia de Castilla, Spain: Rocamador, 1965), pp. 93-96.

59.6 Freire de Matos, Isabel. "Itinerario de un poeta." In Francisco Matos Paoli, Canto de la locura; 2. ed. ampl. y rev. (SJ: Instituto de Culutra Puertorriqueña, 1976), pp. 7-54.

59.7 Gómez Costa, Arturo. "Francisco Matos Paoli." In his Vendimias en prosa (Barcelona: Vosgos, 1976), pp. 78-87.

59.8 González, José Emilio. "[Canto de la locura]." Asomante, 20, 1 (1964), 82-85.

59.9 __________. "[Criatura del rocío]." Asomante, 15, 4 (1959), 81-83.

59.10 __________. "Reflexiones sobre la poesía de Francisco Matos Paoli." In Francisco Matos Paoli, Antología poética (SJ:

Editorial Universitaria, Universidad de Puerto Rico, 1972), pp. 11-32.

59.11 López, Julio César. "Francisco Matos Poali y el vanguardismo literario." In his La patria en dos poetas y un paralelo modernista (Barcelona: Ariel, 1968), pp. 11-22. Also SJ, 1968. Orig. RICP, No. 38 (1968), 9-12.

59.13 Manrique Cabrera, Francisco. "[Criatura del rocío]." Asomante, 15, 4 (1959), 81-83.

59.14 Matos Paoli, Francisco. "Mi experiencia como poeta." BAAC, 11, 1-2 (1975), 88-92.

59.15 Puebla, Manuel de la. "El compromiso poético de Francisco Matos Paoli." SinN, 8, 4 (1978), 10-27.

59.16 Santos Silva, Loreina. "Loor del espacio de Francisco Matos Paoli: una mística materialista." CA, No. 221 (1978), 140-42.

59.17 Torre, José R. de la. "Mundo y trasmundo en el Cancionero de Matos Paoli." SinN, 2, 1 (1971), 49-65.

60

MELÉNDEZ, CONCHA (1895-)

Critical Monographs and Dissertations

60.1 Arnaldi de Olmeda, Cecilia. Concha Meléndez: vida y obra. SJ: Editorial Universitaria de Puerto Rico, 1972.

Critical Essays

60.2 Albuquerque Lima, Sílvio Júlio. "Concha Meléndez." In his Escritores antilhanos (Rio de Janeiro, 1944), pp. 233-67. Signed Júlio Sílvio.

60.3 Asencio-Alvarez Torres, Juan. "La novela indianista en Hispanoamérica, de Concha Meléndez." Brújula, 1, 3-4 (1935), 116.

60.4 ______. "Signos de Iberoamérica, por Concha Meléndez." Brújula, 3, 9-10 (1937), 234.

60.5 Braschi, Wilfredo. "Entrevista a Concha Meléndez, escritora, maestra y símbolo." Educación, 14, 14 (1965), 45-48.

60.6 Brenes Messen, Roberto. "Prólogo." In Concha Meléndez, La novela indianista en Hispamérica (Madrid: Hernando, 1934), pp. 5-8.

60.7 Bueno, Salvador. "De Iberoamérica." RICP, No. 6 (1960), 45.

60.8 Cancel Negrón, Ramón. "Concha Meléndez: dama de la americanidad." RICP, No. 20 (1963), 56-59.

60.9 Castro, Tomás de Jesús. "Concha Meléndez." In his Esbozos críticos (SJ: Baldrich, 1945), pp. 129-34.

60.10 Colberg Petrovich, Juan Enrique. "Concha Meléndez: sobre un eterno verdor de creación." In his Cuatro clásicos contemporáneos de Puerto Rico (Barcelona: Cordillera, 1966), pp. 9-73.

60.11 Córdova de Braschi, Julia. "[La inquietud sosegada, poética de Evaristo Ribera Chevremont]." Asomante, 4, 1 (1948), 104-105. See item no. 71.2.

60.12 Cuchí Coll, Isabel. "Concha Meléndez." In her Oro nativo... (SJ, 1936), pp. 73-82.

60.13 Ferrer Canales, José. "Concha Meléndez: Signos de Iberoamérica." In his Marginalia (SJ?: Venezuela?, 1939), pp. 63-78.

60.14 García Cabrera, Manuel. "La novela indiana en Hispanoamérica [La novela indianista]." AtPR, 1 (1935), 312-13.

60.15 Hernández Aquino, Luis. "[Figuración de Puerto Rico y otros estudios]." La torre, No. 28 (1959), 193-95.

60.16 Laguerre, Enrique A. "Concha Meléndez y los polos de la cultura iberoamericana." In his Polos en la cultura iberoamericana (Boston: Florentia, 1977), pp. 11-20. Orig. RICP, No. 70 (1976), 1-5.

60.17 Larew, Leonor A. "First lady of Puerto Rican letters: Concha Meléndez." Americas, 28, 6-7 (1976) 13-16. Also as "Concha Meléndez. Expresión de Puerto Rico." Américas [Spanish edition], 28, 6-7 (1976), 13-16.

60.18 López González, Julio César. "[Concha Melendez]." In his El ensayo y su enseñza (dos ejemplos puertorriqueños) (Río Piedras: Editorial Universitaria, Universidad de Puerto Rico, 1980), pp. 95-104.

60.19 Martínez Capó, Juan. "[El arte del cuento en Puerto Rico]." Asomante, 18, 4 (1962), 85.

60.20 ________. "[Figuración de Puerto Rico]." Asomante. 16, 1 (1960), 73-77.

60.21 Morales, Angel Luis. "Concha Meléndez y el ensayo de crítica literaria. Notas bibliográficas." RICP, No. 45 (1969), 4-7.

60.22 ________. "La doctora Concha Meléndez." RICP, No. 48 (1970), 27-32.

60.23 Negrón Muñoz, Angela. "Concha Meléndez." In her Mujeres de Puerto Rico (SJ: Venezuela, 1935), pp. 249-51.

60.24 Patout, Paulette. "[Moradas de poesía en Alfonso Reyes]." Caravelle, No. 24 (1975), 103-105.

60.25 Pedreira, Antonio S. "Signos de Iberoamérica." In his Aclaraciones y crítica (Río Piedras: Phi Eta Mu, Universidad de Puerto Rico, 1941), pp. 255-60. Also Río Piedras: Edil, 1969. Also in his Obras completas (SJ: Instituto de Cultura Puertorriqueña, 1970), I, 643-47.

60.26 Rosa-Nieves, Cesáreo. "Concha Meléndez (1895-)." In his Plumas estelares en las letras de Puerto Rico (SJ: Ediciones de la Torre, Universidad de Puerto Rico, 1967), II, 443-60.

60.27 Vientós Gastón, Nilita. "Un libro de Concha Meléndez [El arte del cuento en Puerto Rico]." In her Indice cultural (Río Piedras: Ediciones de la Universidad de Puerto Rico, 1962-71), IV, 205-207.

61

MELÉNDEZ MUÑOZ, MIGUEL (1884-1966)

Critical Monographs and Dissertations

61.1 Cuaderno homenaje a don Miguel Meléndez Muñoz. SJ: Departamento de Instrucción Pública, 1956.

61.2 Duca, Robert Anthony. "The Puerto Rican national identity in the essays of Miguel Meléndez Muñoz." DAI, 37 (1976), 4389A.

61.3 Lube Droz, Josefina. Miguel Meléndez Muñoz: vida y obra. Unpublished thesis, Universidad de Puerto Rico, 1951. Same as item no. 61.19.

61.4 Rosa-Nieves, Cesáreo. Don Miguel Meléndez Muñoz, gran maestro del batey, del cedro y la vereda. SJ, 1957.

Critical Essays

61.5 Arce de Vázquez, Margot. "Significación de la vida y obra de don Miguel Meléndez Muñoz." RICP, No. 34 (1967), 4-5.

61.6 Babín, María Teresa. "Cuentos del cedro." In her Jornadas literarias... (Barcelona: Rvmbos, 1967), pp. 220-27.

61.7 __________. "Puerto Rico en las nuevas obras de Meléndez Muñoz." In her Jornadas literarias... (Barcelona: Rvmbos, 1967), pp. 228-37.

61.8 Braschi, Wilfredo. "Miguel Meléndez Muñoz." In his Perfiles puertorriqueños (SJ: Biblioteca de Autores Puertorriqueños, 1978), pp. 62-64.

61.9 Castro, Tomás de Jesús. "Miguel Meléndez Muñoz." In his Esbozos críticos (SJ: Baldrich, 1945), pp. 48-52.

61.10 Colberg Petrovich, Juan Enrique. "D. Miguel Meléndez Muñoz: vestigios de un alma clara, reflexiva." In his Cuatro autores clásicos contemporáneos de Puerto Rico (SJ: Cordillera, 1966), pp. 75-159.

61.11 Díaz Alfaro, Abelardo. "Miguel Meléndez Muñoz, cedro de la cultura criolla." Prensa, 2a época, No. 4 (1959), 25. Also RICP, No. 34 (1967), 2-3. Also in Miguel Meléndez Muñoz, Obras completas (SJ: Instituto de Cultura Puertorriqueña, 1963), II, 169-73.

61.12 Géigel Polanco, Vicente. "Homenaje a Miguel Meléndez Muñoz." RICP, No. 34 (1967), 30-31.

61.13 __________. "Miguel Meléndez Muñoz (1884-1966)." In Escritores contemporáneos de Puerto Rico (SJ: Sociedad de Autores Puertorriqueños, 1978), pp. 161-64. Also as "Miguel Meléndez Muñoz." In his Valores de Puerto Rico (NY: Arno Press, 1975), pp. 119-23. Orig. SJ: Eugenio María de Hostos, 1943.

61.14 Huyke, Juan B. "Prólogo [a Ensayos]." In Miguel Meléndez Muñoz, Obras completas (SJ: Instituto de Cultura Puertorriqueña, 1962), I, 533-40.

61.15 Laguerre, Enrique A. "En torno a la obra de don Miguel Meléndez Muñoz." RICP, No. 34 (1967), 6-8.

61.16 __________. "Introducción [a Retablo puertorriqueño]." In Miguel Meléndez Muñoz, Obras completas (SJ: Instituto de Cultura Puertorriqueña, 1963), II, 163-68.

61.17 Lube Droz, Josefina. "Miguel Meléndez Muñoz, apuntes para su ensayo." Indice, No. 9 (1929), 147.

61.18 __________. "La obra literaria de Miguel Meléndez Muñoz." RICP, No. 34 (1967), 24-29.

61.19 ________"Prefacio." In Miguel Meléndez Muñoz, Obras completas (SJ: Instituto de Cultura Puertorriqueña, 1963), I, 9-190. Same as item no. 61.3.

61.20 Pagán, Bolívar. "Lecturas puertorriqueñas." In his América y otras páginas (SJ, 1922), pp. 157-60.

61.21 Rosa-Nieves, Cesáreo. "Miguel Meléndez Muñoz (1884-1966)." In his Plumas estelares en las letras de Puerto Rico (SJ: Ediciones de la Torre, Universidad de Puerto Rico, 1967), II, 199-213.

61.22 ________. "Miguel Meléndez Muñoz y sus lecturas puertorriqueñas." In his Ensayos escogidos... (SJ: Academia de Artes y Ciencias de Puerto Rico, 1970?), pp. 161-63. Orig. BAAC, 2, 4 (1966), 813-16.

61.23 Valldejuli Rodríguez, J. "Miguel Meléndez Muñoz." BAAC, 2, 4 (1966), 705-709.

61.24 Zeno Gandía, Manuel. "Juicio crítico [de Lecturas puertorriqueñas]." In Miguel Meléndez Muqoz, Obras completas (SJ: Instituto de Cultura Puertorriqueña, 1963), I, 405-409.

61.25 ________. "Prólogo [a Cuentos del cedro]." In Miguel Meléndez Muñoz, Obras completas (SJ: Instituto de Cultura Puertorriqueña, 1963), I, 631-37. Also in Miguel Meléndez Muñoz, Cuentos del cedro; 2. ed. (SJ: Biblioteca de Autores Puertorriqueños, 1937), pp. 5-15. Also as "Los cuentos del cedro, de don Miguel Meléndez Muñoz." RICP, No. 34 (1967), 15-17.

62

MERCADO, JOSÉ RAMÓN (1863-1911)

Critical Monographs and Dissertations

62.1 Vieta de Miranda, Providencia. Vida y obra de José Mercado (Momo). Unpublished thesis, Universidad de Puerto Rico, 1948.

Critical Essays

62.2 Alegría José S. "José Ramón Mercado 'Momo'." RICP, No. 20 (1963), 34-38.

62.3 Fernández Juncos, Manuel. "José Mercado (Momo)." In

his Antología puertorriqueña (NY: Hinds, Hayden & Eldredge, 1913), pp. 224-30. Various other editions.

62.4 ________. "Prólogo." In José Ramón Mercado, Virutas (SJ: Francisco J. Marxuach, 1900), pp. i-viii.

62.5 Matos Bernier, Félix. "Virutas." In his Isla de arte (SJ: La Primavera, 1907), pp. 74-80.

62.6 Rosa-Nieves, Cesáreo. "José Mercado (1863-1911; seud. Momo)." In his Plumas estelares en las letras de Puerto Rico (SJ: Ediciones de la Torre, Universidad de Puerto Rico, 1967), I, 237-44.

63

MIRANDA, LUIS ANTONIO (1896-)

Critical Essays

63.1 Braschi, Wilfredo. "Luis Antonio Miranda." In his Perfiles puertorriqueños (SJ: Biblioteca de Autores Puertorriqueños, 1978), pp. 136-38.

63.2 Camejo, Rafael W. "Luis Antonio Miranda." In his Florecían los rosales... (Caracas: Hernández, 1952), pp. 205-10.

63.3 "Conversación con Luis Antonio Miranda." Indice, No. 9 (1929), 139-40.

63.4 Dávila, José Antonio. "A Luis Antonio Miranda." In his Prosas: ensayos, artículos y cartas literarias (SJ: Sociedad de Autores Puertorriqueños, 1971), pp. 279-82.

63.5 Díaz Mantí, Vigil. "Secuencias." In Luis Antonio Miranda, Música prohibida (Manatí: Harry C. del Pozo, 1925), pp. 13-21.

63.6 Esteves, José de Jesús. "Atrio." In Luis Antonio Miranda, Abril florido (SJ: Real Hermanos, 1918), pp. 7-9.

63.7 Pagán, Bolívar. "El rosario de doña Inés." In his América y otras páginas (SJ, 1922), pp. 165-66.

63.8 Rosa-Nieves, Cesáreo. "Luis Antonio Miranda (1896-)." In his Plumas estelares en las letras de Puerto Rico (SJ: Ediciones de la Torre, Universidad de Puerto Rico, 1967), II, 265-76.

63.9 Zorrila, Enrique. "Prólogo." In Luis Antonio Miranda, El rosario de doña Inés (SJ, 1919), pp. 7-14.

64

MONTEAGUDO RODRÍGUEZ, JOAQUÍN (1890-1966)

Critical Essays

64.1 Braschi, Wilfredo. "Joaquín Monteagudo." In his Perfiles puertorriqueños (SJ: Biblioteca de Autores Puertorriqueños, 1978), pp. 167-69.

64.2 Camejo, Rafael W. "Joaquín Monteagudo." In his Florecían los rosales (Caracas: Hernández, 1952), pp. 163-70.

64.3 Castro, Tomás de Jesús. "Joaquín Monteagudo." In his Esbozos críticos (Barcelona: Rumbos, 1957), pp. 102-105.

64.4 Fonfrías, Ernesto Juan. "Joaquín Monteagudo." In his Tintillo bravo del quehacer literario (SJ: Club de la Prensa, 1968), pp. 135-38.

64.5 Lluch Mora, Francisco. "La aventura del cambio en la poesía de Joaquín Monteagudo." In Joaquín Monteagudo, El hombre vertical (SJ: Club de la Prensa, 1967), pp. 5-21. Also Atenea, 4, 2 (1967), 27-38.

64.6 Mora, José de. "[Prólogo]." In Joaquín Monteagudo, Acústicas; poemas, 1926-1928 (Santo Domingo: La Provincia, 1928), pagination unknown.

64.7 Poventud, José A. "Nota preliminar." In Joaquín Monteagudo, Dr. Manuel de la Pila Iglesias (SJ: Baldrich, 1953), pp. 7-15.

64.8 Rosa-Nieves, Cesáreo. "Joaquín Monteagudo Rodríguez (seud. Armando Duval: 1890-1966)." In his Plumas estelares en las letras de Puerto Rico (SJ: Ediciones de la Torre, Universidad de Puerto Rico, 1967), II, 225-34.

64.9 Soto Ramos, Julio. "Biografía del doctor Manuel de la Pila Iglesias." In his Una pica en Flandes... (SJ: Club de la Prensa, 1959), pp. 67-72.

65

MORALES, JORGE LUIS (1930-)

Critical Essays

65.1 Belmás, Antonio Oliver. "Prólogo." In Jorge Luis Morales, Discurso a los pájaros (SJ: Moriviví, 1965), pp. 9-10.

65.2 Braschi, Wilfredo. "Prólogo." In Jorge Luis Morales, Antología poética (SJ?: U.P.R., 1968), pp. 7-11.

65.3 Coll y Toste, Cayetano. "José Pablo Morales." In his Puertorriqueños ilustres; segunda selección (Barcelona: Rumbos, 1966), pp. 144-47.

65.4 Gómez Costa, Arturo. "José Luis Morales." In his Vendimias en prosa (Barcelona: Vosgos, 1976), pp. 65-69.

65.5 González, José Emilio. "[Decir del propio ser]." Orfeo, 1 (1954), 43-45.

65.6 __________. "Escorzos de unidad en la obra de Jorge Luis Morales." RICP, No. 43 (1969), 9-10.

65.7 __________. "[Metal y piedra]." Asomante, 9, 3 (1953), 65-68.

65.8 González Torres, Rafael A. "El mundo poético de Jorge Luis Morales." La torre, Nos. 73-74 (1971), 223-36.

65.9 Martín, José Luis. "La trayectoria poética de Jorge Luis Morales." In his Arco y flecha (SJ: Club de la Prensa, 1961), pp. 147-59.

65.10 "[Ventana y yo]." PHisp, No. 255 (1974), 18-19.

66

MUÑOZ RIVERA, LUIS (1859-1916)

Critical Monographs and Dissertations

66.1 Angelis, Pedro de. Luis Muñoz Rivera; su vida y su noble y levantada labor en defensa de las libertades de su patria. SJ: Llabrés, n.d.

66.2 Cruz Monclova, Lidio. Luis Muñoz Rivera; diez años de su vida política. SJ: Instituto de Cultura Puertorriqueña, 1959.

66.3 Dalmau Canet, Sebastián. Luis Muñoz Rivera: su vida, su política, su carácter. SJ: Boletín Mercantil, 1917.

66.4 González Ginorio, José. Luis Muñoz Rivera, a la luz de sus obras y de su vida. Estudio biográfico-crítico-educativo. NY: D. C. Heath, 1919.

66.5 Lagrímas y flores. Homenaje a Luis Muñoz Rivera. Mayagüez: La Bandera Americana, 1916.

66.6 Martínez Acosta, Carmelo. Luis Muñoz Rivera. SJ: Venezuela, 1948.

66.7 Meléndez, Concha. De frente al sol; apuntes sobre la poesía de Luis Muñoz Rivera. SJ: Instituto de Cultura Puertorriqueña, 1960. Same as item no. 66.36.

66.8 Meléndez Muñoz, Miguel. Dos Luises. Ponce: Revista del Caribe, 1957.

Critical Essays

66.9 Abril, Mariano. "Luis Muñoz Rivera [Tropicales]." In his Sensaciones de un cronista (SJ: La Democracia, 1903), pp. 184-94.

66.10 Alegría, José S. "El periodismo lírico de Luis Muñoz Rivera." RICP, No. 4 (1959), 51-53.

66.11 Alegría, Ricardo E. "Muñoz Rivera y de Diego ante la invasión norteamericana." RICP, No. 54 (1972), 19-22. Also in Antología del pensamiento puertorriqueño (1900-1970) (Río Piedras?: Editorial Universitaria, Universidad de Puerto Rico, 1975), pp. 423-27.

66.12 Arana Soto, S. "Luis Muñoz Rivera y la dignidad." RICP, No. 1o (1961), 48-50.

66.13 Arrillaga Roqué, Juan. "Luis Muñoz Rivera." In his Memorias de antaño (Ponce: Baldorioty, 1910), pp. 129-37.

66.14 Balseiro, José A. "Luis Muñoz Rivera: una causa y una época." RICP, No. 11 (1961), 49-54.

66.15 __________. "Un poeta civil de Puerto Rico." In his Expresión de Hispanoamérica; segunda serie (SJ: Instituto de Cultura Puertorriqueña, 1963), pp. 175-85. 2. ed. rev., Madrid: Gredos, 1970; II, 185-96. Also as "Luis Muñoz Rivera, civil poet of Puerto Rico." In his The Americas look at each other (Coral Gables, FL: University of Miami Press, 1969), pp. 146-56.

66.16 Carreras, Carlos N. "Luis Muñoz Rivera." In his Hombres y mujeres de Puerto Rico (M: Orión, 1974), pp. 127-51. Various other editions; orig. 1957.

66.17 Coll Cuchí, Cayetano. "Anécdotas de Muñoz Rivera." In his Historias que parecen cuentos (Río Piedras: Universitaria, 1972), pp. 147-61.

66.18 __________. "Muñoz Rivera íntimo." In his Historias que parecen cuentos (Río Piedras: Universitaria, 1972), pp. 163-84.

66.19 Cruz Monclova, Lidio. "Introducción." In Luis Muñoz Rivera, Obras completas (SJ: Instituto de Cultura Puertorriqueña, 1960-68), II, 15-26.

66.20 Dalmau Canet, Sebastián. "Luis Muñoz Rivera." In his Próceres (SJ: Correo Dominical, 1929), pp. 103-229.

66.21 "Epistolario de Luiz Muñoz Rivera." RICP, No. 4 (1959), 35-36.

66.22 Fernández Méndez, Eugenio. "Introducción." In Luis Muñoz Rivera, Obras completas (SJ: Instituto de Cultura Puertorriqueña, 1960-68), I, 9-20.

66.23 __________. "Luis Muñoz Rivera: maestro de una cultura puertorriqueña de excelencia." RICP, No. 49 (1970), 20-24.

66.24 Fonfrías, Ernesto Juan. "Luis Muñoz Rivera (1859-1916)." In his Sementera; ensayos breves y biografías mínimas (SJ: Club de la Prensa, 1962), pp. 97-125.

66.25 __________. "Luis Muñoz Rivera, político. Síntesis de una conferencia." RICP, No. 4 (1959), 43-48.

66.26 Géigel Polanco, Vicente. "Luis Muñoz Rivera y José de Diego: dos orientadores de nuestro pueblo." In his Valores de Puerto Rico (NY: Arno Press, 1975), pp. 69-85. Orig. SJ: Eugenio María de Hostos, 1943.

66.27 Hostos, Adolfo de. "Luis Muñoz Rivera (1859-1916)." In his Hombres representativos de Puerto Rico (SJ, 1961), pp. 121-24.

66.28 Lefebre, Enrique. "Muñoz Rivera (necrología)." In his Paisajes mentales... (SJ: Cantero, Fernández, 1918), pp. 239-44.

66.29 Matos Bernier, Félix. "Luis Muñoz Rivera." In his Muertos y vivos (SJ: El País, 1905), pp. 191-98.

66.30 __________. "Tropicales (Luis Muñoz Rivera)." In his Isla de arte (SJ: La Primavera, 1907), pp. 104-109.

66.31 Meléndez, Concha. "De frente al sol; apuntes sobre la poesía de Luis Muñoz Rivera." In her Poetas hispanoamericanos diversos (SJ: Cordillera, 1971), pp. 11-30. Also in her Obras completas (SJ: Instituto de Cultura Puertorriqueña, 1970-72), IV, 17-36. Same as item no. 66.7.

66.32 __________. "Un poema alegórico de Luis Muñoz Rivera. 'Sísifo'." RICP, No. 4 (1959), 41-42.

66.33 Meléndez Muñoz, Miguel. "Dos Luises." In his Obras completas (SJ: Instituto de Cultura Puertorriqueña, 1963), II, 491-541. Same as item no. 66.8.

66.34 __________. "Muñoz Rivera y la juventud." RICP, No. 4 (1959), 49-50.

66.35 Morales Carrión, Arturo. "Muñoz Rivera: sentidor de lo puertorriqueño." In his Ojeada al proceso histórico y otros ensayos (SJ: Cordillera, 1971), pp. 97-107.

66.36 Rosa-Nieves, Cesáreo. "Luis Muñoz Rivera (1859-1916)." In his Plumas estelares en las letras de Puerto Rico (SJ: Ediciones de la Torre, Universidad de Puerto Rico, 1967), I, 363-87.

66.37 Ruiz García, Zoilo. "Luis Muñoz Rivera." In his Nuestros hombres de antaño (Mayagüez: Mayagüez Printing Co., 1920), pp. 94-98.

67

PADILLA, JOSÉ GUALBERTO (1829-1896)

Critical Monographs and Dissertations

67.1 Benítez Flores, Manuel. El Caribe. SJ: Cantero, Fernández, 1929.

Critical Essays

67.2 Angelis, Pedro de. "Historiando." In José Gualberto Padilla, and Manuel del Palacio, Para un palacio un Caribe (SJ: Prats, 1906), pp. 50-53. Also Guayama: L. Carminely, 1923. Also SJ: Correo Dominical, 1929.

67.3 "Apreciaciones y comentarios: la personalidad de 'El Caribe'." Indice, No. 4 (1929), 51-52.

67.4 "Biografía sintética: José Gualberto Padilla." Indice, No. 4 (1929), 50.

67.5 "Centenario de 'El Caribe' 1829-1929." Indice, No. 4 (1929), 49.

67.6 Coll y Toste, Cayetano. "...José Gualberto Padilla." BHPR, 6 (1919), 205-207.

67.7 ________. "José Gualberto Padilla." Asomante, 7, 1 (1951), 49-69.

67.8 ________. "Prólogo." In José Gualberto Padilla, Antología (SJ: Ateneo Puertorriqueño, 1961), pp. 5-11.

67.9 Fernández Juncos, Manuel. "José G. Padilla." In his Antología Puertorriqueña (NY: Hinds, Hayden & Eldredge, 1913), pp. 72-73. Various other editions.

67.10 ________. "José Gualberto Padilla (El Caribe)." In his Conferencias dominicales... (SJ: Biblioteca Insular de Puerto Rico, 1914), pp. 123-36.

67.11 ________. "Prólogo." In José Gualberto Padilla, En el combate: poesías completas (Paris: Paul Ollendorff, 1913?), pp. 15-32.

67.12 Hostos, Adolfo de. "José Gualberto Padilla (1829-1896)." In his Hombres representativos de Puerto Rico (SJ: Venezuela, 1961), pp. 100-106.

67.13 Matos Bernier, Félix. "José Gualberto Padilla." In his Muertos y vivos (SJ: El País, 1905), pp. 135-39.

67.14 ________. "Triángulo equilátero (Brau, Padilla, Valle)." In his Isla de arte (SJ: La Primavera, 1907), pp. 224-28.

67.15 Rosa-Nieves, Cesáreo. "José Gualberto Padilla (1829-1896; seud. El Caribe)." In his Plumas estelares en las letras de Puerto Rico (SJ: Ediciones de la Torre, Universidad de Puerto Rico, 1967), I, 403-19.

68

PALÉS MATOS, LUIS (1898-1959)

Bibliographies

68.1 "Bibliografía de Luis Palés Matos." La torre, Nos. 29-30 (1960), 331-36.

68.2 Puebla, Manuel de la. "Notas en torno a la bibliografía sobre Palés." Mairena, No. 1 (1979), 77-91.

68.3 Ward, James H. "Bibliografía de Luis Pales Matos." La torre, Nos. 79-80 (1973), 221-30.

Critical Monographs and Dissertations

68.4 Agrait, Gustavo. Luis Palés Matos, un poeta puertorriqueño. SJ: Biblioteca de Autores Puertorriqueños, 1973.

68.5 Bajeux, Jean-Claude. "Antilia retrouvée: la poésie noire antillaise à travers l'oeuvre de Claude McKay, Luis Palés Matos, Aimé Césaire." DAI, 38 (1977), 780A.

68.6 Blanco, Tomás. Sobre Palés Matos. SJ: Biblioteca de Autores Puertorriqueños, 1950.

68.7 Boulware-Miller, Patricia Kay. "Nature in three negrista poets: Nicolás Guillén, Emilio Ballagas and Luis Palés Matos." DAI, 39 (1978), 5186A-87A.

68.8 Cartey, Wilfred G. "Three Antillian poets: Emilio Ballagas, Luis Palés Matos, and Nicolás Guillén: literary development of the Negro theme in relation to the making of modern Afro-Antillian poetry and the historic evolution of the Negro." DA, 28 (1967), 2203A.

68.9 Clar, Raymond. "Lo antillano en la obra publicada e inédita de Luis Palés Matos: tema e imagen." DAI, 38 (1978), 5455A-56A.

68.10 Coin, Jeanette Bercovici. "Social aspects of black poetry in Luis Palés Matos, Nicolás Guillén and Manuel del Cabral." DAI, 37 (1976), 1581A.

68.11 Colorado, Antonio J. Luis Palés Matos, el hombre y el poeta. SJ: Rodadero, 1964.

68.12 Cruz de Rivera, Lydia. Obra de Luis Palés Matos. Unpublished Ph.D. dissertation, Universidad de Madrid, 1960. Abstract in RUMa, No. 40 (1961), 845-46.

68.13 Diego Padró, José Isaac de. Luis Palés Matos y su trasmundo poético. Río Piedras: Puerto, 1973.

68.14 Enguídanos, Miguel. La poesía de Luis Palés Matos. Río Piedras: Editorial Universitaria, Universidad de Puerto Rico, 1961.

68.15 González Maldonado, Edelmira. Presencia de la muerte en la poesía de Luis Palés Matos. SJ: Departamento de Instrucción Pública, División Editorial, 1972.

68.16 Onís, Federico de. Luis Palés Matos (1898-1959): vida y obra, bibliografía, antología, poesías inéditas. SJ: Ateneo Puertorriqueño, 1960.

68.17 ________. Luis Palés Matos: vida y obra, bibliografía, antología. Santa Clara, Cuba: Universidad Central de las Villas, Instituto de Estudios Hispánicos, 1959.

68.18 Romero de Laguerre, Luz Virginia. El aldeanismo en la poesía de Luis Palés Matos. Río Piedras?: Editorial Universitaria, Universidad de Puerto Rico, 1975.

68.19 Sáenz, Mercedes, and Iris Yolanda Reyes Benítez. Acercamiento a Luis Palés Matos y José de Diego. Río Piedras: Edil, 1976. Pertinent items are listed separately.

68.20 Torres, Lucy. "The black poetry of Luis Palés Matos and its sources." DAI, 31 (1970), 2405A.

68.21 Ward, James H. "The evolution of the thought and poetry of Luis Palés Matos as seen through a study of six themes." DA, 28 (1968), 2660A.

Critical Essays

68.22 Agrait, Gustavo. "Antilla, mujer y amor en la poesía de Luis Palés Matos." Río Piedras, No. 2 (1973), 41-69.

68.23 __________. "Una posible explicación del tema negro en la poesía de Palés Matos." RICP, No. 3 (1959), 39-41.

68.24 Aleixandre, Vicente. "Encuentro con Luis Palés Matos." IAL, No. 45 (1960), 4. Also La torre, Nos. 29-30 (1960), 147-50.

68.25 Anderson Imbert, Enrique. "Luis Pales Matos, desde la Argentina." Asomante, 15, 3 (1959), 39-40.

68.26 Arce de Vázquez, Margot. "Los adjetivos de la 'Danza negra' de Palés Matos." AtPR, 3 (1939), 147-62.

68.27 __________. "Evolución y unidad de la obra poética de Luis Palés Matos." In Luis Palés Matos, Poesía completa y prosa selecta (Caracas: Biblioteca Ayacucho, 1978), pp. ix-xxi.

68.28 __________. "Guayama en la poesía de Luis Palés Matos." RICP, No. 3 (1959), 36-38.

68.29 __________. "'Litoral' de Luis Palés Matos." Asomante, 25, 4 (1969), 9-19.

68.30 __________. "Luis Palés Matos, mago de la palabra." In her Impresiones (SJ: Yaurel, 1950), pp. 77-80.

68.31 __________. "Más sobre los poemas negros de Luis Palés Matos." AtPR, 2 (1936), 35-45. Also RBC, No. 38 (1936), 30-39.

68.32 __________. "Los poemas negros en Luis Palés Matos." AtPR, 1 (1935), 35-52. Also in her Impresiones (SJ: Yaurel, 1950), pp. 43-51.

68.33 __________. "La poesía negra de Guillén y Palés: coincidencias y discrepancias." Mairena, No. 1 (1979), 1-14.

68.34 __________. "Puerta al tiempo en tres voces de Luis Palés Matos." Río Piedras, No. 1 (1972), 9-30.

68.35 __________. "Rectificaciones (al artículos 'Los poemas negros de Luis Palés Matos')." In her Impresiones (SJ: Yaurel, 1950), pp. 53-59. See item no. 68.32.

68.36 __________. "Tres pueblos negros: algunas observaciones sobre el estilo de Luis Palés Matos." La torre, Nos. 29-30 (1960), 163-87.

68.37 __________. "Unidad de la obra poética de Luis Palés Matos." Asomante, 15, 3 (1959), 32-38.

68.38 Arrigoitia, Luis de. "Anotaciones métricas a Poesía (1915-1956) de Luis Palés Matos." Asomante, 25, 4 (1969), 71-84.

68.39 __________. "Cuatro poetas puertorriqueños: José de Diego, Luis Lloréns Torres, Luis Palés Matos, Juan Antonio Corretjer." Caravelle, 18 (1972), 59-76. Also in Instituto de Literatura Iberoamericana, La literatura de la emancipación hispanoamericana y otros ensayos (Lima: Universidad de San Marcos, 1972), pp. 173-78.

68.40 Babín, María Teresa. "Amor y patria en la poesía de Luis Palés Matos." Asomante, 15, 3 (1959), 67-78. Also in her Jornadas literarias (temas de Puerto Rico) (Barcelona: Rvmbos, 1967), pp. 102-16.

68.41 __________. "La búsqueda asesina: glosa a cinco poemas de amor de Luis Palés Matos." La torre, Nos. 29-30 (1960), 217-32. Also in her Jornadas literarias (temas de Puerto Rico) (Barcelona: Rvmbos, 1967), pp. 123-40.

68.42 __________. "Edgar Allan Poe y Palés Matos." In her Jornadas literarias (temas de Puerto Rico) (Barcelona: Rvmbos, 1967), pp. 117-22.

68.43 __________. "Transmutación poética de las influencias 'locales' en la lírica de Luis Palés Matos, Evarista Ribera Chevremont y Manuel Joglar Cacho." In Instituto Internacional de Literatura Iberoamericana, Literatura iberoamericana: influjos locales (M, 1965), pp. 27-33.

68.44 Barradas, Efraín. "José I. de Diego Padró y Luis Palés Matos: recuerdo de una amistad polémica." SinN, 6, 3 (1976), 41-45.

68.45 Barrera, Héctor. "Renovación poética de Luis Palés Matos." Asomante, 7, 2 (1951), 57-67.

68.46 Bayón, Damián Carlos. "Luis Palés Matos o la creación de un mundo a partir de la poesía." La torre, Nos. 29-30 (1960), 105-72.

68.47 Beauchamp, José Juan. "Cuestionario sobre Luis Palés Matos." Mairena, No. 1 (1979), 59-65.

68.48 Belaval, Emilio S. "Algunas topografías palesianas." Asomante, 15, 3 (1959), 41-50.

68.49 Bellini, Giuseppe. "Luis Palés Matos." In his Poeti antillani (Milano: Cisalpino, 1957), pp. 33-47.

68.50 ________. "Luis Palés Matos: intérprete del alma antillana." RICP, No. 38 (1968), 47-70. Also Asomante, 15, 3 (1959), 20-31.

68.51 Benítez, Jaime. "Homenaje a Palés. Introducción." La torre, Nos. 29-30 (1960), 13-21.

68.52 ________. "Luis Palés Matos y el pesimismo en Puerto Rico." RBC, No. 50 (1942), 388-407. Also in Antología del pensamiento puertorriqueño (1900-1970) (Río Piedras?: Editorial Universitaria, Universidad de Puerto Rico, 1975), pp. 547-64.

68.53 ________. "Luis Palés Matos y el pesimismo en Puerto Rico, doce años después." In Luis Palés Matos, Tuntún de pasa y grifería; nueva ed. (SJ: Biblioteca de Autores Puertorriqueños, 1950), pp. 9-37.

68.54 Bianco, José. "Palés Matos desde Buenos Aires." La torre, Nos. 29-30 (1960), 267-75.

68.55 Blanco, Tomás. "Una crítica al poeta Palés Matos." RBC, No. 38 (1936), 286-87.

68.56 ________. "Dos preguntas sobre la poesía de Palés Matos." CaribeSJ, 1, 2 (1941), 20-21.

68.57 ________. "Escorzos de un poeta antillano (Luis Palés Matos)." RBC, No. 42 (1938), 221-40.

68.58 ________. "Poesía y recitación negras." RBC, No. 38 (1936), 24-30. Also AtPR, 3 (1935), 302-309.

68.59 ________. "A Puerto Rican poet: Luis Palés Matos." AM, 21 (1930), 72-75.

68.60 ________. "Reincidencia y ratificación." RICP, No. 1 (1958), 35-37.

68.61 Blanco Lázaro, Enrique T. "El diepalismo de Luis Palés Matos." EstLit, No. 374 (1967), 10-11.

68.62 Braschi, Wilfredo. "Luis Palés Matos." In his Perfiles puertorriqueños (SJ: Biblioteca de Autores Puertorriqueños, 1978), pp. 5-7.

68.63 Camejo, Rafael W. "Luis Palés Matos." In his Florecían los rosales (Caracas: Hernández, 1952), pp. 190-96.

68.64 Campos, Jorge. "Palés Matos desde España: notas de una lectura homenaje." La torre, Nos. 29-30 (1960), 247-58.

68.65 Canino Salgado, Marcelino. "Tres versiones del poema 'San Sabás' de Luis Palés Matos." Mairena, No. 1 (1979), 15-34.

68.66 Cartey, Wilfred G. "Some aspects of the language of Luis Palés Matos." La voz, 3, 12 (1959), 8-9.

68.67 Castro de León, José M. "Tres etapas de la poesía de Luis Palés Matos." El cóndor, 2, 2 (1977), 60-67.

68.68 Corretjer, Juan Antonio. "Lo que no fue Palés." RICP, No. 2 (1959), 35.

68.69 Cuchí Coll, Isabel. "Luis Palés Matos." In her Oro nativo... (SJ: Venezuela, 1936), pp. 83-91.

68.70 Cumpiano, Elisa I. "El paisaje interior en la poesía de Luis Palés Matos." Mairena, No. 1 (1979), 51-58.

68.71 Curet de De Anda, Miriam. "Zoología en Palés." REH-PR, Nos. 1-4 (1972), 191-222.

68.72 Davis, Paul A. "The black man and the Caribbean as seen by Nicolás Guillén and Luis Palés Matos." CarQ, 25, 1-2 (1979), 72-79.

68.73 Davis, William Myron. "Animals in the Afro-Antillean poems of Luis Palés Matos." AION-SR, 10 (1968), 377-97.

68.74 Del Pozo, Ivania. "Language and silence in contemporary Spanish-American literature: as treated by the Puerto Rican poet, Luis Palés Matos." Centerpoint, 1, 1 (1974), 85-89.

68.75 __________. "Raíces modernistas en un texto en prosa de Luis Palés Matos: sobre 'El traje de Medea' (1927)." In José Olivio Jiménez, Estudios críticos sobre la prosa modernista hispanoamericana (NY: Eliseo Torres, 1975), pp. 293-303.

68.76 Díaz Quiñones, Arcadio. "Luis Palés Matos en la Biblioteca Ayacucho." SinN, 10, 2 (1979), 7-13. See item no. 68.27.

68.77 __________. "Notas para el estudio de Tuntún de pasa y grifería." Insula, Nos. 356-57 (1976), 4.

68.78 __________. "El Palés de Consuelo Gotay." SinN, 6, 4 (1976), 82-87.

68.79 __________. "La poesía negra de Luis Palés Matos." SinN, 1, 1 (1970), 7-25. Also CAm, No. 70 (1972), 84-93.

68.80 __________. "Testimonio autobiográfico de Luis Palés Matos." RICP, No. 26 (1965), 1-7. Also Isla, No. 10-12 (1971), 19-21.

68.81 Diego, Gerardo. "La palabra poética de Luis Palés Matos." La torre, Nos. 29-30 (1960), 81-94.

68.82 Diego Padró, José Isaac de. "Alfarero de la Groglia [fragmentos de la obra inédita, Luis Palés Matos y su trasmindo poético]." RICP, No. 45 (1969), 10-20.

68.83 Diez de Andino, Juan. "Poeta de noble y humana comprensión." Isla, Nos. 10-12 (1971), 18-21.

68.84 Domínguez, Ivo. "En torno a la poesía afro-hispanoamericana." CHA, No. 319 (1976), 125-31.

68.85 Doreste, Ventura. "El mundo poético de Palés Matos." La torre, Nos. 29-30 (1960), 67-79.

68.86 Enguídanos, Miguel. "El encuentro de Edgar Allan Poe y Luis Palés Matos." Insula, No. 170 (1962), 7. Also as "El encuentro de Edgar Allan Poe y Luis Palés Matos en la tierra de los sueños." In Instituto Internacional de Literatura Iberoamericana, Influencias extranjeras en la literatura iberoamericana y otros temas (M, 1963), pp. 67-74.

68.87 __________. "Lo que Palés Matos añadió a Puerto Rico." La torre, Nos. 29-30 (1960), 49-65.

68.88 __________. "Poesía como vida: Luis Palés Matos." PSA, No. 36 (1959), 241-78.

68.89 Figueira, Gastón. "Luis Palés Matos, poeta y artista." La torre, Nos. 29-30 (1960), 233-43.

68.90 Figueroa Berrios, Edwin. "Un poema de Luis Palés Matos: 'Mulata-Antilla'." RICP, No. 22 (1964), 24-27.

68.91 Florit, Eugenio. "El mar en los versos de Palés Matos." Asomante, 15, 3 (1959), 57-62.

68.92 __________. "Los versos de Palés Matos [Poesía, 1915-1956]." RHM, 24 (1958), 216-17.

68.93 González, José Emilio. "La individualidad poética de Luis Palés Matos." La torre, Nos. 29-30 (1960), 291-329.

68.94 __________. "El negro en la poesía de Luis Palés Matos." KRQ, 18 (1971), 37-63.

68.95 ________. "Tres danzas negras de Luis Palés Matos." Asomante, 25, 4 (1969), 20-33.

68.96 González-Cruz, Luis F. "Nature and the black reality in three Caribbean poets: a new look at the concept of negritude." PLL, 5 (1979), 138-40. Pales Matos inter alios.

68.97 Guereña, Jacinto Luis. "Circuito con Luis Palés Matos." La torre, No. 44 (1963), 151-59.

68.98 Gullón, Ricardo. "Situación de Palés Matos." La torre, Nos. 29-30 (1960), 35-46.

68.99 Henríquez Ureña, Max. "Recuerdos y apreciaciones en torno a Luis Palés Matos." La torre, Nos. 29-30 (1960), 129-43.

68.100 Hernández Novas, Raúl. "Luis Palés Matos: poeta antillano." CAm, No. 89 (1975), 28-37.

68.101 ________. "Prólogo." In Luis Palés Matos, Poesía (La Habana: Casa de las Américas, 1975), pp. vi-xxxi.

68.102 "Homenaje a Luis Palés Matos." RHM, 17 (1951), 373-76.

68.103 Isaza Calderón, Baltasar. "Una interpretación de Luis Palés Matos." RIB, 25 (1975), 285-91. See item no. 68.4.

68.104 Johnson, Lemuel. "El tema negro: the nature of primitivism in the poetry of Luis Palés Matos." In Miriam DeCosta, Blacks in Hispanic literature: critical essays (Port Washington, NY: Kennikat, 1977), pp. 123-36.

68.105 Labarthe, Pedro Juan. "La poesía afro-antillana: Luis Palés Matos." In Actas del Primer Congreso Internacional de Hispanistas (Oxford: Dolphin, 1964), pp. 335-41.

68.106 ________. "El tema negroide en la poesía de Luis Palés Matos." Hispania, 31 (1948), 30-42.

68.107 Lavandero, Ramón. "Luis Palés Matos y el negrismo poético antillano." AtPR, 2 (1936), 48-50.

68.108 ________. "Negrismo poético y Eusebia Cosme." RBC, No. 38 (1936), 39-45. Also AtPR, 2 (1936), 46-53.

68.109 Lloréns, Washington. "La jitanjáfora en Luis Palés Matos." AyL, No. 10 (1954), 3, 5.

68.110 Lluch Mora, Francisco. "Cuatro estudios del sentimiento religioso en la poesía de Luis Palés Matos." PLit, No. 25 (1966), 8-9, 14, 17-18. Also in his Miradero: ensayos de crítica literaria (SJ: Cordillera, 1966), pp. 111-31.

68.111 ________. "En la muerte de Luis Palés Matos." Asomante, 15, 3 (1959), 54-55.

68.112 Martínez Dávila, Manuel A. "Palabras prelimares." In Luis Palés Matos, Azaleas (Guayama: Rodríguez, 1951), pp. 5-8.

68.113 Matos Freire, Susana. "Luis Palés Matos, poeta del tedio." Mairena, No. 1 (1979), 67-76.

68.114 Matos Paoli, Francisco. "De poeta a poeta." Mairena, No. 1 (1979), 35-39.

68.115 Medina, José Ramón. "Luis Palés Matos en la poesía hispanoamericana." La torre, Nos. 29-30 (1960), 259-65.

68.116 Meléndez, Concha. "Alegorías de Luis Palés Matos." La torre, Nos. 29-30 (1960), 203-16. Also in her Obras completas (SJ: Instituto de Cultura Puertorriqueña, 1970-72), IV, 37-52. Also in her Poetas hispanoamericanos diversos (SJ: Cordillera, 1971), pp. 31-46.

68.117 __________. "Presencia jesucristiana en la poesía de Luis Palés Matos." Asomante, 15, 3 (1959), 63-66. Also in her Obras completas (SJ: Instituto de Cultura Puertorriqueña, 1970-72), IV, 53-59. Also in her Poetas hispanoamericanos diversos (SJ: Cordillera, 1971), pp. 47-53.

68.118 Morales, Angel Luis. "Julio Herrera Reissig y Luis Palés Matos." Asomante, 25, 4 (1969), 34-53. Also in Instituto Internacional de Literatura Iberoamericana, Literatura iberoamericana: influjos locales (M, 1961), pp. 85-95.

68.119 __________. "Puerta al tiempo en tres voces." RI, No. 44 (1957), 311-22. Also Mairena, No. 1 (1979), 41-49.

68.120 Morales Oliver, Luis. "Dos aspectos en la poesía de Luis Palés Matos." RICP, No. 33 (1966), 11-17.

68.121 Oliver Belmás, Antonio. "Luis Palés Matos y su 'Danza negra'." RICP, No. 38 (1968), 47-50.

68.122 Onís, Federico de. "Introducción." In Luis Palés Matos, Poesía (1915-1956) (Río Piedras: Ediciones de la Universidad de Puerto Rico, 1957), pp. 9-35.

68.123 __________. "Luis Palés Matos." In his España en América... (Río Piedras?: Ediciones de la Universidad de Puerto Rico, 1955), pp. 672-73. Also 1968.

68.124 __________. "Luis Palés Matos." Islas, 1, 3 (1959), 593-664.

68.125 __________. "Programa silvestre: reconstrucción de un tema de Luis Palés Matos." La torre, Nos. 29-30 (1960), 189-202.

68.126 __________. "El velorio que oyó Palés de niño en Guayama." RICP, No. 5 (1959), 15-19.

68.127 Ortiz, Fernando. "Tuntún de pasa y grifería. Poemas afroantillanos." EAF, 1, 1 (1937), 156-59.

68.128 Pérez Marchand, Monelisa L. "Luis Palés Matos, una conciencia lúdica." Asomante, 25, 4 (1969), 55-70.

68.129 Polit, Carlos E. "Imagen inocente del negro en cuatro poetas antillanos." SinN, 5, 2 (1974), 43-60. Palés Matos inter alios.

68.130 Putte, Igma van. "De 'Dreamland' de Poe a 'La tierra de los sueños' de Palés." Norte, 13, 3 (1972), 75-81.

68.131 Ramírez de Arellano, Diana. "'Majestad negra' de Luis Palés Matos." In Homenaje a Andrés Iduarte... (Clear Creek, IN: American Hispanist, 1976), pp. 301-10.

68.132 Reyes Benítez, Iris Yolanda. "Las Antillas en la poesía de Luis Palés Matos." In Mercedes Sáenz, and Iris Yolanda Reyes Benítez, Acercamiento a Luis Palés Matos..., q.v., pp. 27-50.

68.133 Rojas, Víctor J. "Sobre el negro en la poesía de Luis Palés Matos y de Jorge de Lima." SinN, 2, 3 (1972), 75-88.

68.134 Rosa-Nieves, Cesáreo. "Luis Palés Matos (1898-1959)." In his Plumas estelares en las letras de Puerto Rico (SJ: Ediciones de la Torre, Universidad de Puerto Rico, 1967), II, 301-17.

68.135 __________. "Luis Palés Matos: poeta del hastío, el pesimismo y la ironía." Prensa, 2a época, No. 8 (1959), 19-21. Also in his Ensayos escogidos... (SJ: Academia de Artes y Ciencias de Puerto Rico, 1970?), pp. 165-76.

68.136 Rosario, Charles. "Palés en su mundo." La torre, Nos. 29-30 (1960), 177-89.

68.137 Russell, Dora Isella. "Isla, trópico, negro y universo en la poesía de Luis Palés Matos." RICP, No. 2 (1963), 7-10.

68.138 __________. "La poesía de Luis Palés Matos." CCLC, No. 97 (1965), 81-84.

68.139 Sáenz, Mercedes. "Temas y estilo en algunos poemas de Palés." In Mercedes Sáenz, and Iris Yolanda Reyes Benítez, Acercamiento a Luis Palés Matos..., q.v., pp. 9-26.

68.140 Sanavía, Pietro. "La coscienza nel trópico." InventarioF, 18 (1963), 117-22.

68.141 Sánchez, Luis Alberto. "Luis Palés Matos." In his Escritores representativos de América; segunda serie; 2. ed. (Madrid: Gredos, 1972), III, 147-59.

68.142 Santos Silva, Loreina. "Poe y Palés." Atenea, 10, 3 (1973), 37-68.

68.143 Torre, Guillermo de. "La poesía negra de Luis Palés Matos." La torre, Nos. 29-30 (1960), 151-61. Also in his Tres conceptos de la literatura hispanoamericana (BA: Losada, 1963), pp. 179-89.

68.144 Valbuena Prat, Angel. "Sobre la poesía de Luis Palés Matos y los temas negros." La voz, 4, 5-6 (1959), 14-16. Also in Luis Palés Matos, Tuntún de pasa y grifería (SJ: Biblioteca de Autores Puertorriqueños, 1937), pp. 9-21. 2. ed., 1950.

68.145 Valdés-Cruz, Rosa E. "Luis Palés Matos." In her La poesía negroide en América (NY: Las Américas, 1970), pp. 133-49.

68.146 Vandercammen, Edmond. "La magia concreta en la obra de Luis Palés Matos." La torre, Nos. 29-30 (1960), 95-103.

68.147 Vientós Gastón, Nilita. "Una antología de Luis Palés Matos." In her Indice cultural (Río Piedras: Ediciones de la Universidad de Puerto Rico, 1962-71), II, 201-203.

68.148 __________. "Dedicación del homenaje." Asomante, 15, 3 (1959), 7-8.

68.149 __________. "Luis Palés Matos (1898-1959)." In her Indice cultural (Río Piedras: Ediciones de la Universidad de Puerto Rico, 1962-71), III, 25-26.

68.150 __________. "Poe y Palés Matos." In her Indice cultural (Río Piedras: Ediciones de la Universidad de Puerto Rico, 1962-71), IV, 33-34.

68.151 Williams, Eric. "Four poets of the greater Antilles." CarQ, 3, 4 (1951-52), 8-19. Palés Matos inter alios.

69

PEDREIRA, ANTONIO S. (1899-1939)

Critical Monographs and Dissertations

69.1 Barceló de Barasorda, María Angélica. Interpretación de Puerto Rico en la obra de Antonio S. Pedreira. Unpublished thesis, Universidad de Puerto Rico, 1957.

69.2 Flores, Juan. Insularismo e ideología burguesa. Río

Piedras: Huracán, 1979. Also La Habana: Casa de las Américas, 1979.

69.2 Maldonado Ortiz, Cándida. Antonio S. Pedreira: vida y obra. Río Piedras?: Editorial Universitaria, Universidad de Puerto Rico, 1974.

69.3 Sierra Berdecía, Fernando. Antonio S. Pedreira, buceador de la personalidad puertorriqueña; 2. ed. rev. SJ: Biblioteca de Autores Puertorriqueños, 1942.

Critical Essays

69.4 Agrait, Gustavo. "Semblanza de Antonio S. Pedreira." RICP, No. 16 (1962), 11-13.

69.5 ________. "Tres recuerdos y uno apócrifo de Antonio S. Pedreira." AtPR, 3, 3 (1939), 250-54.

69.6 "Antonio S. Pedreira. Notas biográficas." RAMG, 2, 2 (1940), 5-6.

69.7 "Apreciaciones y críticas. Antonio S. Pedreira y sus obras." RAMG, 2, 2 (1940), 15-16.

69.8 Arce de Vázquez, Margot. "Antonio S. Pedreira, hispanista." In her Impresiones (SJ: Yaurel, 1950), pp. 29-34.

69.10 ________. "Reflexiones en torno a Insularismo." In Antología del pensamiento puertorriqueño (1900-1970) (Río Piedras?: Editorial Universitaria, Universidad de Puerto Rico, 1975), pp. 622-33. Orig. RAMG, 5, 1 (1943), 20-26.

69.11 Babín, María Teresa. "Antonio S. Pedreira, maestro de juventudes." RAMG, 2, 2 (1940), 25.

69.12 Barceló, Puruca. "Don Antonio, maestro de la juventud." RAMG, 2, 2 (1940), 9-10.

69.13 Barceló de Barasorda, María A. "Definición y afirmación de lo puertorriqueño en la obra de Antonio S. Pedreira." RICP, No. 14 (1962), 6-9.

69.14 ________. "Prólogo [a Insularismo]." In Antonio S, Pedreira, Obras completas (SJ: Instituto de Cultura Puertorriqueña, 1970), I, 15-22. Orig. in Antonio S. Pedreira, Insularismo; ensayos de interpretación puertorriqueña (SJ: Edil, 1968), pp. 7-13.

69.15 Belaval, Emilio S. "Pedreira, un promotor de la cultura de su país." AtPR, 3, 3 (1939), 222-36. Also in Antología del pensamiento puertorriqueño (1900-1970) (Río Piedras?: Editorial Universitaria, Universidad de Puerto Rico, 1975), I, 611-21.

69.16 Bosch, Juan. "Duelo en las islas." AtPR, 3, 3 (1939), 240-42.

69.17 Braschi, Wilfredo "Antonio S. Pedreira." In his Perfiles puertorriqueños (SJ: Biblioteca de Autores Puertorriqueños, 1978), pp. 54-56.

69.18 Cuchí Coll, Isabel. "Antonio S. Pedreira." In her Oro nativo... (SJ, 1936), pp. 65-72.

69.19 Dávila, José Antonio. "Aclaraciones y crítica de Antonio S. Pedreira." In his Prosa: ensayos, artículos y cartas literarias (SJ: Sociedad de Autores Puertorriqueños, 1971), pp. 123-26.

69.20 ________. "Pedreira y la ironía." AtPR, 3, 3 (1939), 243-47. Also in his Prosa: ensayos, artículos y cartas literarias (SJ: Sociedad de Autores Puertorriqueños, 1971), pp. 127-30.

69.21 Ferrer Canales, José. "Discurso por Pedreira." In his Acentos cívicos... (Río Piedras: Edil, 1972), pp. 139-55.

69.22 Franco Oppenheimer, Félix. "Antonio S. Pedreira: un hombre de Puerto Rico." In his Contornos... (SJ: Yaurel, 1960), pp. 51-67.

69.23 Gallardo, José M. "Antonio S. Pedreira, un hombre y un nombre." AtPR, 3, 3 (1939), 256-59.

69.24 Géigel Polanco, Vicente. "Antonio S. Pedreira." In his Valores de Puerto Rico (NY: Arno Press, 1975), pp. 111-17. Orig. SJ: Eugenio María de Hostos, 1943.

69.25 ________. "Homenaje del Ateneo al doctor Antonio S. Pedreira." AtPR, 3, 3 (1939), 203-208.

69.26 Grismer, Raymond Leonard, and César Arroyo. "Antonio S. Pedreira." In their Vida y obras de autores puertorriqueños (La Habana: "Alfa", 1941-), I, 11-14. Also Ann Arbor: University Microfilms, 1976. Also 1978. Only vol. I ever published.

69.27 Hostos, Adolfo de. "Pedreira, hostiano." AtPR, 3, 3 (1939), 262-78.

69.28 Isales, Carmen. "Problemas sociales en La charca, La llamarada e Insularismo." RSS, 1, 2 (1939), 16-17.

69.29 Lluch Mora, Francisco. "Sobre Antonio S. Pedreira." In his Miradero: ensayos de crítica literaria (SJ: Cordillera, 1966), pp. 51-54.

69.30 Labarthe, Pedro Juan. "Pedreira, el amigo, el maestro, el animador." AtPR, 3, 3 (1939), 288-92.

69.31 Maldonado-Denis, Manuel. "Visión y revisión de _Insularismo_." _Asomante_, 19, 1 (1963), 7-18.

69.32 Meléndez, Concha. "Antonio S. Pedreira." _RAm_, 27 (1940), 200, 202.

69.33 __________. "Antonio S. Pedreira: vida y expresión." _AtPR_, 3, 3 (1939), 216-21. Also in her _Asomante_ (SJ: Cordillera, 1970), pp. 47-52. Orig. SJ: Universidad de Puerto Rico, 1943. Also in her _Obras completas_ (SJ: Instituto de Cultura Puertorriqueña, 1970-72), II, 47-52.

69.34 __________. "Pedreira: autorretrato en su autocrítica." In her _Figuración de Puerto Rico y otros estudios_ (SJ: Instituto de Cultura Puertorriqueña, 1958), pp. 29-33. Also in her _Obras completas_ (SJ: Instituto de Cultura Puertorriqueña, 1970-72), II, 357-62. Also in Antonio S. Pedreira, _Tres ensayos_ (Río Piedras: Edil, 1969), pp. 7-12. Also in Antonio S. Pedreira, _El año terrible del 87, sus antecedentes y sus consecuencias_ (SJ: Edil, 1968), pp. 7-12. Also in Antonio S. Pedreira, _Hostos, ciudadano de América_ (SJ: Edil, 1968), pp. 7-12.

69.35 __________. "Pedreira: discurso a la juventud." In her _Figuración de Puerto Rico y otros ensayos_ (SJ: Instituto de Cultura Puertorriqueña, 1958), pp. 35-38. Also in her _Obras completas_ (SJ: Instituto de Cultura Puertorriquela, 1970-72), II, 363-66.

69.36 __________. "Prólogo." In Antonio S. Pedreira, _Aclaraciones y crítica_ (Río Piedras: Phi Eta Mu, Universidad de Puerto Rico, 1941), pp. 9-12. Also Río Piedras: Edil, 1969. Also in Antonio S. Pedreira, _Obras completas_ (SJ: Instituto de Cultura Puertorriqueña, 1970), I, 453-55.

69.37 __________. "Prólogo a las obras de Antonio S. Pedreira." In Antonio S. Pedreira, _Obras completas_ (SJ: Instituto de Cultura Puertorriqueña, 1970), I, 5-12.

69.38 __________. "Recordación de Pedreira." In her _Palabras para oyentes_ (SJ: Cordillera, 1971), pp. 21-31.

69.39 Osuna, J. J. "Antonio S. Pedreira, una apreciación personal." _AtPR_, 3, 3 (1939), 260-61.

69.40 Pasarell, Emilio J. "La bibliografía de Pedreira." In his _Ensayos y artículos_ (SJ: Cordillera, 1969), pp. 179-81. See item no. A.19.

69.41 Pedeira, Antonio S. "_Insularismo_." In his _Obras completas_ (SJ: Instituto de Cultura Puertorriqueña, 1970), I, 579-82.

69.42 Picó, Rafael. "El hombre y el medio de dos obras puertorriqueñas [_Insularismo_ y _La llamarada_]." _CaribeSJ_, 1, 1 (1941), 33-35, 43.

69.43 Quiñones, Samuel R. "Filiación de Antonio S. Pedreira." AtPR, 3, 3 (1939), 209-15. Also in his Temas y letras; 3. ed. (SJ: Biblioteca de Autores Puertorriqueños, 1955), pp. 51-59. Also RICP, No. 71 (1976), 7-9.

69.44 Rodríguez Demorizi, Emilio. "Antonio S. Pedreira." AtPR, 3, 3 (1939), 248-49.

69.45 Rodríguez López, Josefina. "Valor puertorriqueño de la obra de Pedreira." Isla, 2, 1 (1940), 4-6. Also in Antología del pensamiento puertorriqueño (1900-1970) (Río Piedras?: Editorial Universitaria, Universidad de Puerto Rico, 1975), pp. 607-10. Also RAMG, 2, 2 (1940), 7-8, 26.

69.46 Rosa-Nieves, Cesáreo. "Antonio S. Pedreira (seud. Assur Bani Pal: 1899-1939)." In his Plumas estelares en las letras de Puerto Rico (SJ: Ediciones de la Torre, Universidad de Puerto Rico, 1967), II, 341-60.

69.47 Sierra Berdecía, Fernando. "Antonio S. Pedreira: buceador de la personalidad puertorriqueña." In Antología del pensamiento puertorriqueño (1900-1970) (Río Piedras?: Editorial Universitaria, Universidad de Puerto Rico, 1975), pp. 597-606. Same as item no. 69.3.

69.48 Silva, Ana Margarita. "Antonio S. Pedreira, mi amigo y maestro." RAMG, 2, 2 (1940), 11.

69.49 Soto Ramos, Julio. "Antonio S. Pedreira." In his Una pica en Flandes... (SJ: Club de la Prensa, 1959), pp. 183-88.

69.50 Toro Cuebas, Emilio del. "Pedreira y la universidad." AtPR, 3, 3 (1939), 255.

69.51 Vientós Gastón, Nilita. "Insularismo." RAMG, 2, 2 (1940), 17.

69.52 Villaronga, Luis. "Pedreira es de la estirpe de los Hostos, Martí y Rodó." AtPR, 3, 3 (1939), 279-84.

69.53 Vizcarrondo, Carmelina. "Notas sobre Insularismo." AtPR, 3, 3 (1939), 285-87.

70

PÉREZ PIERRET, ANTONIO (1885-1937)

Critical Monographs and Dissertations

70.1 Feliciano de Mendoza, Ester. *Antonio Pérez Pierret: vida y obra*. SJ: Coquí, 1968. Orig. an unpublished thesis, Universidad de Puerto Rico, 1960.

Critical Essays

70.2 Diez de Andino, Juan. "Recordando al poeta." In his *Voces de la farándula* (Barcelona: Rvmbos, 1959), pp. 89-92.

70.3 Ferrer, Rafael. "Antonio Pérez-Pierret." In his *Lienzos* (SJ, 1965), pp. 109-11.

70.4 ________. "Perfiles: Antonio Pérez Pierret." *RAnt*, 2, 6 (1914), 65-67.

70.5 Franco Oppenheimer, Félix. "Bronces líricos en la poesía de Antonio Pérez Pierret." In Antonio Pérez Pierret, *Antología* (SJ: Ateneo Puertorriqueño, 1914), pp. ix-xxiv. Also 1959; pp. 7-16. Also in his *Contornos* (SJ: Yaurel, 1960), pp. 69-78.

70.6 Guerrera Mondragón, Miguel. "El poeta." In Antonio Pérez Pierret, *Bronces* (SJ: Antillana, 1914), pp. ix-xxiv.

70.7 ________. "El poeta. Antonio Pérez Pierret." *Asomante*, 8, 3 (1952), 53-64.

70.8 Medrano, Higinio J. "*Bronces*. Crítica sobre un libro de versos de Antonio Pérez-Pierret." *RAnt*, 2, 8 (1914), 47-49.

70.9 Nolasco, Sócrates. "Antonio Pérez Pierret, Canales y el equilibrio en el arte." In his *Escritores de Puerto Rico* (Manzanillo, Cuba: "El Arte", 1953), pp. 25-43.

70.10 Rosa-Nieves, Cesáreo. "Antonio Pérez-Pierret (1885-1937)." In his *Plumas estelares en las letras de Puerto Rico* (SJ: Ediciones de la Torre, Universidad de Puerto Rico, 1967), II, 99-107.

71

RIBERA CHEVREMONT, EVARISTO (1896-)

Critical Monographs and Dissertations

71.1 Gallego Otero, Laura. Las ideas literarias de Evaristo Ribera Chevremont. Unpublished thesis, Universidad de Puerto Rico, 1962.

71.2 Meléndez, Concha. La inquietud sosegada; poética de Evaristo Ribera Chevremont. SJ: Junta Editora, Universidad de Puerto Rico, 1946. Also SJ: Biblioteca de Autores Puertorriqueños, 1956. Also as La inquietud sosegada. SJ: Cordillera, 1970. Same as item no. 71.33.

71.3 Ribera Chevremont, Evaristo. La naturaleza en Color. SJ: Venezuela, 1943. Same as item no. 71.43.

Critical Essays

71.4 Albornoz, Aurora de. "El canto logrado: poesía y madurez de Evaristo Ribera Chevremont." In Evaristo Ribera Chevremont, Punto final (SJ: Venezuela, 1963), pp. 91-96. Orig. as "El canto logrado (poesía de madurez de Evaristo Ribera Chevremont." La torre, No. 37 (1962), 131-38.

71.5 "Algunas opiniones sobre la obra poética de Evaristo Ribera Chevremont." BAAC, 4, 1 (1968), 51-58.

71.6 Arroyo, Anita. "Prólogo: cantor de Puerto Rico." In Evaristo Ribera Chevremont, Canto de mi tierra (Río Piedras: Editorial Universitaria, Universidad de Puerto Rico, 1971), pp. 5-16.

71.7 __________. "Puerto Rico en su poesía. Evaristo Ribera Chevremont y el color loval." RICP, No. 44 (1969), 1-3.

71.8 Babín, María Teresa. "Evaristo Ribera Chevremont." RevL, 1 (1969), 36-40.

71.9 __________. "Evaristo Ribera Chevremont y sus 'Siete sonetos sanjuaneros' o 'Arcoiris de poniente y noche'." Mairena, No. 4 (1980), 35-40.

71.10 __________. "Transmutación poética de las influencias 'locales' en la lírica de Luis Palés Matos, Evaristo Ribera Chevremont y Manuel Joglar Cacho." In Instituto Internacional de Literatura Iberoamericana, Literatura iberoamericana: influjos locales (M, 1965), pp. 27-33.

71.11 Braschi, Wilfredo. "Don Evaristo: poeta integral." Mairena, No. 4 (1980), 44-45.

71.12 __________. Evaristo Ribera Chevremont." In his *Perfiles puertorriqueños* (SJ: Biblioteca de Autores Puertorriqueños, 1978), pp. 35-38.

71.13 Buñuel, Miguel. "Evaristo Ribera Chevremont." *IndiceM*, Nos. 100-101 (1957), 20-21.

71.14 Cabañas, Pablo. "La poesía de Evaristo Ribera Chevremont." In Evaristo Ribera Chevremont, *Memorial de arena* (SJ: Venezuela, 1962), pp. 65-69.

71.15 __________. "La poesía de Ribera Chevremont." *CLit*, Nos. 10-12 (1948), 231-36.

71.16 __________. "Presentación." In Evaristo Ribera Chevremont, *La llama pensativa* (Madrid: Cultura Hispánica, 1955), pp. 5-10.

71.17 Camejo, Rafael W. "Evaristo Ribera Chevremont." In his *Florecían los rosales* (Caracas: Hernández, 1952), pp. 245-54.

71.18 Canino Salgado, Marcelino. "Los 'Tres sonetos a la muerte' de Evaristo Ribera Chevremont." *Mairena*, No. 4 (1980), 29-34.

71.19 Castro, Tomás de Jesús. "Evaristo Ribera Chevremont." In his *Esbozos críticos* (SJ: Baldrich, 1945), pp. 64-66.

71.20 Dávila, José Antonio. "*Color* de Ribera Chevremont." In his *Prosa: ensayos, artículos y cartas literarias* (SJ: Sociedad de Autores Puertorriqueños, 1971), pp. 149-53. See also "Carta," pp. 259-60.

71.21 Fernández Gill, Alicia. "Ribera Chevremont ante la crítica." *Mairena*, No. 4 (1980), 81-99.

71.22 Ferrer, Rafael. "Evaristo Ribera Chevremont." In his *Lienzos* (SJ, 1965), pp. 217-21.

71.23 Gallego, Laura. "El concepto de poeta y de poesía en Ribera Chevremont." *Mairena*, No. 4 (1980), 71-79.

71.24 Géigel Polanco, Vicente. "Evaristo Ribera Chevremont." In his *Valores de Puerto Rico* (NY: Arno Press, 1975), pp. 139-51. Orig. SJ: Eugenio María de Hostos, 1943.

71.25 González, José Emilio. "Espiritualidad religiosa y arte en *El semblante*, de Evaristo Ribera Chevremont." *La torre*, No. 60 (1968), 143-96.

71.26 __________. "El mar de Puerto Rico en la poesía de Evaristo Ribera Chevremont." *RICP*, No. 25 (1964), 47-51.

71.27 __________. "La personalidad y la obra de Evaristo Ribera Chevremont." *Mairena*, No. 4 (1980), 5-12.

71.28 Hernández Aquino, Luis. "Evaristo Ribera Chevremont y su paso por el vanguardismo." Mairena, No. 4 (1980), 65-70.

71.29 Marxuach, Carmen Irene. "Vicente Huidobro y Evaristo Ribera Chevremont." Mairena, No. 4 (1980), 13-24.

71.30 Matos Paoli, Francisco. "Evaristo Ribera Chevremont y su poesía." ILit, 3a época, Nos. 2-3 (1969), 47-48.

71.31 _________. "Memorial de arena." In Evaristo Ribera Chevremont, Punto final (SJ: Venezuela, 1963), pp. 111-13.

71.32 Meléndez, Concha. "El hondero lanzó la piedra." In Evaristo Ribera Chevremont, El hondero lanzó la piedra (SJ: Cordillera, 1975), pp. v-xii.

71.33 _________. "La inquietud sosegado: poética de Evaristo Ribera Chevremont." In her Obras completas (SJ: Instituto de Cultura Puertorriqueña, 1970-72), II, 175-316. Same as item no. 71.2.

71.34 _________. "Prólogo: universo del canto: regreso a la poesía de Evaristo Ribera Chevremont." In Evaristo Ribera Chevremont, El semblante (Río Piedras: Editorial Universitaria, 1964), pp. 7-33.

71.35 _________. "Río volcado: segunda consideración." La torre, No. 61 (1968), 150-61. Also as "Río volcado: segunda contemplación." In Evaristo Ribera Chevremont, Río volcado (SJ: Universitaria, 1968), pp. 5-12.

71.36 _________. "Universo del canto: regreso a la poesía de Evaristo Ribera Chevremont." RICP, No. 15 (1962), 5-12.

71.37 Miranda, Luis Antonio. "Del poeta y su obra." In Evaristo Ribera Chevremont, Nueva antología (SJ: Cordillera, 1966), pp. 7-19.

71.38 Neggers, Gladys. "Clara Lair y Julia de Burgos: reminiscencias de Evaristo Ribera Chevremont y Jorge Font Saldaña." RevI, 4 (1974), 258-63.

71.39 Negrón Fernández, Luis. "Premio Nobel de literatura para Evaristo Rivera [sic] Chevremont." ILit, 3a época, No. 1 (1969), 35.

71.40 Onís, Federico. "Introducción." In Evaristo Ribera Chevremont, Antología poética (1924-1950) (Río Piedras: Ediciones "La Torre", 1957), pp. 7-27.

71.41 Pedreira, Antonio S. "Lámpara azul." In his Aclaraciones y crítica (Río Piedras: Phi Eta Mu, Universidad de Puerto Rico, 1941), pp. 77-83. Also Río Piedras: Edil, 1969. Also in his Obras completas (SJ: Instituto de Cultura Puertorriqueña, 1970), I, 509-13.

71.42 Puebla, Manuel de la. "Tiempo y creación: cronología de un poeta." Mairena, No. 4 (1980), 47-63.

71.43 Ribera Chevremont, Evaristo. "La naturaleza en Color." BAAC, 11, 3 (1975), 5-32. Same as item no. 71.3.

71.44 Rivera Alvarez, Josefina. "Evaristo Ribera Chevremont." RICP, No. 71 (1976), 16-22.

71.45 Rivera Santiago, Rafael. "Un poeta de raza." In his Comprensión y análisis (SJ: Venezuela, 1938), pp. 70-76.

71.46 Rosa-Nieves, Cesáreo. "Evaristo Ribera Chevremont (1896-)." In his Plumas estelares en las letras de Puerto Rico (SJ: Ediciones de la Torre, Universidad de Puerto Rico, 1967), II, 245-63.

71.47 Russell, Dora Isella. "El permanente diálogo de Evaristo Ribera Chevremont con la poesía." In Evaristo Ribera Chevremont, Memorial de arena (SJ: Venezuela, 1962), pp. 70-73. Orig. RICP, No. 13 (1951), 9-11. Also as "El permanente diálogo. Ribera Chevremont y la poesía." PLit. 3, 9 (1965), 8-9.

71.48 Soto Ramos, Julio. "Antología poética de E. Ribera Chevremont." In his Una pica en Flandes... (SJ: Club de la Prensa, 1959), pp. 73-77.

72

RODRÍGUEZ DE TIÓ, LOLA (1843-1924)

Critical Monographs and Dissertations

72.1 Cuevas, Carmen Leila. Lola de América. Hato Rey: Ramallo, 1969.

Critical Essays

72.2 Acosta, Cecilio. "Juicio sobre la oda de la señora Lola Rodríguez de Tió, intitulada 'La vuelta del pastor'." In Lola Rodríguez de Tió, Claros y nieblas (Mayagüez: Tipografía Comercial, 1885), pp. 321-29.

72.3 Algarín Feliciano, Luz María. "Lola Rodríguez de Tió. Su personalidad y su obra." Asomante, 4, 3 (1948), 48-53. Also RBC, No. 42 (1948), 244-50.

72.4 Angelis, María Luisa de. "Lola Rodríguez de Tió." In her _Mujeres puertorriqueñas que se han distinguido en el cultivo de las ciencias, las letras y las artes desde el siglo XVII hasta nuestros días_ (SJ: Boletín Mercantil, 1908), pp. 71-81.

72.5 Carreras, Carlos N. "Lola Rodríguez de Tió." In his _Hombras y mujeres de Puerto Rico_ (M: Orión, 1974), pp. 53-67. Orig. 1957. Various other editions.

72.6 Cuevas, Carmen Leila. "Lola Rodríguez de Tió: la primera puertorriqueña liberada." _Ceiba_, 3, 6 (1975), 43-63.

72.7 Fernández Juncos, Manuel. "Lola Rodríguez de Tió." _Las Antillas_, 3, 2 (1921), 134.

72.8 Meléndez, Concha. "Nuevo vendor florece." _La torre_, No. 8 (1954), 55-79. Also as "Nuevo vendor florece: homenaje a Lola Rodríguez de Tió." In her _Figuración de Puerto Rico y otros ensayos_ (SJ: Instituto de Cultura Puertorriqueña, 1958), pp. 7-28. Also in her _Obras completas_ (SJ: Instituto de Cultura Puertorriqueña, 1970-72), II, 331-56.

72.9 Negrón Muñoz, Angela. "Lola Rodríguez de Tió." In her _Mujeres de Puerto Rico_ (SJ: Venezuela, 1935), pp. 67-79.

72.10 Peñaranda, Carlos. "Prólogo." In Lola Rodríguez de Tió, _Claros y nieblas_ (Mayagüez: Tipografía Comercial, 1885), pp. ix-xxix.

72.11 Romeu, José A. "Lola Rodríguez de Tió: conciencia contra la tiranía." In Martín Guadier, _La borinqueña_ (Barcelona: Rumbos, 1959), pp. 9-12.

72.12 Rosa-Nieves, Cesáreo. "Lola Rodríguez de Tió (1843-1924)." In his _Plumas estelares en las letras de Puerto Rico_ (SJ: Ediciones de la Torre, Universidad de Puerto Rico, 1967), I, 169-84.

72.13 __________. "Lola Rodríguez de Tió (1843-1924)." In his _Ensayos escogidos_... (SJ: Academia de Artes y Ciencias de Puerto Rico, 1970?), pp. 67-91.

72.14 Ruiz Orozco, Pablo. "Loal Rodríguez de Tió: discurso de ingreso a la Academia de Artes y Ciencias de Puerto Rico." _BAAC_, 14, 3-4 (1978), 95-110. See item no. 71.16.

72.15 Sánchez, Luis Alberto. "Prólogo." In Ricardo Palma, _Diecisiete cartas inéditas con otras éditas cambiadas con doña Lola Rodríguez de Tió (1894-1907)_ (Lima: Universidad Nacional Mayor de San Marcos, 1968), pp. 5-16.

72.16 Tió, Aurelio. "Contestación al discurso del dr. Pablo Ruiz Orozco." _BAAC_, 14, 3-4 (1978), 111-18. See item no. 71.14.

72.17 ________. "Juicios sobre la obra de Lola Rodríguez de Tió." BAAC, 2, 1 (1966), 97-114.

72.18 ________. "Prólogo." In Lola Rodríguez de Tió, Obras completas (SJ: Instituto de Cultura Puertorriqueña, 1968-), I, v-xxxii.

72.19 ________. "Semblanza de Lola Rodríguez de Tió." BAPH, 2, 7 (1971), 99-119.

73

ROSA-NIEVES, CESÁREO (1901-1974)

Critical Monographs and Dissertations

73.1 Figueroa de Cifredo, Patria. Apuntes biográficos en torno a la vida y obra de Cesáreo Rosa-Nieves. SJ: Cordillera, 1965.

73.2 ________. Nuevo encuentro con la estética de Rosa-Nieves. SJ, 1969.

Critical Essays

73.3 Castro, Tomás de Jesús. "Cesáreo Rosa-Nieves." In his Esbozos críticos (SJ: Baldrich, 1945), pp. 113-24.

73.4 Colberg Petrovich, Enrique. "Cesáreo Rosa-Nieves: ideal paradigma." In his Cuatro autores clásicos contemporáneos de Puerto Rico (SJ: Cordillera, 1966), pp. 213-53.

73.5 Dávila, José Antonio. "A Cesáreo Rosa-Nieves." In his Prosa: ensayos, artículos y cartas literarias (SJ: Sociedad de Autores Puertorriqueños, 1971), p. 265.

73.6 Ferrer Canales, José. "Cesáreo Rosa-Nieves." In his Marginalia (SJ: Venezuela?, 1939), pp. 129-31.

73.7 Figueroa de Cifredo, Patria. "Cesáreo Rosa-Nieves." In Escritores contemporáneos de Puerto Rico (SJ: Sociedad de Autores Puertorriqueños, 1978), pp. 47-57.

73.8 ________. "El universo estético de Cesáreo Rosa-Nieves." RICP, No. 33 (1966), 3-6.

73.9 Franco Oppenheimer, Félix. "Conversando con el Dr. Cesáreo Rosa-Nieves." In his Contornos (SJ: Yaurel, 1960), pp. 91-98.

73.10 __________. "Prólogo: una novela de sabor puertorriqueño." In Cesáreo Rosa-Nieves, El mar bajo de la montaña; relato de una mujer sin historia (SJ: Yaurel, 1963), pp. 7-10.

73.11 Grismer, Raymond Leonard, and César Arroyo. "Cesáreo Rosa Nieves." In their Vida y obras de autores puertorriqueños (La Habana: "Alfa", 1941-), I, 18-19. Also Ann Arbor: University Microfilms, 1976. Also 1978. Only vol. I ever published.

73.12 Lluch Mora, Francisco. "Jurisdicción de los hibiscos y Diapasón negro de Cesáreo Rosa-Nieves." In his Miradero... (SJ: Cordillera, 1966), pp. 209-23.

73.13 __________. "Palabras sobre dos libros de Cesáreo Rosa-Nieves." In Cesáreo Rosa-Nieves, Diapasón negro (SJ: Campos, 1960), pp. 75-85.

73.14 Losada, Ana María. "Prólogo." In Cesáreo Rosa-Nieves, Siete caminos en luna de sueños (SJ: Biblioteca de Autores Puertorriqueños, 1957), pp. iii-x.

73.15 Martín, José Luis. "Acercándonos al libro de ensayos La lámpara del faro (variaciones críticas sobre temas puertorriqueños) tomo I, del Dr. Cesáreo Rosa-Nieves." Prensa, 2a época, No. 9 (1959), 19.

73.16 __________. "Cesáreo Rosa-Nieves y su Antología poética puertorriqueña." In his Arco y flecha... (SJ: Club de la Prensa, 1961), pp. 85-95.

73.17 Rodríguez Escudero, Néstor A. "El proletarismo en la poesía de Cesáreo Rosa-Nieves." In his El mar en la literatura puertorriqueña... (Barcelona: Rumbos, 1967), pp. 101-11.

73.18 Soto Ramos, Julio. "Historia panorámica de la literatura puertorriqueña." In his Yo soy yo y mi verdad... (SJ: Cordillera, 1973), pp. 31-48.

73.19 __________. "Poética ensueñista; ¡Borinquen!" In his Una pica en Flandes... (SJ: Club de la Prensa, 1959), pp. 83-87.

74

SÁEZ, ANTONIA (1889-1964)

Critical Essays

74.1 Acevedo, Herminia. "[La lectura, arte del lenguaje]." Asomante, 4, 4 (1948), 81.

74.2 Arce de Vázquez, Margot. "La lectura, arte del lenguaje." Educación, 9, 1 (1961), 87-89. Also La torre, No. 37 (1962), 197-99.

74.3 ________. "La salvación por el lenguaje." In her Impresiones; notas puertorriqueñas... (SJ: Yaurel, 1950), pp. 145-48.

74.4 Arriví, Francisco. "Cita y glosa de sus recuerdos, doña Antonia Sáez, ceiba." Educación, 15, 16 (1965), 66-81.

74.5 ________. "Doña Antonia Sáez, ceiba (1889-1964)." RICP, No. 25 (1964), 11-19.

74.6 Belaval, Emilio S. "El teatro en Puerto Rico, de Antonia Sáez." In his Areyto (SJ: Biblioteca de Autores Puertorriqueños, 1948), pp. 39-51.

74.7 Braschi, Wilfredo. "Antonia Sáez." In her Perfiles puertorriqueños (SJ: Biblioteca de Autores Puertorriqueños, 1978), pp. 66-68.

74.8 Córdova de Braschi, Julia. "Antonia Sáez: razón y sentido de una vocación." RICP, No. 6 (1960), 15-16.

74.9 ________. "Las artes del lenguaje en la escuela elemental." Asomante, 1, 2 (1945), 93-94.

74.10 ________. "[La lectura, arte del lenguaje]." Asomante, 5, 1 (1949), 91-93.

74.11 ________. "[El teatro en Puerto Rico]." Asomante, 6, 2 (1950), 97-99.

74.12 Ferrer Canales, José. "Voz de doña Antonia Sáez." In his Acentos cívicos... (Río Piedras: Edil, 1972), pp. 131-37.

74.13 Figueroa de Cifredo, Patria. "Presencia de tres mujeres en la investigación en Puerto Rico." BAAC, 14, 3-4 (1978), 121-39. Sáez inter alias.

74.14 Gallego, Laura. "Antonia Sáez, voluntad y carácter." Educación, 15, 16 (1965), 63-64.

74.15 Meléndez, Concha. "Memorias de Antonia Sáez." RICP, No. 25 (1964), 1-3. Also in her Personas y libros (SJ: Cordillera, 1970), pp. 89-95. Also in her Obras completas (SJ:

Instituto de Cultura Puertorriqueña, 1970-72), IV, 311-17. Also in Antonia Sáez, Caminos del recuerdo (SJ: Instituto de Cultura Puertorriqueña, 1967), pp. 7-14.

74.16 Negrón Muñoz, Angela. "Antonia Sáez." In her Mujeres de Puerto Rico (SJ: Venezuela, 1935), pp. 218-19.

75

SÁNCHEZ, LUIS RAFAEL (1936-)

Bibliographies

75.1 Hernández Vargas, Nélida. "Luis Rafael Sánchez: guía bibliográfica." REH-PR, 5 (1978), 167-96.

Critical Monographs and Dissertations

75.2 Waldman, Gloria Feiman. "Luis Rafael Sánchez and the new Latin American theater." DAI, 39 (1979), 6154A-55A.

Critical Essays

75.3 Arrigoitia, Luis de. "Una novela escrita en puertorriqueño: La guaracha del Macho Camacho de Luis Rafael Sánchez." REH-PR, 5 (1978), 71-89.

75.4 Arce de Vázquez, Margot. "Acotaciones a una lectura de La guaracha del Macho Camacho." RPIS, 1, 2 (1977), 18-25.

75.5 Barradas, Efraín. "[La guaracha del Macho Camacho]." RI, Nos. 102-103 (1978), 231-34.

75.6 __________. "La pasión según Antígona Pérez: mito latinoamericano y realidad puertorriqueña." SinN, 10, 1 (1979), 10-22.

75.7 Beauchamp, José Juan. "La guaracha del Macho Camacho: lectura política y visión de mundo." REH-PR, 5 (1978), 91-128.

75.8 Bun-Ur, Lorraine Elena. "Hacia la novela del Caribe: Guillermo Cabrera Infante y Luis Rafael Sánchez." REH-PR, 5 (1978), 129-38.

75.9 ________. "Myth montage in a contemporary Puerto Rican tragedy: La pasión según Antígona Pérez (The passion according to Antigone Pérez)." LALR, No. 7 (1975), 15-21.

75.10 Bravo-Elizondo, Pedro. "La pasión según Antígona Pérez: radiografía de la dictadura." In his Teatro hispanoamericano de crítica social (Madrid: Playor, 1975), pp. 95-108.

75.11 Calaf de Agüera, Helen. "Entrevista: Luis Rafael Sánchez." Hispamérica, Nos. 23-24 (1979), 71-80. A fragment also appeared as "Luis Rafael Sánchez speaks about Macho Camacho's beat." Review, No. 23 (1981), 39-41.

75.12 ________. "La guaracha del Macho Camacho: intertextualidad y ruptura." Caribe, 2, 2 (1977), 5-16.

75.13 Caraballo de Abreu, Daisy. "Una lectura de La hiel nuestra de cada día." REH-PR, 5 (1978), 139-44.

75.14 Escajadillo, Tomás Gustavo. "[La guaracha del Macho Camacho]." RCLL, No. 5 (1977), 121-24.

75.15 Fiet, Lowell A. "Luis Rafael Sánchez's The passion of Antígona Pérez: Puerto Rican drama in North American performance." LATR, 10, 1 (1976), 97-101.

75.16 García Castro, Ramón. "La guaracha del Macho Camacho de Luis Rafael Sánchez y '/que sepa abrir la puerta para ir a jugar'." Chasqui, 9, 2-3 (1980), 71-74.

75.17 González, José Emilio. "El primer libro de cuentos de Luis Rafael Sánchez [En cuerpo de camisa]." RICP, No. 44 (1969), 7-15.

75.18 Kuehne, Alyce de. "The Antigone theme in Anouilh, Marechal and Luis Rafael Sánchez." In Papers on French-Spanish, Luso-Brazilian, Spanish American literary relations (Brockport, NY: State University of New York, Department of Foreign Languages, 1970), pp. 50-70.

75.19 López-Baralt, Luce. "[La guaracha del Macho Camacho]." SinN, 8, 1 (1977), 62-68.

75.20 ________. "La prosa de Luis Rafael Sánchez, escrita 'en puertorriqueño'." Insula, Nos. 356-57 (1976), 9.

75.21 Monleón, José. "Con Luis Rafael Sánchez (WYCO)." In his América latina: teatro y revolución (Caracas: El Ateneo de Caracas, 1978), pp. 167-79.

75.22 Montes Huidobro, Matías. "Luis Rafael Sánchez: lenguaje e identidad en el teatro puertorriqueño." TAH, Nos. 30-31 (1978), 22-25.

75.23 Morales, Luis Angel. "Consideraciones sobre La guaracha del Macho Camacho de Luis Rafael Sánchez." REH-PR, 5 (1978), 7-25.

75.24 Morán, Carlos Roberto. "Los lenguajes, la dependencia, el intento liberador." SinN, 8, 1 (1977), 57-61.

75.25 Moretti, Darcia. "Luis Rafael Sánchez." In her Gente importante (NY: Plus Ultra, 1973), pp. 95-101.

75.26 Morfi, Angelina. "El teatro de Luis Rafael Sánchez." RICP, No. 52 (1971), 39-49.

75.27 Pilditch, Charles. "O casi el alma: a bilingual production." LATR, 9, 1 (1975), 85-86.

75.28 Pope, Randolph D. "La guaracha del Macho Camacho y la contaminación de la mente." BR/RB, 5, 1-2 (1978), 152-55.

75.29 Ramos, Julio. "¡A bailar la guaracha!" Reintegro, 1, 2 (1980), 26-27.

75.30 Robatto, Matilde Albert. "Antígona Pérez: heroicidad y fatalismo." REH-PR, 5 (1978), 141-48.

75.31 Rodríguez, María Cristina. "Poor-black, rich-white: women in La guaracha del Macho Camacho." SAHL, 2-3 (1978-79), 244-54.

75.32 Rosa, María Inés. "Los ensayos de Luis Rafael Sánchez." REH-PR, 5 (1978), 149-65.

75.33 Sánchez, Enriquillo. "Alexis Gómez: pluróscopo. Conretismos y pluralemas." ¡Ahora!, No. 693 (1977), 41-48.

75.34 Solá Márquez, María. "Puerto Rico entre amos y guaracha: novelas de Enrique Laguerre y Luis Rafael Sánchez." SinN, 10, 2 (1979), 84-97.

75.35 Vaquero de Ramírez, María. "Interpretación de un código lingüístico: La guaracha del Macho Camacho." REH-PR, 5 (1978), 27-69.

75.36 Waldman, Gloria Feiman. "Luis Rafael Sánchez: an interview." RevI, 9 (1979), 9-23.

75.37 Zalacaín, Daniel. "La Antígona de Sánchez: recreación puertorriqueña del mito." ExTL, 9 (1981), 111-18.

76

SOTO, PEDRO JUAN (1928-)

Bibliographies

76.1 Ortiz Guzmán, Rosaura. "Pedro Juan Soto: treinta años de producción literaria (1948-1978). Guía bibliográfica." REH-PR, 6 (1979), 251-83.

Critical Monographs and Dissertations

76.2 Berrocal Torres, Bettie. La narrativa de Pedro Juan Soto. Unpublished doctoral dissertation, Universidad Complutense de Madrid, 1977.

76.3 Casanova-Sánchez, Olga. "La nueva novela puertorriqueña contemporánea: Pedro Juan Soto y Emilio Díaz Valcárcel." DAI, 38 (1977), 298A-99A.

76.4 Mur, Rose-Marie. Le problème de l'identité nationale à Porto Rico d'après l'oeuvre de Pedro Juan Soto. Unpublished thesis, Université de Toulouse, 1971.

76.5 Ortiz Guzmán, Rosaura. Aproximación a los relatos de Spiks. Unpublished thesis, Universidad de Puerto Rico, 1978.

76.6 Soto, Pedro Juan. A solas con Pedro Juan Soto. Río Piedras: Puerto, 1973.

76.7 Umpierre-Herrera, Luz María. "Un compromiso en la literatura: corrientes ideológicas en tres novelistas puertorriqueños: Manuel Zeno Gandía, Enrique A. Laguerre y Pedro Juan Soto." DAI, 39 (1979), 5539A.

Critical Essays

76.8 Alvarez, Ernesto. "El compromiso del arte en El francotirador de Pedro Juan Soto." BR/RB, 1 (1974), 252-58.

76.9 Arana de Love, Francisca. "Las novelas de Pedro Juan Soto: Usmaíl y Ardiente suelo, fría estación." In her La novela de Puerto Rico durante la primera década del Estado Libre Asociado (Barcelona: Vosgos, 1976), pp. 74-82.

76.10 Arellano Salgado, Olga. "El cuento y su influencia objetiva y subjetiva en el niño." NRP, Nos. 13-14 (1979), 1-5. Soto inter alios.

76.11 Boring, Phyllis Z. "Escape from reality in the fiction of Pedro Juan Soto." PLL, 8 (1972), 287-96.

76.12 ________. "Usmaíl: the Puerto Rican Joe Christmas." CLAJ, 16 (1973), 324-33.

76.13 Casanova-Sánchez, Olga. "Racismo y existencialismo en Usmaíl de Pedro Juan Soto." SAHL, 2-3 (1978-79), 90-105.

76.14 Casey, Calvert. "[Usmaíl]." CAm, No. 2 (1960), 87-88.

76.15 Dalmau de Sánchez, María M. "Ardiente suelo, fría estación, por Pedro Juan Soto." BSBPR, 1, 3 (1962), 64-66.

76.16 Febles, Jorge M. "Campeones de Pedro Juan Soto y el ambiente corrosivo del Harlem hispano." RC-R, 2 (1974), 41-49.

76.17 González, José Emilio. "[Spiks]." Asomante, 13, 4 (1957), 89-93.

76.18 Lago de Pope, María Inés. "Una alegoría del neocolonialismo [Temporada de duendes]." BR/RB, 1, 2 (1974), 208-11.

76.19 Martín, José Luis. "La yuxtaposición tiempo-espacial en El francotirador, de Pedro Juan Soto." NNH, 2, 2 (1972), 187-94.

76.20 Ortiz, Victoria. "Introduction." In Pedro Juan Soto, Spiks (NY: Monthly Review Press, 1973), pp. 11-17.

76.21 Seda Bonilla, Eduardo. "On the vicissitudes of being 'Puerto Rican': an exploration of Pedro Juan Soto's Hot land, cold season." RevI, 8 (1978), 116-28. Also MELUS, 6, 3 (1979), 27-40.

76.22 Torre, José Ramón de la. "La nueva novela en Puerto Rico: El francotirador." RUM, 24, 11 (1970), 2-7. Also Penélope, 1, 1 (1972), 41-55.

76.23 Vientós Gastón, Nilita. "El primer libro de Pedro Juan Soto [Spiks]." In her Indice cultural (Río Piedras: Ediciones de la Universidad de Puerto Rico, 1962-71), II, 17-18.

76.24 Waldman, Gloria Feiman. "El tema de Puerto Rico en Abelardo Díaz Alfaro, René Marqués y Pedro Juan Soto." RICP, No. 69 (1975), 16-22.

77

TAPIA Y RIVERA, ALEJANDRO (1826-1882)

Critical Monographs and Dissertations

77.1 Beauchamp, José Juan. Imagen del puertorriqueño en la novela (en Alejandro Tapia y Rivera, Manuel Zeno Gandía y Enrique A. Laguerre). Río Piedras?: Universidad de Puerto Rico, 1976.

77.2 Castro Pérez, Elsa. Tapia: señalador de caminos. SJ: Coquí, 1964.

77.3 García Díaz, Manuel. Alejandro Tapia y Rivera: su vida y su obra. Unpublished thesis, Universidad de Puerto Rico, 1933. Also SJ: Coquí, 1964.

77.4 Martín, José Luis. Alejandro Tapia y su poema La sataniada. Río Piedras: Ateneo Universitario, Universidad de Puerto Rico, 1957.

77.5 ________. Análisis estilístico de La sataniada de Tapia. Unpublished thesis, Universidad de Puerto Rico, 1953. Also SJ: Instituto de Cultura Puertorriqueña, 1958.

77.6 Serrano de Matos, Magdalena. El teatro de Alejandro Tapia y Rivera. Unpublished thesis, Universidad de Puerto Rico, 1953.

Critical Essays

77.7 Acosta, José J. "Juicio sobre el drama Roberto D'Evreux." In Alejandro Tapia y Ribera, Roberto D'Evreux; 3. ed. (SJ: Venezuela, 1944), pp. 92-110.

77.8 "Al margen de La sataniada." Indice, No. 11 (1930), 169.

77.9 Baldorioty de Castro, R. "Juicio crítico sobre el drama Bernardo de Palissy." In Alejandro Tapia y Rivera, Bernardo de Palissy (SJ: Venezuela, 1944), pp. 139-47.

77.10 Brau, Salvador. "Alejandro Tapia y Rivera." In his Ecos de la batalla; primera serie (SJ: J. González Font, 1886), pp. 136-41.

77.11 Coll y Toste, Cayetano. "Proemio." In Alejandro Tapia y Rivera, Mis memorias, o Puerto Rico cómo lo encontré y cómo lo dejo (NY: De Lasine & Rossboro, 1928?), pp. 3-5.

77.12 ________. "Puertorriqueños ilustres. Tapia." BHPR, 7 (1920), 321-32. Also as "Alejandro Tapia y Rivera." In his Puertorriqueños ilustres; primera selección (NY: Las Américas, 1952), pp. 187-91. Also in his Puertorriqueños ilustres; segunda selección (Barcelona: Rumbos, 1963), pp. 123-26. Also 1966; pp. 140-43.

77.13 _________. "Las reliquias de Tapia." BHPR, 12 (1925), 312-13.

77.14 Collado Martell, Alfredo. "Tapia--¿novelista?" Indice, No. 11 (1930), 170.

77.15 Collante de Tapia, Lola de. "Dr. Alejandro Tapia: figuras del proscenio." Lotería, No. 201 (1972), 49-52.

77.16 Fernández Juncos, Manuel. "Alejandro Tapia." In his Antología puertorriqueña (NY: Hinds, Hayden & Eldredge, 1913), pp. 48-50. Various other editions.

77.17 _________. "Alejandro Tapia y Rivera." In his Varias cosas (SJ: Tipografía de las Bellas Artes, 1884), pp. 181-201.

77.18 _________. "Alejandro Tapia y Rivera." In his Semblanzas puertorriqueñas (SJ: González Font, 1888), pp. 57-95.

77.19 Figueroa, Sotero. "Alejandro Tapia y Rivera (1827-1882)." In his Ensayo biográfico de los que más han contribuído al proceso de Puerto Rico (Ponce: El Vapor, 1888), pp. 285-97.

77.20 Fránquiz, José A. "Prefacio a la obra de don Alejandro Tapia y Rivera." In Alejandro Tapia y Rivera, Conferencias sobre estética y literatura; 2. ed. (SJ: Venezuela, 1945), pp. 9-19. Also as "Conferencias sobre estética y literatura." In Alejandro Tapia y Rivera, Conferencias sobre estética y literatura (Barcelona: Rumbos, 1968), pp. 9-19.

77.21 _________. "Tapia." In Alejandro Tapia y Rivera, La sataniada, grandiosa epopeya (Barcelona: Rvmbos, 1967), pp. 9-13. Orig. 1945.

77.22 García Díaz, Manuel. "Alejandro Tapia y Rivera." In Alejandro Tapia y Rivera, La palma del cacique; 2. ed. (M: Orión, 1952), pp. 7-20.

77.23 González, Aníbal. "La cuarentona and slave society in Cuba and Puerto Rico." LALR, No. 16 (1980), 47-54.

77.24 Hernández Norman, Isabel. "Alejandro Tapia y Ribera (1826-1882)." In her La novela romántica en las Antillas (NY: Ateneo Puertorriqueño de Nueva York, 1969, c1967), pp. 195-215.

77.25 _________. "...Alejandro Tapia y Rivera (1826-1882)." In her La novela criolla en las Antillas (NY: Plus Ultra, 1977), pp. 195-215.

77.26 Hostos, Adolfo de. "Alejandro Tapia y Rivera (1826-1882)." In his Hombres representativos de Puerto Rico (SJ, 1961), pp. 78-100.

77.27 Martín, José Luis. "Alejandro Tapia y su poema La sataniada." Asomante, 12, 2 (1956), 78-94. Also in his Arco y flecha... (SJ: Club de la Prensa, 1961), pp. 51-76.

77.28 ________. "Enardo y Rosael, publican en inglés una obra de Tapia." In his Arco y flecha... (SJ: Club de la Prensa, 1961), pp. 77-83.

77.29 Matos Bernier, Félix. "Alejandro Tapia y Rivera." In his Pedazos de roca (Ponce: "La Libertad", 1894), pp. 178-82.

77.30 Medina y González, Zenón. "Alejandro Tapia y Rivera." In his Pinceladas (SJ: V. de González, 1895), pp. 36-37.

77.31 Morales Carrión, Arturo. "Tapia y su Biblioteca Histórica." Asomante, 2, 2 (1946), 104-106. Also as "Significación de la Biblioteca Histórica de Tapia." In his Ojeada al proceso histórico y otros ensayos (SJ: Cordillera, 1971), pp. 111-15. Also 1974.

77.32 Morfi, Angelina. "Alejandro Tapia y La cuarterona." In her Temas del teatro (Santo Domingo: Caribe, 1969), pp. 93-100.

77.33 Pagán, Juan Bautista. "Don Alejandro Tapia y Rivera." In his Dionisios (SJ: Biblioteca de Autores Puertorriqueños, 1957), pp. 134-54.

77.34 ________. "Sobre el padre de nuestras letras: don Alejandro Tapia y Rivera." AyL, 1, 3 (1953), 12-18.

77.35 Pedreira, Antonio S. "Tapia: mis memorias." REH-PR, 1, 4 (1928), 393-95.

77.36 Rosa-Nieves, Cesáreo. "Alejandro Tapia y Rivera (1826-1882)." In his Plumas estelares en las letras de Puerto Rico (SJ: Ediciones de la Torre, Universidad de Puerto Rico, 1967), I, 83-102.

77.37 Sáez, Antonia. "Tapia dramaturgo." Indice, No. 11 (1930), 168.

78

VIDARTE, SANTIAGO (1827-1848)

Critical Monographs and Dissertations

78.1 Medina, Ramón Felipe. *Santiago Vidarte: vida y obra.* Unpublished thesis, Universidad de Puerto Rico, 1965.

Critical Essays

78.2 Coll y Toste, Cayetano. "Puertorriqueños ilustres. Santiago Vidarte (1827-1848)." *BHPR*, 4, 2 (1917), 74-76. Also as "Santiago Vidarte (1827-1848)." In his *Puertorriqueños ilustres; primera selección* (NY; Las Américas, 1952), pp. 149-53. Also in his *Puertorriqueños ilustres; segunda selección* (Barcelona: Rumbos, 1963), pp. 93-96. Also 1966; pp. 110-13.

78.3 Fernández Juncos, Manuel. "Santiago Vidarte." In his *Antología puertorriqueña* (NY: Hindes, Noble & Eldridge, 1913), pp. 56-57. Various other editions.

78.4 Figueroa, Sotero. "Santiago Vidarte (1827-1848)." In his *Ensayo biográfico de los que más han contribuído al progreso de Puerto Rico* (Ponce: "El Vapor", 1888), pp. 95-104.

78.5 Hernández Aquino, Luis. "Dos cantores de Puerto Rico. Vidarte y Gautier." *AyL*, 2a época, No. 17 (1958), 3-6.

78.6 Neumann Gandía, Eduardo. "Santiago Vidarte." In his *Benefactores y hombres notables de Puerto Rico* (Ponce: "Listín Comercial", 1899), II, 51-54.

78.7 Rosa-Nieves, Cesáreo. "Santiago Vidarte (1828-1848)." In his *Plumas estelares en las letras de Puerto Rico* (SJ: Ediciones de la Torre, Universidad de Puerto Rico, 1967), I, 27-40.

78.8 ________. "Santiago Vidarte, un poeta romántico." *Prensa*, 2a época, No. 4 (1959), 13-14.

79

VIZCARRONDO, CARMELINA (1906-)

Critical Monographs and Dissertations

79.1 Ramírez Mattei, Aída Elsa. Carmelina Vizcarrondo: vida, obra y antología. SJ: Editorial Universitaria, Universidad de Puerto Rico, 1972. Orig. an unpublished thesis, Universidad de Puerto Rico, 1965.

Critical Essays

79.2 Albuquerque Lima, Sílvio Júlio. "Carmelina Vizcarrondo." In his Escritores altilhanos (Rio de Janeiro, 1944), pp. 222-33. Signed Júlio Sílvio.

79.3 Arce de Vázquez, Margot. "Carmelina Vizcarrondo y su poesía." In Carmelina Vizcarrondo, Pregón en llamas (SJ: Venezuela, 1935), pp. 7-13.

79.4 Cadilla, Carmen Alicia. "Destino del cuento en Carmelina Vizcarrondo." RAMG, 2, 1 (1939), 24.

79.5 Castro, Tomás de Jesús. "Carmelina Vizcarrondo." In his Esbozos críticos (SJ: Baldrich, 1945), pp. 110-12.

79.6 Dávila, José Antonio. "A Carmelina Vizcarrondo." In his Prosa: ensayos, artículos y cartas literarias (SJ: Sociedad de Autores Puertorriqueños, 1971), pp. 253-57.

79.7 __________. "Clara Lair y Carmelina Vizcarrondo." In his Prosa: ensayos, artículos y cartas literarias (SJ: Sociedad de Autores Puertorriqueños, 1971), pp. 155-57.

79.8 Ferrer Canales, José. "Carmelina Vizcarrondo, la infancia y Poemas para mi niño." In his Marginalia (SJ?: Venezuela?, 1939), pp. 19-31.

79.9 Hernández Aquino, Luis. "Minutero en sombras." InsulaP, 1, 5 (1942), 19-23.

79.10 Laguerre, Enrique A. "Prólogo." In Carmelina Vizcarrondo, Minutero en sombras (SJ: Venezuela, 1941), pp. 13-16.

79.11 Lloréns, Washington. "La poesía de Carmelina Vizcarrondo." In his Críticas profanas (SJ: Progreso, 1936), pp. 28-32.

79.12 Nuñez, Serafina. "Dos voces líricas de Puerto Rico." RBC, 44, 2 (1939), 316-17. Vizcarrondo and Padilla.

79.13 Pedreira, Antonio S. "Pregón en llamas." In his Aclaraciones y crítica (SJ: Phi Eta Mu, Universidad de Puerto Rico, 1941), pp. 197-201. Also Río Piedras: Edil, 1969. Also in his Obras completas (SJ: Instituto de Cultura Puertorriqueña, 1970), pp. 597-600.

79.14 Préndez Saldías, Carlos. "[El pregón en llamas]." AteneaC, No. 121 (1935), 186-87.

79.15 Sánchez Trincado, José Luis. "Poemas para mi niño. Juicios de la crítica española." RevP, No. 184 (1938), pagination unknown.

80

ZENO GANDÍA, MANUEL A. (1855-1930)

Bibliographies

80.1 Arce de Vázquez, Margot. "Bibliografía de Manuel Zeno Gandía." Asomante, 11, 4 (1955), 72-74.

Critical Monographs and Dissertations

80.2 Algarín, Pedro J. "El naturalismo en Manuel Zeno Gandía." DAI, 33 (1973), 5668A.

80.3 Alvarez-Valle, Ernesto. "Manuel Zeno Gandía: estética y sociedad." DAI, 39 (1978), 3611A-12A.

80.4 Beauchamp, José Juan. Imagen del puertorriqueño en la novela (en Alejandro Tapia y Rivera, Manuel Zeno Gandía y Enrique A. Laguerre). Río Piedras: Editorial Universitaria, Universidad de Puerto Rico, 1976.

80.5 Colón, José M. La naturaleza en Manuel Zeno Gandía y Enrique Laguerre. Unpublished thesis, Unversidad de Puerto Rico, 1949.

80.6 Darbouze, Gilbert. "Dégénérescence et regénéscence dans les romans d'Emile Zola et de Manuel Zeno Gandía: étude comparative." DAI, 41 (1980), 1626A-27A.

80.7 Fernández Montes, José. El naturalismo y el romanticismo: La charca comentada. Ponce: M. López, 1897.

80.8 Gardón Franceschi, Margarita. Manuel Zeno Gandía: vida y poesía. SJ: Coquí, 1969. Orig. an unpublished dissertation, Universidad de Puerto Rico, 1962.

80.9 ________. La poesía de Manuel Zeno Gandía. SJ: Departamento de Instrucción Pública, 1968.

80.10 Guzmán, Julia M. *Apuntes sobre la novelística puertorriqueña. Manuel Zeno Gandía: del romanticismo al naturalismo*. Madrid: Rauser y Menet, 1960.

80.11 Lluch Mora, Francisco. *La naturaleza en La charca de Manuel Zeno Gandía*. SJ: Club de la Prensa, 1960.

80.12 Palmer de Dueño, Rosa M. *Sentido, forma y estilo de Redentores de Manuel Zeno Gandía*. Río Piedras: Editorial Universitaria, Universidad de Puerto Rico. Orig. as *Análisis estilístico de Redentores de Manuel Zeno Gandía*. Unpublished dissertation, Universidad de Puerto Rico, 1966.

80.13 Quiñones, Samuel R. *Manuel Zeno Gandía y la novela en Puerto Rico*. M: Orión, 1955. Same as item no. 80.41.

80.14 Soto, Venus Lidia. *El arte de novelar en Garduña de Manuel Zeno Gandía*. SJ: Departamento de Instrucción Pública, 1967.

80.15 Umpierre-Herrera, Luz María. "Un compromiso en la literatura: corrientes ideológicas en tres novelistas puertorriqueños: Manuel Zeno Gandía, Enrique A. Laguerre y Pedro Juan Soto." *DAI*, 39 (1979), 5539A.

80.16 Zeno de Matos, Elena. *Manuel Zeno Gandía: documentos biográficos y críticos, su vida y su obra reproducida por eminentes críticos de Puerto Rico y del extranjero*. SJ, 1956, c1955.

Critical Essays

80.17 Alba-Bufill, Elio. "Loveira y Zeno Gandía: representantes del naturalismo en las Antillas." In *Estudios literarios sobre Hispanoamérica (homenaje a Carlos M. Raggi y Ageo)* (San José, CR: Círculo de Cultura Panamericana, 1976), pp. 85-96.

80.18 Aponte Alsina, Marta. "Notas para un estudio ideológico de las novelas de Manuel Zeno Gandía." *SinN*, 5, 1 (1974), 30-42.

80.19 Barradas, Efraín. "La naturaleza en *La charca*: tema y estilo." *SinN*, 5, 1 (1974), 30-42.

80.20 Barrera, Héctor. "*La charca* (osario de vivos o generación de fantasmas)." *Asomante*, 11, 4 (1955), 59-71.

80.21 Cadilla Colón, Francisco M. "Manuel Zeno Gandía." In his *Los ochocentistas* (Barcelona: Rumbos, 1961), pp. 221-31.

80.22 Cano, Lamberto A. "La montaña, génesis del cromatismo en *La charca*." *RICP*, No. 32 (1966), 7-11.

80.23 Carrión Maduro, Tomás. "*La charca* (crónica de un mundo enfermo, por el Dr. Manuel Zeno Gandía)." In his *Ten con ten; impresiones de un viaje a América del Norte* (SJ: La República Española, 1906), pp. 139-200.

80.24 Colón, José M. "La naturaleza en *La charca*." *Asomante*, 5, 2 (1949), 50-59.

80.25 Dalmau Canet, Sebastián. "Manuel Zeno Gandía." In his *Crepúsculos literarios* (SJ: Boletín Mercantil, 1903), pp. 25-26.

80.26 Galaos, José Antonio. "Zeno Gandía y sus crónicas de un mundo enfermo." *CHA*, No. 177 (1964), 415-20.

80.27 González, José Luis. "Tres fundadores de la literatura puertorriqueña [Hostos, Brau, Zeno Gandía]." *Humanismo*, Nos. 48-49 (1958), 96-115.

80.28 Hostos, Adolfo de. "Manuel Zeno Gandía (1855-1930)." In his *Hombres representativos de Puerto Rico* (SJ: Venezuela, 1961), pp. 140-52.

80.29 Huyke, Juan B. "Manuel Zeno Gandía." In his *Triunfadores* (SJ: Negociado de Materiales, Imprenta y Transporte, 1927), II, 93-102.

80.30 Laguerre, Enrique A. "El arte de novelar en Zeno Gandía." *Asomante*, 11, 4 (1955), 48-53.

80.31 __________. "Prólogo." In Manuel A. Zeno Gandía, *La charca* (Caracas: Biblioteca Ayacucho, 1978), pp. ix-li.

80.32 Lloréns, Washington. "*La charca*--novela de Manuel Zeno Gandía." In his *Críticas profanas* (SJ: Progeso, 1936), pp. 78-85.

80.33 Lluch Mora, Francisco. "La naturaleza en *La charca* de Manuel Zeno Gandía." In his *Miradero*... (SJ: Cordillera, 1966), pp. 37-49.

80.34 López, Mariano. "El perfil humano de *La charca*." *SinN*, 9, 4 (1979), 46-61.

80.35 Machuca, Julio. "Una novela de Manuel Zeno Gandía (*El negocio*)." In his *Ensayos (literatura, sociología, pedagogía)* (SJ: Venezuela, 1943), pp. 87-102.

80.36 Manrique Cabrera, Francisco. "*La charca*." In Manuel A. Zeno Gandía, *La charca* (SJ: Instituto de Cultura Puertorriqueña, 1968), pp. xiii-xviii. Various other editions.

80.37 __________. "Manuel Zeno Gandía: poeta del novelar isleño." *Asomante*, 11, 4 (1955), 19-47. Also in Elena Zeno de Matos, *Manuel Zeno Gandía*, q.v., pp. 9-35.

80.38 Mariñez, Pablo A. "Manuel Zeno Gandía: novelista de todos los tiempos." ¡Ahora!, No. 226 (1968), 62-64, 76.

80.39 Matos Bernier, Félix. "Gandía (Manuel Zeno Gandía)." In his Isla de arte (SJ: La Primavera, 1907), pp. 25-29.

80.40 __________. "Manuel Zeno Gandía." In his Cromos ponceños (Ponce: Imprenta de la Libertad, 1896), pp. 30-31.

80.41 Quiñones, Samuel R. "Manuel Zeno Gandía y la novela en Puerto Rico." In his Temas y letras; 3. ed. (SJ: Biblioteca de Autores Puertorriqueños, 1955), pp. 9-38. Also in Manuel A. Zeno Gandía, La charca (M: Orión, 1957), pp. 7-36. Various other editions. Also in Mariana Robles de Cardona, Búsqueda y plasmación de nuestra personalidad... (SJ: Club de la Prensa, 1958), pp. 301-15.

80.42 __________. "Nuestro novelista de la tierra:--M. Zeno Gandía." Indice, No. 12 (1930), 183-84.

80.43 Rosa-Nieves, Cesáreo. "La charca, una gran novela de América." In his Ensayos escogidos... (SJ: Academia de Artes y Ciencias de Puerto Rico, 1970?), pp. 109-16.

80.44 __________. "Manuel Antonio Zeno y Gandía (1855-1930)." In his Plumas estelares en las letras de Puerto Rico (SJ: Ediciones de la Torre, Universidad de Puerto Rico, 1967), I, 249-72.

80.45 __________. "Presencia de Manuel Zeno Gandía." In his La lámpara del faro... (SJ: Club de la Prensa, 1957-60), I, 67-73. Orig. Asomante, 11, 4 (1955), 54-58.

80.46 Vientós Gastón, Nilita. "Editorial [número de homenaje a Zeno Gandía]." Asomante, 11, 4 (1955), 7.

INDEX TO AUTHORS OF CRITICAL WORKS

www.ingramcontent.com/pod-product-compliance
Lightning Source LLC
Chambersburg PA
CBHW060529310726
48982CB00002B/479

* 9 7 8 0 3 1 3 2 3 4 1 9 4 *